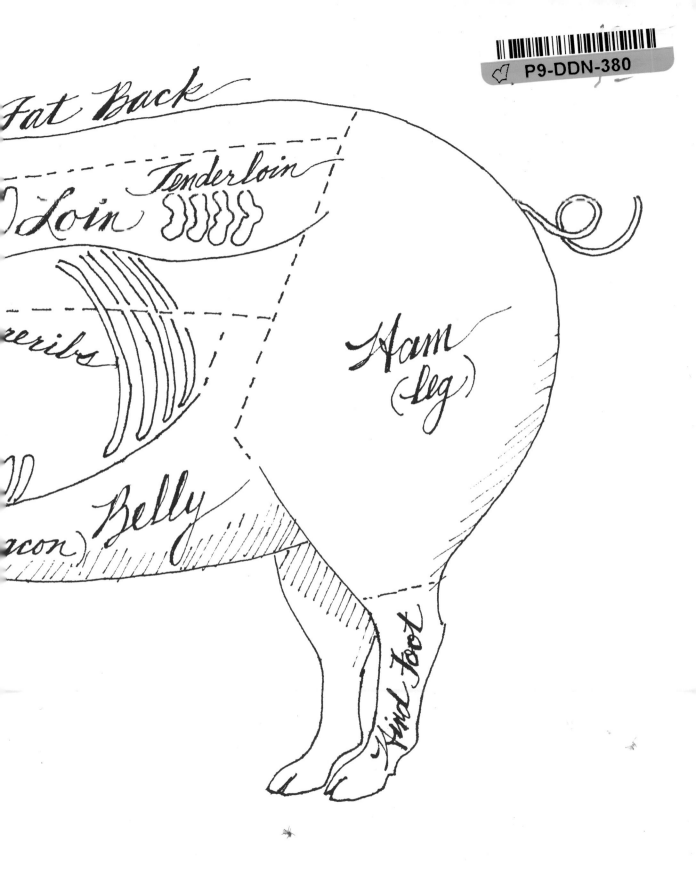

Fat Back

Loin Tenderloin

Loin

reribs

Ham
(leg)

con) Belly

Hind Foot

THE
USEFUL
PIG

THE USEFUL PIG

150 Succulent Pork Recipes

ROBERTA WOLFE
SMOLER

HarperCollins*Publishers*

For Julie Fallowfield.
This book is the result of her unwavering enthusiasm.
And for Arthur,
my partner at the table for over twenty years.

The photographs on pages 33, 50, and 153 courtesy of the Roughwood Collection.

The photographs on pages 113, 140, 162, 167, 253, and 270 courtesy of the Bettmann Archives.

FIRST EDITION

DESIGNED BY JOEL AVIROM

Library of Congress Cataloging-in-Publication Data

Smoler, Roberta Wolfe.
    The useful pig/Roberta Wolfe Smoler.—1st ed.
        p.   cm.
    ISBN 0-06-016197-3
    1. Cookery (Pork) I. Title.
TX749.5.P67S66 1990   89-46558
641.6′64—dc20

90 91 92 93 94 DT/RRD 10 9 8 7 6 5 4 3 2 1

C · O · N · T · E · N · T · S

A·C·K·N·O·W·L·E·D·G·M·E·N·T·S

I wish to thank the many producers of fine hams all across the country who enthusiastically responded to my queries with envelopes chock full of interesting information and mouth-watering details that made me want to drop everything and order their hams and bacon right on the spot.

Joe Leathers, of the Pork Producers Council, and Robin Kline, director of consumer affairs for the Pork Producers Council, deserve special thanks for not only returning my calls but providing a network of information. Through them I contacted Julie Shapero, director of public relations and special events for John Morrell & Company, who fervently regaled me with stories of "flying pigs" over Cincinnati.

I am especially grateful to Stephen Bonadies, who opened the door to Porkopolis, and for the help I received from the Cincinnati Historical Society, who sent me an abundance of information on the role of the pig in Cincinnati's history.

A word of thanks goes to Linda Keen of Leonia, New Jersey, for assisting me in my quest for the origin of the word *bacon,* and I thank Bill of Kocher's Pork Store in Ridgefield, New Jersey, my accommodating butcher for almost twenty years.

A Brief History of the Useful Pig

There is no farm animal that has given the world so much—from the treasures of its lore to the nourishment of its people. Whether it be the adorable squirming piglet or the prized hog, the pig has always been the source of fables, superstitions and sustenance.

Early history

The earliest written record of the pig dates to about 7000 B.C. in China, along with the development of permanent settlements and the beginning of farming in the neolithic period. (Pigs were also found to have existed in Mesopotamia in 6750 B.C. and 6000 B.C. in ancient Greece.) The Stone Age pig's appearance was that of a semidomesticated wild boar. It is speculated, but not documented, that wild hogs were present on Earth as far back as 40 million years ago.

The pig became a farm animal at the same time man learned to cultivate his first crops, mainly grains, such as barley, wheat and lentils. The pig was probably the first animal to share man's food. Prior to farming, man's principal domesticated animals were goats and sheep, which are better suited to the nomadic way of life; pigs could not travel long distances.

The pig is referred to again and again throughout history. Homer wrote of pork and pigs in the *Iliad* and the *Odyssey:* Achilles offered pork to the Greek generals; Circe changed men into swine but was forced by Odysseus to change them back again. The Spartans and Athenians were known to have enjoyed pork in stews, puddings and sausages; and by 600 B.C., pork was an important food in Roman charcuteries. In Julius Caesar's time (100 to 44 B.C.) pork was a principal dish at formal banquets.

During the rule of the Roman Emperor Trajanus (A.D. 98 to 117), the role of pork as the centerpiece of any lofty occasion had escalated to a level of bizarre indulgence. Apicius, a pseudonym adopted by several culinary writers in Roman times, describes a recipe for *Porcus Trajanus* in which the cavity of the pig, after being washed with wine, was stuffed with small game birds and assorted fowl, egg yolks, hens' belly sacs full of tiny unborn eggs, the teats and vulvas of nursing sows, and other "delicacies," and trussed. The pig would then be roasted to a beautiful shade of golden brown. The reaction of Trajanus's guests was not recorded but the Roman Senate eventually passed a law forbidding such scandalous extravagances.

The pig in Europe

During the Middle Ages in France, the Church controlled the sale of pork and imposed a tithe on it. The Church hierarchy would stage ham fairs; the first recorded was held in front of Notre Dame. The original term for this "pig market" was *bacon* and the fair was called *la foire de bacon.* The word *bacon* is thought to be a variant of the Old Norman and Saxon word *baco* or *baccho,* from *back*—meaning hindquarter, haunch or ham; or Old High German, where it might have been *bakko.*[1] From the sound of these words, I find it easy to hear its transformation to the French word for ham, *jambon,* and the Spanish *jamon.* Until the English adapted the word *bacon* to mean the smoked belly we know today, it simply meant the meat of the pig.

The pig is still celebrated and highly valued by rich and poor alike in Europe. Unlike cattle, pigs are not dependent on pasture, and pork is often the predominant meat where the landscape is harsh.

On farms in many parts of France, you can still find a *Fête du Cochon,* a Sunday ritual following the slaughtering of the pig; it is the occasion for a gathering of family and friends. At this event, each dish of the meal (except dessert) will contain some part of the pig—from pâtés, cold sausages, soups and salads, through casseroles, ragouts, hot sausages, roasts and vegetables. The French have an expression: *"Tout est bon dans le cochon!"* (All of the pig—from head to tail—is good!) In America, a meat packer used the slogan "We use everything but the oink."

[1] Eric Partridge, *Origins: A Short Etymological Dictionary of Modern English,* 2d ed. (New York: Macmillan, 1959).

The first pigs in America

There is no evidence to suggest there was ever a pig truly native to North America. The first pigs in early America arrived on ships with the first explorers. Pigs were popular as part of the standard provisions of any voyage. Being omnivorous, they were easy to feed, and with their ability to produce two litters a year, proliferation was rapid. Another advantage of having pigs on board was that as they were butchered, the meat could be packed in salt and stored for future consumption.

In the early 1500s de Soto brought pigs to Florida, leaving them with various Indian tribes as he moved on. Some of the pigs wandered away, and since the tropical environment was hospitable, these feral pigs thrived and bred. Explorers also left pigs in the Caribbean and in Hawaii, where they also flourished.

The nature of pigs

The pig has certain unique charms. It is easily domesticated and possesses lovable attributes. Pigs and piglets are even treated as pets in certain countries; they are often given the run of the house in China. In New Guinea orphan pigs are sometimes suckled by nursing mothers.

The pig's ideal habitat is near water. Having no sweat glands, pigs need to wallow to keep cool. Lakes, ponds, riverbanks and puddles all suit this purpose.

Pigs also need dense cover for shade. They seek shelter in forests, thickets, brush and high grasses and make snug dens not only in caves, but also in such places as the hollows between large roots of old trees. Their poor eyesight is more than compensated for by a keen sense of smell, which helps them to find food by rooting in the ground. This is what makes them such distinguished truffle hunters. Highly gregarious, pigs live and travel in groups; they sometimes form colonies of their own. They are remarkable swimmers and have been known to populate uninhabited islands some distance from any mainland.

The beginning of curing

Although there is little documentation, it is believed that around 2000 to 1500 B.C. the Chinese developed a method for salting and preserving pork. Pork was and still is their main meat and, in some ways, practically their only meat since beef and lamb were—and are—scarce, and birds have to be consumed as soon as they are killed. In China, the word *meat* is virtually synonymous with pork.

On the other side of the world, Europeans developed their own methods of salting and curing. The Gauls managed large numbers of pigs, which they let forage for themselves in the vast Celtic forests. Living well off the abundance of acorns and scrub, the pigs were both easy to care for and virtually cost free. The enterprising French began to produce hams and were soon exporting them. The Romans had a great appreciation for these hams, especially the Gauls' method of salting, smoking and oiling them—a process they had refined to an art. (These hams were very salty, and as the Romans did not normally drink while they ate, thirst-inducing hams and other charcuterie were usually consumed at the end of the meal.)

Curing hams in early America and the legendary country hams of the South

Hams have been produced in America ever since the settling of Jamestown in the early 1600s. Although some of the first colonists may have brought the knowledge of curing with them from England, it is generally accepted that the settlers learned to cure hams from the Indians, who knew how to cure venison.

The curing and exporting of hams was one of the first forms of trade in early America. As early as 1779, Smithfield hams were exported to the West Indies and Bermuda, where they were called "tropical-cured hams." Since the hams could be kept without refrigeration, they were extremely popular with the islanders. Although it was easy enough for them to raise pigs, the Caribbean climate was too warm for curing meat.

In the South, this enterprise of curing and exporting hams coincided with the profitable cultivation of peanuts. It was the practice to let pigs roam the peanut fields, foraging for nuts missed during harvesting. (The peanut industry has long since declined and it is no longer profitable for farmers to raise hogs on peanuts. Today, most of the pigs in the United States are raised in the Midwest and are corn-fed.) The diet of oil-rich nuts resulted in meat of remarkable flavor and texture. Smithfield hams, thought to be unique, were coveted by English royalty. Queen Victoria's name appears on a historic customer list belonging to the heirs of Mallory Todd, originally of Smithfield and one of America's oldest producers of hams.

Ideal weather conditions, crucial for curing a fine country ham, were unique to the South—particularly Maryland, Virginia, North Carolina, Kentucky, Tennessee and Georgia. The process of creating a fine ham went on over three seasons. The hams were packed in salt in the winter, then taken out of the salt and hung in well-ventilated storage rooms to let the salt "equalize," aided by the rising temperatures and low humidity of the spring months. The aging process was completed in summer. Today the climate can be controlled by technology, but some small producers still cure their hams by the original method in which weather is a critical factor.

For those who do their own slaughtering, frosty mornings and frosty nights are what they like. Cooling the meat and rubbing it with its salt cure must be done in temperatures above freezing but below 40°F. The salt is toxic to most bacterium and the aging kills any trichinae that may be present, if at all. This is important as some people might like to eat the ham uncooked—as is the custom in Europe where raw hams are highly regarded.

These old-fashioned producers are watched over by a USDA inspector who will visit their facilities at least once a week. The weather temperature is carefully recorded daily and if it is not in the range specified by the USDA, depending on the stage of the cure, the hams must remain in the salt or aging room for an additional number of days to compensate for the variance.

Porkopolis

Cincinnati, Ohio, also known as Porkopolis, rivaled Smithfield, Virginia, in the early 1800s as a producer of hams. Cincinnati's source of strength was its location on the Ohio River. Before the railroads became the major means of transportation, the river and its tributaries formed a natural system of cheap transportation. In winter the river provided ice for refrigeration; salt was transported by boat from Virginia's Kanawha Valley by way of the river's tributaries; and the wood needed to make the pork barrels came by the river. Most important, the river enabled the meat packers to transport their pork products rapidly to consumers.

The pork barrels the packers used were the genuine article. Later, after the invention of refrigeration, the term *pork barrel* took on a political connotation. Just as the literal pork barrel was a symbol of security because it contained an abundant supply of salted meat to be portioned out over the winter or to see people through hard times, the political pork barrel came to symbolize projects or appropriations that would yield fat benefits (the pork) for a specific locality and legislator's constituents.

Other terms of slang using pork with political connotations include *porkchopper,* meaning a political appointee, union official, relative or friend of a politician who is put on the payroll as a favor in return for past service. The pork-chopper receives payment for little or no work. Another term is *home-porking*. As recently as June 15, 1989, a *Wall Street Journal* article referred to home-porking. " 'Politicians love home-porking,' adds Kenneth Hagan, a naval historian. 'They get jobs for the home folks. The Navy loves it too. They get a political base for a bigger fleet.' "

Cincinnati was also located in the heart of the corn belt—the land of nourishment for pigs and cattle alike. Originally pigs in the Miami and Scioto valleys were raised in the same way the Gauls cared for their pigs—they were allowed to roam free in the local forests, foraging for themselves. As these valleys produced large amounts of corn it was soon discovered that feeding it to the hogs produced larger animals with a higher quality of meat.

Other conditions also favored both the farmers and the meat-packing industry: many farms were close enough to the city for the pigs to be walked to the market. This created rumors, partially true, of droves of menacing pigs roaming the streets, and it *is* true that strays would be picked up by families and fattened for their own consumption.

The rise of the meat-packing industry

The tremendous growth of the meat-packing industry was described in the *Boston Courier,* Monday, January 19, 1835,[2] where a journalist who had recently visited the slaughterhouses in Cincinnati observed:

"Cincinnati is the greatest 'Pork market' in the known world. The number of hogs slaughtered annually, and the perfection and science to which the art of 'hog-killing' has been brought, is indeed astonishing. The business of butchering is carried on distinct from that of packing, and by different persons."

The journalist singled out the awesome slaughterhouse of one John Coleman, who owned the most extensive establishment of its kind, having laid 100,864 hogs to rest in the year 1834. Coleman's place of business was described as a lot of eight acres with four separate buildings and the grounds divided totally into pens.

Each building had scalding tubs at either end so the number of pigs slaughtered in each building was doubled. The unsuspecting hogs would be moved into two smaller pens leading to the doorways at each end of the

[2] Courtesy of the Cincinnati Historical Society.

building. From there they quickly met their maker. Then they were bled and washed in the tubs of scalding water. (Perhaps after the hogs were washed, the water left in the tubs was called "hogwash.") Next, the hogs were scraped and shaved clean with special tools designed for this purpose, after which, with the help of a pulley, they were strung up by a hind foot and dressed. The hogs, 2,600 a day from the four buildings, were then transferred to a cool room to hang until morning.

This entire procedure, from start to finish, was all accomplished within about one minute! The men who did the work were paid $1.25 a day. Among these workers was a sort of "king among the hog-killers" who could remove the offal and dress three hogs in a minute. This man received $2.50 per day.

The profits for Mr. Coleman derived from the offal—rough fat, soap-grease and bristles. This was usually worth twenty to twenty-five cents net per hog, and it was estimated that Mr. Coleman cleared fifteen to twenty thousand dollars in a three-month season.

The following morning, the carcasses would be loaded into large wagons and taken to the various packinghouses. This same journalist describes the operation of Miller & Lee:

> These men are very enterprising, have high reputation for the uniform excellence of their Pork, as also for their superior Hams, their "sugar hams" are said to be as good as any cured in any part of the Union.
>
> It is, indeed, astonishing, the rapidity with which they put a hog out of sight, when they once get fair hold of him. As at the slaughter house, a perfect system is kept up, every man has his alloted duty to perform, and there is consequently no interference with each other; everything goes on "like clock work."

The procedure of the packinghouse was first to weigh in the hogs, then lay them out on blocks, where the carcasses were attacked by the meat cutters who made quick work of dispatching the various parts to their destinations. Two-hundred-pound barrels were used as salt boxes to store the meat, with fifty pounds of coarse salt added to each barrel of pork. The cooper then closed the barrels, holes were bored and the barrels filled with water to make a strong brine. After this, the holes were plugged, and the barrels were labeled and ready for shipping.

The handling of the lard was a separate operation. It was sorted into two classes—leaf lard and rough lard—then rendered in kettles over wood-fired furnaces. Eight to ten men would be assigned to this task, producing about two hundred kegs, or nine thousand pounds daily.

Another operation was the production of bulk meat. This included the smoking of hams, which were taken from the smaller hogs. At this time it was said (in Cincinnati, of course) that "better hams cannot be procured than those smoked in Cincinnati."

By the late 1860s and 1870s, Cincinnati meat packers were averaging nearly two million hams and shoulders a year. The hogs were raised all over the Western states—many running free and feeding on beechnuts, hickory nuts, fodder and corn. Some hogs were attached to large distilleries and fattened on the warm slop from the still and mash tubs. (I wonder how these self-marinated pigs must have tasted!)

The slaughter- and packinghouses were even further streamlined. Hogs would arrive not only on foot, but by steamboat, flat boat and train in crates especially constructed for this purpose. Often the hogs would be transferred from the trains to temporary holding pens along the railroad tracks before being moved on to pens at the slaughterhouses.

As the number of hogs being processed increased, changes were made —all geared toward efficiency. In large establishments, the curing process now took place in two stories of cellars. These rooms were cold and damp and the floor was covered with salt. As the meat was sent by chute into the room, it was rubbed with salt and laid in piles three feet high—in the style of masonry. In a few days the meat stacks were taken down, and the meat was resalted and restacked. This was done repeatedly until the meat reached a height of ten feet.

For "sugar curing," the hams were treated with a small amount of salt-peter and left to lie for twenty-four hours. They were then put in a mixture of brine and molasses, which was renewed in ten days. Sugar-cured hams were finished in many different ways, depending on the market for which they were destined.

The pig's popularity commercially

Other businesses were founded from the by-products of the meat-packing industry. The pig's bones became buttons, Stearns & Foster used the pig's hair and bristles for making furniture, and Procter & Gamble began the manufacture of soaps and candles—an industry built on the pig's fats and oils. Other by-products that had no obvious uses were turned into fertilizer. At one time, the prosperity for which the pig was a symbol even caused it to be used as currency. (In Kentucky, during the pig's heyday, hogs were actually used in place of money in buying real estate.)

Changes in breeding practices

With the flourishing of the meat-packing industry and the coming of railroads, breeding practices of the pig changed. Many Americans who were born before World War II became aware of these changes as they grew up, noticing a discernible difference in leanness and quality.

In early America, the pig was originally bred to be able to walk to market. After railroads were established, this was no longer important and in the mid to late 1800s, pigs were bred to have a high fat content. A brown spotted hog known as the Poland China, for example, was developed in Ohio's Miami Valley. Because it came to be marketed on the eve of the Civil War, its impact on the meat-packing industry was only marginal. The number of pigs slaughtered between the 1820s and the 1840s jumped from about 12,000 to roughly 300,000, and by 1872 to 450,000. At this time the Poland China pig was finally officially recognized as a separate breed. It was this fatter breed that helped attain Cincinnati's world recognition. These fatter pigs, classified as the "lard type," had more fat in proportion to meat than other breeds. (In pictures, their small legs are almost obscured by the bulk of their bellies.) These were the pigs Americans were accustomed to eating until the 1940s. When a fat pig was the standard of perfection, it was said that 4-H Club members would sit with their prized pigs under heat lamps all night before a judging. The warmth of the lamps would make the pig appear soft and malleable to the touch—emphasizing a great wealth of fat beneath the skin.

During this same period, pigs in western Europe were being bred for longer bodies, uniform belly thickness and less fat. These pigs were called the "bacon type." Careful and selective crossbreeding resulted in the development of fatter or leaner pigs, depending on demand. In 1823 the English Berkshire, which had little excess fat, was the popular breed and in 1934 the favorite was the long-bodied Danish Landrace—the name sounding more like a sports car than a pig.

An increased demand for leaner meat and substitutions for pig fat motivated American breeders to produce a leaner, longer-bodied pig. This they achieved by crossing lard types with bacon types. Originally the pig was as prized for its fat and by-products as its meat: the fat was transformed into soaps and candles, lubricants for industrial use and even fertilizer, as well as lard for cooking; the pig's hair and bristles were used to stuff furniture and mattresses, as well as for brushes for grooming. However, by 1950 vegetable oils were being used in increasing amounts in cooking and for soap; petroleum products were used as lubricants; and man-made fibers had replaced the demand for hair and bristles. Only the use of the pig's skin remains undiminished.

Edible Parts of the Pig

From our useful pig, the head gives us brains—delicious in brown butter, dotted with capers—tongue, throat, jowl, ears, lips, and muzzle (snout), all wonderful pickled in fragrant brine laced with spices and molded into headcheese, a French *salade de museau,* or a jellied German *Sülze.* The feet (trotters), hocks (knuckles), shanks and tail can be stewed and used in salads or gilded with mustard and bread crumbs and grilled until crisp. Head, tail and feet, joined together in cooking with herbs and other aromatics, compose *brawn,* a special headcheese, favored by the English.

Within the pig lies the heart, liver and kidneys, the secret ingredients of many a fine pâté; the bladder—raised to fame by Paul Bocuse, who liked to poach a chicken in it *(en vessie);* the stomach (tripe) used for French *andouillettes* and other delectable sausages; and the intestines, which are used as casings in the more than two hundred kinds of sausages found in meat counters across America.

A wealth of sustenance before we even begin to consider the eminently edible cuts of meat. (The names of these cuts of meat come from the guide to retail cuts published by the National Live Stock and Meat Board.)

Shoulder

The upper shoulder provides clear plate and fat trimmings, the Boston butt, blade steak, boneless rolled Boston butt and smoked shoulder butt. Ground pork for a multitude of uses, particularly sausages, is often taken from this part of the pig.

Whether in one piece or cut into cubes, meat from the shoulder is succulent and moist, perfect for barbecuing, long-simmering soups and stews. Cut into strips, raw or cooked, it can be tossed in a wok with vegetables and a spicy sauce.

The lower part of the shoulder (one of the less expensive cuts of the pig) is called the picnic. Picnic is not quite as lean and tender as the upper part of the shoulder, but it can be used in much the same manner. Retail cuts labeled fresh picnic, smoked picnic, boneless rolled picnic, canned picnic and canned luncheon meat all come from the lower shoulder. Add fresh and smoked hocks and the pig's feet and this section of the pig is complete.

Loin

The most expensive meat of the pig comes from the loin area, which, in relation to the pig's knuckles and feet, is very definitely high on the hog, as in the expression, "living high on the hog." This cut was symbolic of meat for the wealthy, and to be able to enjoy the loin was a sign of good times and living well.

The loin runs along the backbone, protected by a layer of fatback. It supplies the blade loin roast and chops, center loin roast with rib and loin chops, top loin chops, butterfly chops, boneless rolled loin roast and tenderloin. The loin is delicious barbecued and the meat is equally good hot or cold; it is most often associated with traditional recipes cooked with love and care for special occasions. A loin of pork roasted on a bed of potatoes makes the perfect Sunday dinner for the family on a winter's day, and a roast pork stuffed with prunes and apricots, accompanied by a robust wine sauce, has all the elegance required for the centerpiece of a formal dinner party. Also from the loin area is the sirloin roast, sirloin chop, smoked loin chop and Canadian-style bacon (the only bacon not from the belly), as well as country-style spareribs and back ribs.

Belly

Beneath the loin is the belly. The lean and fatty sections of meat are cut away from the ribs and sold as bacon and salt pork. The bones that are left are spareribs, to barbecue to our heart's delight. Bacon and salt pork, though low on the scale of meats from the pig, should not be sold short (unless you are a commodities broker). Any competent cook knows their worth and, in some instances, subtle as their contribution might be, our fine pâtés could hardly do without them.

Ham

Last, but not least, is the economical leg or ham, the hind leg of a hog.

A leg that is not cured is called a fresh ham. It could also be called a leg of fresh pork, nothing whatsoever having been done to the meat, but fresh ham is the term generally used.

There are basically four kinds of cured ham: the dry aged country hams of the South with their strong salty tang; ham cured with its natural juices; ham with water added (most common in supermarkets across the country); and ham with water and by-products added. Each kind is cured and processed differently.

The dry aged country hams of the South are renowned, particulary those of Smithfield. The art of curing country hams has changed very little since the first settlers of Jamestown made their hams. A few of the oldest firms, who regard their "recipe" as almost sacred, have not changed their curing methods in three hundred years. The length of time, the temperature and humidity at each stage of the curing process are all significant factors in the final taste and texture of the finished ham. It is still strongly believed that the true secret of a fine ham relies on the human element: the sense of touch, smell and sight—the way a ham looks—judgments that can be made only by a skilled individual. The art of curing a ham has been compared to that of a wine maker blending wine.

The State of Virginia Charter declares that a ham bearing the name of Smithfield must be cured for at least six months and within the town limits. The law has been changed only once: in 1966 the legislature dropped a provision requiring that the hogs be raised in Smithfield and that they be peanut-fed. Cost and harvesting techniques have made it impractical for pigs to forage in peanut fields, and the use of pesticides put an end to this practice. Today there are only four producers left within the Smithfield town limits.

Today most of the hogs that provide the hams of the South are corn-fed in the Midwest. The hams are selected for their leanness, but what is of special importance to producers is the way the hogs are slaughtered. A long shank, which serves as a handle, is needed for hanging the hams, and some firms that do not have their own slaughtering facilities look as far away as Canada for the butchering expertise that will give the hams their characteristic long shank and untrimmed butt end.

Country hams are packed in salt, sometimes rubbed with sugar and other seasonings, and stored at a constant temperature of 39° to 40° F. for a varying number of weeks (about seven weeks for Smithfield hams). Before hanging they are given a good rubbing of pepper. The practice of rubbing Virginia hams with black pepper was originally employed to ward off insects, not to flavor the meat. The use of pepper has continued only because without it, a Smithfield or Virginia ham would surely be suspect. Next the hams are hung in smokehouses (about two weeks for Smithfield hams) to take on flavor from the smoldering hardwood ashes of a combination of apple, oak and hickory logs. The hams are then aged at least six months and, on occasion, several years. The latter are expensive: they can lose a third of their original weight from dehydration, which intensifies their flavor.

While modern technology makes it possible to control the temperature and humidity in the atmosphere surrounding the hams, there are still operations scattered throughout the South—such as Henson and Courtner's in Tennessee and Newsom's in Kentucky—that rely totally on the traditional three-seasons approach, risking the vicissitudes of weather. (The Newsom's "recipe" came from an old family will dating back to the 1600s.)

Checking hams for spoilage before they are shipped is still somewhat primitive, a test unchanged and unimproved upon by modern methods. A skilled worker punctures the aging ham with an ice pick and with a sniff of the pick, knows in an instant if a ham has gone bad. After many years' experience, some specialists can tell if a ham has spoiled simply by thumping it with the handle of the pick.

Not all country hams are smoked. Smoking the ham to dry it, as a way of preservation, is the specialty in humid coastal areas—where a ham isn't considered a ham unless it *is* smoked. But inland, within some of these same states (Virginia, Kentucky and Tennessee), high up along the Appalachians, there is little humidity and the air is dry enough to preserve the hams without smoke.

These salt-cured country hams *always* need a good scrubbing and a long soaking before they are cooked. Most hams should be soaked at least twenty-four hours to free them of some of their saltiness, but for the longer-aged and saltier hams, three days is not unreasonable. When soaking a ham, change the water daily or, if possible, more often. Be forewarned: It will be several days after purchasing a ham before it makes its appearance on the dinner table. *Always* read the producer's instructions as soon as you buy the ham, if not before.

A much misunderstood characteristic of these hams is the frequent presence of a blue-gray or green mold. This is perfectly normal and simply a reaction of the moisture of the ham to the temperature and humidity of the air. It will disappear when the ham is scrubbed.

The ham will surely be salty; it should therefore be cut in slices as close to paper-thin as possible (similar to prosciutto). Country ham is served (in delicate portions) most often with biscuits or other somewhat bland foods, which act as a foil for the salt. A country ham is properly served as a garnish or a second meat. Tradition calls for serving it as a second meat because of the need to balance the saltiness. Few people will consume more than an ounce or two of country ham at a meal.

You will usually find the ham as part of a buffet table. If the occasion is a brunch, it will be served with scrambled eggs and, normally, there will be a somewhat bland but popular seafood dish such as oysters or crab in a cream-based sauce. Turkey or chicken would also be served, with condiments of a sweet-sour nature like pickled fruits.

Country ham can also be found combined with seafood or poultry in dishes like jambalaya or oysters and ham in patty shells. In the South, it is often used in eggs Benedict.

A country ham is perfect fare for a cocktail party, brunch or reception. Serving a country ham during the Christmas holiday season is a tradition in the South.

Specialty Hams

Specialty hams, which rely on their own natural juices for moistness, can be found in many parts of the United States. Most of these hams include sugar in their cure. This has several advantages: sugar speeds up the cure and contributes flavor. If the sugar cure is in the form of a liquid solution (molasses, honey, maple syrup, etc.) rather than a dry mixture of salt and sugar, the need for soaking before cooking can usually be eliminated. A country ham, despite an addition of sugar, is predominately a dry salt cure and will still need soaking. The proportion of sugar mixed with salt in the cure of a country ham is roughly 1 to 5 or, as Colonel Newsom's daughter Nancy says, "just enough sugar to knock the edge off the salt."

When smoked, these hams will gather flavor from the kind of wood that is used, which varies in different parts of the country. Arkansas and Kentucky use green hickory, alone or combined with sassafras; Vermont uses corncobs and applewood or hickory; Nueske's in Wisconsin is noted for its applewood, although they also smoke ham over embers of pecan, cherry and plum wood; and in the Sierra Nevada mountains of California, Roi Ballard uses 300-year-old fallen mahogany logs for smoking.

Other specialty hams take their names from the country of origin but are produced in the United States.

Domestic prosciutto is our version of the world-famous dry-cured unsmoked ham of Italy. It is cured purely with salt, not nitrite or nitrate, and aged for about a year. Prosciutto is usually sold boneless and pressed (today, this is done by machine with a special mold) to achieve its traditional flat shape and to make slicing easier. Prosciutto is less salty than our country ham and the best prosciutto is mild and sweet tasting.

Westphalian ham is a dry-cured boneless German-style ham, not as salty as country ham and similar to prosciutto, but smoked. It takes its flavor from juniper twigs and berries added to a beechwood fire; sometimes juniper berries are incorporated into the salt cure.

Black Forest ham is boneless ham much like Westphalian ham, except more heavily smoked. Its characteristic black color comes from smoking over soft wood containing tar resins, which adhere to the ham. The color may also be achieved by other means, such as a dipping in beef blood or soaking in a caramel solution.

Polish ham is a boneless round ham covered with a layer of fat and skin. After smoking, it is cooked in water to lower the salt content.

Other Kinds of Ham in America

These are the hams common in supermarkets. Although often labeled "ready to eat," most will profit from a long slow baking or further cooking by other methods.

Regular ham is sold with the bone in, the skin on or partially skinned, in portions of half or whole hams and has been partially cooked to an internal temperature of 137°F.

Cooked ham is most frequently called "boiled ham" (however, the USDA will not allow it to be labeled as such because it is not literally boiled). It is water or steam cooked in a mold to a temperature of 148°F. (considered cooked) or to 155°F. This bland unsmoked ham is commonly used for so-called luncheon meat.

Baked ham   is a term that can be applied only to a ham cooked by direct dry heat. The internal temperature, by government standards, must reach 170°F.

Water added   means the ham may, by law, contain up to 10 percent additional water but no more than that. This is injected during the curing process and is often smoke flavored. During cooking some of the moisture of a ham is lost. If only enough water is added to return the ham to its original weight, it can still be labeled HAM. If the result, however, is anywhere between 1 percent and 10 percent more than the original weight, the ham must be labeled HAM, WATER ADDED.

Ham with water by-products   means that along with water, parts of the pig other than the ham have been added. (By law, the label must state the percentage of "added ingredients.")

Sectioned (or chunked) and formed ham   is a boneless ham that is taken apart and tenderized by tumbling or massaging, then reassembled in a casing or mold. It is usually defatted during this process.

Skinless-shankless ham   has all of the skin and shank removed, but the leg bone and aitchbone remain.

Smoked ham   is either smoked naturally or has had an application of regenerated liquid smoke.

Smoke flavoring added   means that liquid smoke is incorporated during the curing process.

Canned ham   is boneless with up to 7 percent water added. It is usually not smoked. After curing, the hams are vacuum-sealed in cans, then cooked. Gelatin is added to help retain the natural juices. Canned hams are perishable and are marked PERISHABLE—KEEP REFRIGERATED.

Picnic hams   are not true hams since they are cut from the lower part of the shoulder and a ham is the hind leg of the hog. Technically, there is no such thing as a picnic ham, but under this designation it is sold fresh or cured and smoked, with or without bone. Because of their size, picnic hams come in handy at times when a large true ham might be daunting.

The butt or Boston butt   is a moist and tender cut from the upper part of the shoulder and is sold both fresh or cured and smoked. Clearly not a ham, it is listed here because when cured and smoked, the meat can sometimes be substituted for ham when a small amount is needed.

Raw Ham

There is a very special *raw* ham, which is never served cooked, although bits and pieces of the meat may be used to add character to a dish based on other ingredients. This air-dried ham is cured to be eaten as is with good crusty bread and butter. For a sampling of this marvelous ham, look for the newly imported Parma ham of Italy, back in our markets, at last, after an absence of almost twenty-two years. Until its recent availability in the United States, the closest approximation we had to the famous raw hams of Europe was domestic prosciutto, or prosciutto imported from Canada or Switzerland.

The Italian hogs used for Parma hams are almost twice the size of American hogs and are fattened on a diet of whey, a by-product of the manufacture of Parmesan cheese. The hams are cured with sea salt only and then hung for over a year to age. Their fine quality is attributed to the remarkable climate of the Po Valley.

Since the early 1800s England has produced the famed York (i.e., Yorkshire) ham; Spain is known for its fine Asturian and *serrano* hams; in Portugal there is *presunto;* the Black Forest and Westphalian hams of Germany are famous; and there are Hungarian hams, Prague hams, Polish hams, Belgium's Ardennes ham and, my favorite, the *jambons crus* of France—the oldest and best-known being *jambon de Bayonne.* Crisscrossing France, I have tried them all from Normandy, Brittany, Toulouse, the Auvergne, the Morvan, Burgundy, Lorraine, Alsace, the Vosges and the Savoy. I love these as well as all the local hams *(jambon de pays),* which make a perfect lunch or picnic on the road.

Special Fats from the Pig

Pork belly   designates that part of the pig between the rib cage and the pelvis. This part of the pig is the source of fats as well as meats, varying from surprisingly lean sections to areas of pure fat with barely a streak of meat, if any. (Pork bellies are a volatile commodity, attracting more than average attention on the Chicago Mercantile Exchange.)

Corned belly   is a fresh piece of belly cured with salt for preservation. Corned belly and salt pork are the same thing. When a recipe calls for salt pork, unless otherwise specified, I mean for the reader to use good-quality belly that is as streaky with meat as possible, not the salt-encrusted, virtually meatless white blob sold in many supermarkets. In European meat markets, all types of belly, from somewhat fatty to the very leanest, are commonly available. In the United States, I find German butchers, particularly those who make sausages, the most reliable and accommodating source for both good-quality lean slab belly and bacon.

When curing is followed by smoking, the result is bacon. Except for Canadian bacon, all bacon is from the belly.

Top-quality belly is meaty enough to be served on its own. A lean slab of belly can be sliced like bacon and cooked in the same way. (When slicing thin strips of belly yourself, the task is much easier if the meat is partially frozen.) Thinly sliced, the leanest belly resembles prosciutto. It makes a delicious wrapping for roasted or grilled game birds and a thick slab is frequently included in a classic *choucroute garnie* or the long-simmered mélange of vegetables, cabbage and beans known as *potée*. Cooked with lentils, it is the foundation of a *petit salé*.

Pancetta   is cured belly formed into a roll. It is sold cut in round slices. It is not smoked.

Lardons   are small strips of smoked bacon or salt pork. They are usually sautéed as an addition or enrichment to other dishes (including salads), but are also used for larding very lean meats. In this case, the strips are more often called *lardoons* and cut as long as needed. Lardons for sautéing should be lean and meaty and are cut from a slab into thick strips, roughly ¼ inch wide x 1 inch long.

Canadian bacon   comes from the loin. It is not true bacon and is considerably leaner than bacon from the belly.

Fatback   is exactly what its name implies. The firm high-quality fat runs along the back, above the loin, from the clear plate at the shoulder to the tail. It is good for melting and is malleable enough to make it perfect for lining the terrines in which fine pâtés are made. It is also used for barding and larding extra-lean meats and game birds. Sometimes sheets of fat from the jowl, not quite so delicate, are used as a substitute.

Leaf lard   is found in the interior of the loin and surrounding the kidneys; it is the purest, most delicate fat of the pig. It is soft and melts easily, and is most often used for pâtés and preserving meats, an example being French *confits*. Rendered, it makes the finest lard.

Lard   is the fluid or semisolid rendered fat of the pig, refined to a state that can be used for cooking or the enrichment of sausages or pastry dough.

Caul fat   is the membrane enclosing the stomach. The weblike sheets are most often used to wrap liver, heart, kidneys and delicate meats that supply no fat of their own. Since it melts rapidly when cooked, it is useful as a method of basting and is frequently employed in brochets. Leaves of sage, rosemary and thyme are sometimes tucked between the meat and the fat.

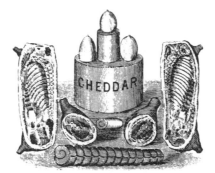

Foreign Products

Larger and better-stocked Oriental and Asian supermarkets carry a multitude of products from China, Japan, Korea, Thailand, the Philippines, India and virtually all the countries of Asia and Southeast Asia where trade is permissible.

Black beans are labeled as fermented, spiced, or salted—all mean the same thing. The beans are soft, heavily salted and partially dried. After their cellophane package is opened, they will keep forever in the refrigerator. Soak before using to remove some of the salt.

Chinese chili pastes are highly concentrated and sold in eight-ounce jars. Their composition varies; the pastes I use are Chili Paste with Black Bean and Chili Paste with Garlic. I use Lan Chi brand, made in Taiwan, China.

Coconut milk. For information on how to make coconut milk, see page 81.

Fish sauce is an important ingredient in Thai cooking. It is manufactured in countries besides Thailand and each has its name for the product, printed in its own language. Somewhere on the label, in English, the ingredients will list fish extract or anchovy extract, water and salt. The sauce I like best is made in Hong Kong by the Pin Dhian Fishgravy Company.

Korean hot bean mash is sold in jars ranging from one pint to a giant eight cups. It is more like a thick sauce than a paste and is sometimes simply called ''hot sauce.'' There are two kinds; both are composed of soy bean mash and chiles, but the more expensive one also includes sesame seeds in the ingredients. Examining the two jars, which usually carry the same label, will show the difference. I use several brands; all are manufactured in Long Island City, New York.

Oriental egg noodles, fresh or frozen, can be found in stores that stock Asian products. They are sold cooked and uncooked. The weight is about the same either way, but if only dry noodles are available, use less. Cooked noodles are coated with oil, but follow the same procedure for preparation as for fresh noodles: drop them into boiling water, but for no longer than one minute, or just long enough to rinse away the oil. If the noodles are frozen, they should be defrosted first so they cook evenly. Fresh homemade or store-bought pasta can also be used, or, if absolutely necessary, substitute dry American and Italian brand egg noodles.

Pomegranate juice is sold in stores that carry Middle Eastern products. Sometimes it is called "grenadine molasses." Pomegranate juice and tamarind liquid are usually interchangeable in recipes. If unobtainable, substitute fresh lime juice.

Pressed bean curd. For information on pressed bean curd, see page 145.

Rice vinegar is available in several varieties. Japanese brands are superior to others. Mild rice vinegar is sweet and sometimes flavored, and not at all harsh. Strong rice vinegar is full strength, with the same acidity as most vinegars.

Soy sauce is also available in several varieties. I alternate between three kinds: mild soy sauce, which is slightly lower in sodium and less salty (not to be confused with "light soy sauce," where light refers to color); regular soy sauce, which is somewhere in the middle—a basic all-purpose soy sauce; and dark (or black) soy sauce, which is very intense and syrupy. Always buy a good-quality imported soy sauce rather than a domestic brand.

Tamarind is sold in both Middle Eastern and Asian markets. Tamarind liquid is made by soaking a walnut-size piece of tamarind pulp in a half-cup of hot water for one hour or longer. Strain the liquid through a fine sieve, pressing down hard on the tamarind.

Vietnamese chili sauces are the fieriest I know. It is the flavor underlying the heat that makes them so appealing. Two that I use most are *túóng ót tói Vietnam,* a loose-textured chili garlic sauce, bright red-orange in color (particles of chile pepper provide both an attractive red-speckled texture and a noticeable boost of spice); and *tia chieu sa-té,* a darker, highly concentrated pepper saté, as intensely flavorful as it is fiery. Both are made in Rosemead, California, by Huy Fong Foods, Inc.

THE
PREPRANDIAL
PIG

Vietnamese Pork and Shrimp Balls in Lettuce Leaves
·
Thai Spicy Herb Sauce
·
Tuscan Pork and Chicken Liver Spread for Grilled Toast
·
Clams in Wine with Ham and Parsley Sauce
·
Mireille's Prunes Wrapped in Bacon
·
Wontons
·
Wontons in Chili and Scallion Sauce
·
Yorkshire Pudding with Cheese and Sausage
·
Clams Stuffed with Bacon and Herbs
·
Prosciutto with Figs

Chile-Pork Empanadas

·

Spring Rolls

·

Indonesian Pork Balls with Coconut

·

Vietnamese Spring Rolls Wrapped in Rice Paper

·

Ham and Cheese Pastry with Chile Peppers

·

Periwinkles and Lardons with Wine and Tomatoes

·

Parsleyed Ham in Wine Aspic

·

Pheasant or Chicken Pâté with Fresh Herbs

·

Country Pâté with Pork Liver

·

Terrine of Jellied Pork and Rabbit

·

Coarse Country Pâté with Duck, Pork, Green Peppercorns and Pistachios

·

Country Pâté with Saddle of Rabbit

Call it an appetizer, hors d'oeuvre, amuse-gueule or tapas. It is that "little something"—a preamble to the meal—to quell the pangs of hunger, whet the appetite or fortify in the event of strong libation. Partaken informally before the meal or seated at the table to herald its beginning, the selection of such delectables is infinite, be it a plate of purple figs with prosciutto in the old-world elegance of a London hotel or platters of empanadas on the shore of a lake with the clan in wet bathing suits.

That little something can comprise almost anything: warm prunes wrapped in bacon, hot pastries flavored with ham and cheese, delicate spring rolls, pork and shrimp balls, clams in wine with ham and parsley sauce. For special occasions, there are pâtés and terrines—classics composed of rabbit, pheasant, duck, liver and ham—dense with meats bound together by a pork forcemeat and redolent of herbs and spices.

Vietnamese Pork and Shrimp Balls
in Lettuce Leaves

With garden lettuces used for wrapping and the fresh herbs of summer for flavoring, these meatballs make a welcome and highly attractive platter. Tucked into separate leaves, the balls may also be used as a garnish for other dishes. Do not serve them piping hot, as the flavor will be masked; warm is preferable.

As a variation, try using the meat mixture as a filling for wontons.

SERVES 6 TO 8 AS AN APPETIZER

¾ pound ground pork
1 extra-large egg, lightly beaten
1 tablespoon cornstarch
1 tablespoon dry sherry
¼ teaspoon sugar
1 tablespoon mild imported soy sauce
1 scant cup (½ ounce) dried shiitake mushrooms, soaked, squeezed dry and chopped
½ pound shrimp, peeled, deveined and chopped
4 large whole scallions, finely chopped (about ⅔ cup)
8 canned water chestnuts, finely chopped
2 tablespoons finely chopped fresh ginger

2 large cloves garlic, finely chopped
2 tablespoons chopped fresh basil leaves
2 tablespoons chopped fresh mint leaves
2 tablespoons chopped fresh coriander leaves
1 tablespoon imported sesame oil
Tender lettuce leaves, such as Boston or Bibb
A handful each fresh basil, fresh mint and fresh coriander leaves, cut into shreds or coarsely chopped
Sweet red onion slices or scallion brushes
Thai Spicy Herb Sauce (page 35)

Combine all the ingredients except the sesame oil, lettuce, shredded herbs, onion slices and herb sauce. Mix well and refrigerate for at least 1 hour before cooking. (This can also be done a day in advance.)

Preheat the oven to 350°F. Line a baking sheet with foil and grease the foil with sesame oil.

With moist fingers, form small meatballs, about an inch in diameter and arrange them on the baking sheet.

Bake the meatballs for 30 to 40 minutes, or until lightly browned. Turn them once or twice during cooking. Before serving, run them under the broiler briefly, until nicely browned.

TO SERVE

Line a large platter with lettuce leaves, arranged like scoops. Scatter half the combined herbs over the lettuce, taking care that each leaf contains some of each. Depending on the size of the leaves, nest 1 or 2 meatballs in each, then scatter the rest of the herbs over all. Intersperse a garnish of onion slices or scallion brushes around the platter.

Spoon a little sauce over each portion, then fold the lettuce around the meatballs; pass the remaining sauce separately. Eat with your fingers or chopsticks.

Thai Spicy Herb Sauce

Make this sauce in advance but on the same day it is to be served; otherwise, the herbs will lose their bright green color.

MAKES ABOUT 1 CUP

¼ cup fish sauce from Thailand
¼ cup freshly squeezed lime juice
¼ teaspoon sugar
2 tablespoons finely chopped hot green chile pepper
1 tablespoon minced garlic
1 tablespoon minced fresh ginger
1 tablespoon, or more, finely chopped fresh basil leaves

1 tablespoon, or more, finely chopped fresh mint leaves
1 large whole scallion, finely chopped
2 tablespoons chopped fresh coriander leaves
4 tablespoons water

Combine all the ingredients in a bowl, then taste the sauce. More lime juice may be desired, tempered with another dash of sugar. If the sauce is too harsh, thin with a little more water.

Tuscan Pork and Chicken Liver Spread
for Grilled Toast
CROSTINI

Crostini are served hot or warm, with the cooked pureed meats spread on thick slices of grilled toast. The bread should be slightly stale so it will withstand being dipped into broth before toasting. A coarse-grained round French or Italian country loaf is perfect for this.

SERVES 12 AS AN APPETIZER OR 6 AS A FIRST COURSE

4 tablespoons olive oil
1 cup chopped onion
1 small inner-stalk celery with leaves, chopped
1 small carrot, chopped
½ teaspoon fresh thyme leaves *or* a pinch of dried thyme
1 pound ground pork
½ pound chicken livers, cut into small pieces
½ cup (about ½ ounce) imported dried cèpes or porcini mushrooms, soaked, squeezed dry and chopped
1 rounded tablespoon finely chopped garlic
1 pound ripe tomatoes, peeled, seeded and chopped *or* 2 cups chopped canned Italian plum tomatoes, well drained

Freshly grated nutmeg
Freshly ground pepper
½ cup dry white wine
About ¾ cup strong beef stock
Coarse salt (optional)
1 tablespoon cognac or brandy
2 tablespoons butter
2 tablespoons finely chopped fresh parsley
2 teaspoons chopped fresh tarragon leaves *or* 1 teaspoon dried tarragon, crumbled
Olive oil for the baking sheet
1-pound loaf slightly stale French or Italian bread, cut into thick slices, then into 2½-inch squares

Heat the oil in a large skillet and add the onion, celery and carrot. Sauté over medium heat, stirring frequently, until the onion is soft and lightly colored. Add the thyme, then the pork, and cook, stirring to break up the meat. When the pork is fully cooked, push it to the side and add the chicken livers.

As the livers brown, combine them with the pork. Then remove the meats and add the mushrooms and garlic to the skillet. Cook a few minutes, stirring continuously; add the tomatoes and raise the heat. When tomato juices have reduced, return the livers and pork. Sprinkle generously with nutmeg and pepper and cook a few minutes longer, stirring frequently.

Pour the wine into the skillet and reduce until the liquid is almost cooked away. Add ¼ to ⅓ cup of stock, just enough to moisten the mixture. Taste for seasoning and add salt, if needed. Off heat, add the cognac and butter. Stir until the butter is thoroughly incorporated, then mix in the parsley and tarragon.

Cool the mixture slightly, then puree it in a food processor or blender. The consistency should be coarse; this is best achieved by pureeing it in several batches.

Preheat the broiler. Pour enough olive oil onto a large baking sheet to coat the bottom liberally. (Use 2 baking sheets, if necessary.) Pour the remaining stock into a soup plate. Take slices of bread, one at a time, and dip each side quickly in and out of the broth. Then, after wiping each side in the oil, arrange on the baking sheet. Slide the baking sheet under the broiler for just long enough to brown the bread lightly. Then turn the slices and brown the other side.

A few minutes before serving, spread the puree lavishly on the toast, then return it to the broiler only until the puree is hot.

Clams in Wine with Ham and Parsley Sauce

ALMEJAS Y JAMÓN A LA MARINERA

In Spain, the clams for this dish would be very small and the quantity much greater. Such tiny clams are almost impossible to find in this country outside of the Pacific Northwest, but the smallest size littlenecks are a very good substitute.

Accompanied by lots of good crusty bread to soak up the sauce, this appetizer could also constitute a meal for two.

SERVES 4 TO 8 AS AN APPETIZER

2 dozen very small littleneck clams
Salt
⅓ cup olive oil
½ teaspoon crushed dried red chile peppers *or* 1 fresh chile pepper, seeded and finely chopped
1 cup chopped onion
4 to 5 large cloves garlic, chopped
2 large fresh plum tomatoes, cut into large dice

Freshly ground pepper
1 or 2 sprigs fresh oregano, leaves stripped from the stems *or* 1 teaspoon dried oregano
1 small bay leaf
⅔ cup dry white wine
½ cup finely chopped fresh parsley
2 ounces cooked ham or prosciutto, coarsely chopped (about ½ cup)

Several hours before cooking, scrub the clams and soak them in a large basin of cold salted water. Change the water and wash the clams several times, until the water remains clear and free of sediment when stirred.

Heat the olive oil in a casserole large enough to hold the clams in one layer. Add the chile pepper and onion. When the onion softens, add half the garlic. Cook briefly, then add the tomatoes, a generous grinding of pepper, the rest of the garlic, the oregano and bay leaf. When the tomatoes are bubbling nicely, pour in the white wine and bring to a boil.

Reduce the sauce slightly, lower the heat and stir in half the parsley. Then add the ham, mixing to combine, followed by the clams, arranged side by side. Sprinkle with a little more parsley, saving some to add when the clams have opened.

Cover the casserole and simmer about 10 minutes, or until all the clams have opened. As they cook, check them frequently, each time spooning the sauce over them. When the clams have opened, sprinkle with the remaining parsley. Discard any that do not open.

Serve from the casserole or, if this is to be a first course, capture the flavor of Spain by serving the clams in small individual terra-cotta casseroles. Be sure to accompany the clams with a basket of good crusty bread.

Mireille's Prunes Wrapped in Bacon

Mireille MacCarthy is a French friend of mine, married to an American. Whenever we dine at her house, I look forward to her appetizers, which almost always include these delicious prunes. Served piping hot with drinks before dinner, they are one of my favorite *amuse gueules*.

This is a simple appetizer that can serve any number of people. Depending on the size of the prunes, two or three per person would be enough. Allow half a slice of bacon for each prune.

Large pitted prunes
Hot freshly brewed tea
1 small strip orange zest

Walnut halves, split into **2** pieces
Lean meaty bacon, thinly sliced

One or 2 hours in advance of serving, place the prunes in a bowl with enough hot tea to cover. Add the orange zest and let steep until swelled.

Drain the prunes, insert a segment of walnut in the center of each one, and wrap it in half a slice of bacon, or enough to encircle the prune with the ends slightly overlapping. Secure the bacon with a toothpick and arrange the prunes, spread out, on a baking sheet.

Preheat the oven to 425°F. Shortly before serving, place the prunes in the oven and bake about 15 minutes. Turn them once or twice so the bacon is nicely crisped on all sides.

When done, transfer the prunes to a plate and serve.

Wontons

Wontons freeze nicely so it is worthwhile making a large quantity. They are tasty fried as an appetizer with dipping sauces or served in a pool of delectable chili and scallion sauce (page 42). They also create a hearty soup.

Many supermarkets and all Oriental grocery stores sell wonton skins.

MAKES 40 TO 60 WONTONS

FILLING

½ pound ground pork
1 egg, lightly beaten
⅛ teaspoon sugar
⅛ teaspoon freshly ground white pepper
1 tablespoon dry sherry

1 tablespoon imported soy sauce
1 tablespoon finely chopped fresh ginger
1 clove garlic, finely chopped
4 whole scallions, finely chopped
2 teaspoons imported sesame oil

40 to 60 wonton skins, preferably square
Salt

Peanut or corn oil for frying

Combine all the filling ingredients with a fork and let sit at room temperature for 1 hour before using.

FILLING THE WONTONS

Lightly moisten the edges of each wonton skin with cold water. Place a scant teaspoon of filling in the center and fold the skin in half. Press the edges together and fold in half again, making only a crease. Then take the 2 corners from the first fold and bring them together, crossing over each other slightly.

Press together, using a drop of water to help them stick. The result should resemble an old-fashioned nurse's cap, but as long as the filling is securely enclosed, the style of the fold is not that important.

COOKING

Fill a stockpot with salted water and bring to a vigorous boil. Drop in 8 to 10 wontons, all at once. Cook a few minutes, or until they all rise to the surface and remain there. Add 1 cup cold water and return to a boil. Use a strainer or slotted spoon to remove the wontons, drain, and spread out on 1 or 2 large baking sheets. Proceed with the next batch.

The wontons are now ready to use. If you plan to freeze some of them, wrap them, side by side, in a sheet of heavy aluminum foil.

TO FRY THE WONTONS

Heat 3 to 4 cups peanut or corn oil to 375°F. and drop in small batches of precooked wontons. As they become crisp and golden, remove, drain briefly on paper towels and serve at once.

TO MAKE A SIMPLE WONTON SOUP

Heat chicken broth to a boil and add wontons with sliced whole scallions. When the soup returns to a boil, it is ready. Serve with a basket of Fried Noodles (page 78). See also Hearty Wonton Soup (page 90).

Dipping Sauces

English or Chinese Mustard

Place several tablespoons of powdered mustard in a small round-bottomed dish. Stir in cold water, a little at a time, dissolving the mustard and thinning it to make a smooth paste. A drop of mild rice vinegar can be added if desired.

Soy Dipping Sauce

Combine 4 tablespoons imported soy sauce with 1 teaspoon strong or mild rice vinegar and 1 teaspoon imported sesame oil. Stir in 1 teaspoon minced fresh ginger and, if desired, a dash of dry sherry. Taste for seasoning.

Plum Sauce

Combine ½ cup plum sauce with 2 tablespoons imported soy sauce and 1 tablespoon strong rice vinegar or balsamic or cider vinegar. Stir together and warm the mixture slightly before serving.

Wontons in Chili and Scallion Sauce

Wontons prepared this way make a super first course. The dish can be assembled in advance and only needs reheating. How many wontons depends on the rest of the meal. Be forewarned: They will all be eaten!

SERVES 4 TO 6 AS A FIRST COURSE

2 cups Spicy Chicken Stock (page 77)
1 tablespoon sesame paste
1 tablespoon Vietnamese chili garlic
    sauce
1 tablespoon long, thin slivers fresh
    ginger

1 tablespoon long, threadlike strips
    orange zest, without pith
20 to 24 precooked wontons
    (pages 40–41)
3 to 4 whole scallions, very thinly sliced
Fresh coriander leaves (optional)

Bring the chicken stock to a simmer in a shallow casserole about 9½ inches in diameter. Stir in the sesame paste; when it is dissolved, add the chili garlic sauce and ginger.

Simmer briefly and add the orange zest, followed by the wontons. Carefully turn the wontons in the sauce until hot, then add the scallions, reserving a heaping tablespoon of the green tops. Spoon the sauce over the wontons only until the scallions are evenly distributed. Cover the casserole and remove from heat until ready to serve. (This should be within the hour.)

When ready, gently reheat the wontons and serve from the casserole or a deep serving dish. At the last moment, sprinkle with the reserved scallion tops and scatter a few coriander leaves over all. Tilt the casserole and spoon a little sauce over the surface of the wontons, then serve at once.

Yorkshire Pudding with Cheese and Sausage

Divided into thin wedges and served piping hot, this light and airy concoction based on Yorkshire pudding makes a terrific appetizer. The slices have enough body to be picked up and eaten with the fingers—an advantage at a cocktail party. Accompanied by a salad, it could also make an easy meal for two.
SERVES 6 TO 8 AS AN APPETIZER

2 extra-large eggs
¼ teaspoon finely ground white pepper
1 cup milk
1 scant cup flour, sifted with
    ½ teaspoon salt
2 tablespoons chopped fresh chives *or*
    fresh basil

1 clove garlic, flattened and peeled
About 2 tablespoons olive oil
1 or 2 large sweet Italian sausages (6 to
    8 ounces), cooked and thinly sliced
¼ pound Gruyère cheese, shredded

Preheat the oven to 450°F. Beat the eggs vigorously, then add the pepper and about half the milk. Continuing to beat, add the flour and the rest of the milk. When the batter is well blended, stir in the chives or basil, depending on your preference.

Rub a 13-inch tart or quiche pan with garlic, then discard the clove. Add enough olive oil to liberally coat the bottom and sides of the pan. Pour in the batter and arrange the slices of sausage evenly over the surface. Scatter the cheese over all.

Place the pan in the hot oven and bake 10 minutes, then lower the heat to 375°F. and cook 10 minutes longer. At this point, give the pan a 180° turn so that the pastry colors evenly. Bake 10 minutes longer, or until nicely browned.

Remove the pan from the oven. At first, this puffed creation will resemble a quiche, but then it collapses and looks more like a pizza. Serve hot, cut into large or small slices.

Clams Stuffed with Bacon and Herbs

SERVES 10 AS AN APPETIZER OR 5 AS A FIRST COURSE

18 cherrystone clams
¼ pound lean bacon, preferably in
   one piece
2 tablespoons olive oil
½ cup finely chopped onion
1 rounded tablespoon finely chopped
   shallot
1 tiny fresh hot chile pepper, seeded
   and minced

1 large garlic clove, finely chopped
1 large vine-ripened tomato (about 8
   ounces), peeled and chopped, or
   about 1¼ cups peeled and chopped
   plum tomatoes
Freshly ground pepper
½ cup homemade bread crumbs
½ cup chopped fresh herbs (see note)

ADVANCE PREPARATION

Scrub clams well with a stiff brush, then soak in cold salted water for at least 2 hours, changing the water several times. Give the clams a final scrubbing, then arrange in a large casserole, allowing plenty of room for them to open. Add 1 inch of water, cover and bring to a boil.

Lower the heat slightly, but make sure the clams continue to steam. Cook until all have opened, redistributing them occasionally. Discard any that do not open. Shuck the clams when cool enough to handle, and drop them into a bowl. Save the shells and broth.

Select 10 large, perfect shells; scrub them thoroughly and soak in scalding water. Later, scrub them again and wipe dry before stuffing with the clam mixture.

Strain the broth through a cloth. Submerge the shucked clams in the broth to keep them moist. If desired, save and freeze the excess broth.

STUFFING AND BAKING THE CLAMS

Preheat the oven to 475°F. Remove the rind from the bacon and chop the meat and fat into fine dice. Place in a skillet moistened with olive oil, and cook over low heat until lightly browned, stirring frequently.

Add the onion and shallot and continue to cook over low heat until softened. Add the chile pepper and garlic. Cook briefly, then raise the heat and add the tomato, discarding any accumulated juice. Add freshly ground pepper and cook only long enough for the excess juices to evaporate. Keep the mixture barely moist.

Drain the clams, then coarsely chop them by hand into pieces as small as possible. Stir the clams into the skillet and remove from the heat. Mix with the bread crumbs and fresh herbs. Taste for seasoning. Salt should not be needed.

Divide the stuffing among the shells and arrange them on a baking sheet. When ready to serve, place in the hot oven for barely 10 minutes, or just until sizzling hot. Because the shells are a wonderful conductor of heat, they can wait a few minutes, if necessary, before serving.

NOTE Depending on availability, combine parsley with thyme, oregano or basil, but allow parsley to predominate.

Prosciutto with Figs

SERVES 1

3 full slices imported prosciutto   **3 ripe figs**

For each serving, arrange 3 full slices of prosciutto side by side on a dinner plate.

Take 3 perfectly ripe figs and, working from the stem end down toward the base, quarter them, stopping about ½ inch above the base. Part the quarters without separating them.

Arrange the 3 figs, centered side by side across the slices of prosciutto. Spread them open just slightly, tulip-fashion.

Chile-Pork Empanadas

PICADILLO DE CERDO

I like to accompany this Mexican specialty with Thai Spicy Herb Sauce—a contrast of cuisines that, in this case, balance very well.

Tho dough for thoco ompanadas is also good for unsweetened pastry shells. It has the advantage of being easy to work with in warm weather.

MAKES ABOUT 15 EMPANADAS

SOUR CREAM PASTRY DOUGH

2 cups flour, sifted
1 teaspoon salt
1 teaspoon baking powder

8 tablespoons (1 stick) cold butter, cut into small pieces
½ cup sour cream

CHILE-PORK FILLING

3 tablespoons olive or peanut oil
1 cup finely chopped onion
2 to 3 fresh hot green chile peppers, seeded and thinly sliced
2 cloves garlic, finely chopped
1 pound lean ground pork
½ teaspoon coarse salt
1 tablespoon fresh oregano leaves *or* 1 teaspoon dried oregano
1 rounded tablespoon best-quality chili powder
1 tablespoon paprika
2 teaspoons ground cumin

1 egg mixed with 1 teaspoon cold water for a wash

¼ teaspoon ground allspice
¼ teaspoon ground cloves
Scant ¼ cup pine nuts, lightly toasted
½ cup water
2 tablespoons tomato paste
½ cup yellow raisins, soaked for 1 hour in lukewarm water, drained and patted dry with a towel
2 tablespoons capers, drained and chopped, if large
1 ripe plum tomato, peeled and chopped
12 small green pimiento-stuffed olives, cut in half

Thai Spicy Herb Sauce (page 35), optional

PREPARING THE DOUGH

Combine the flour, salt and baking powder in a food processor or by hand. Cut the butter into the flour until the texture resembles coarse meal, then add the sour cream and mix until the dough is smooth and well combined. Refrigerate 30 minutes, or until ready to use.

PREPARING THE FILLING

Heat the oil in a large skillet and add the onion. Cook, stirring frequently, until the onion has softened. Add the chile peppers and garlic. Cook briefly and add the ground pork, stirring to break it up.

When the meat loses its rosiness, add the salt, oregano and spices. When well incorporated, add the pine nuts and water. Cook briefly, stirring frequently; add a little more water if the juices reduce too quickly. Add the tomato paste, raisins, capers and chopped tomato and combine with the meat. Add more water, if necessary. Cook a few minutes longer and taste for seasoning. Add the olives and remove from heat. Let cool completely.

FINISHING THE EMPANADAS

Cut the chilled ball of dough into quarters. On a floured work surface, roll each portion out as thin as possible. Each piece should yield three 5-inch circles, with scraps remaining. Cut the circles, using a saucer as a guide. Combine the scraps and reroll; you should have 3 more circles.

Brush a narrow border of egg wash around each piece of dough, then place a rounded tablespoon of filling in the center, including as much sauce as possible. Fold the dough, bringing the edges together to form a half-circle. Press to seal, then crimp the edges with the tines of a fork. Refrigerate 15 minutes before baking.

Preheat the oven to 425°F. Before baking, brush each empanada lightly with egg wash. Bake 20 minutes.

Serve the empanadas piping hot or at least still warm.

Spring Rolls

Spring rolls are smaller and crisper than egg rolls. These spring rolls are a fair amount of work, but well worth it.

Since the preparation can be a bit tedious, try to space it out. Make the filling early in the day, then do the wrapping and frying later. There will be quite a lot of filling, but the rolls are so good, it is wise to allow at least two per person. I have known my family to consume five each and skip the rest of the meal.

MAKES ABOUT 30 SPRING ROLLS

½ pound medium shrimp, peeled, deveined and coarsely chopped
1 extra-large egg white
1 teaspoon dry sherry
Finely ground white pepper

6 to 8 ounces lean ground or hand-minced pork
⅛ teaspoon sugar
1 teaspoon cornstarch

SAUCE

1 teaspoon cornstarch
1 tablespoon dry sherry
2 tablespoons imported soy sauce

1 tablespoon fish sauce from Thailand
2 teaspoons imported sesame oil

About 6 tablespoons peanut oil
1¾ cups (about 1 ounce) dried shiitake mushrooms, soaked and squeezed dry, caps cut into thin slivers
7 or 8 scallions, finely chopped (about 1 cup)
2 cloves garlic, finely chopped
1 or 2 fresh hot chile peppers, seeded and finely chopped
1 tablespoon finely chopped fresh ginger
¾ cup chopped canned water chestnuts
1 small Chinese cabbage (about 1½ pounds), cut into thin shreds (about 8 cups)

3 tablespoons strong rice, cider or balsamic vinegar
1 rounded tablespoon coarsely chopped fresh basil leaves (optional)
30 large square spring-roll skins *or* extra-thin *egg-roll skins*
English or Chinese Mustard (page 41)
Thai Spicy Herb Sauce (page 35)
Plum Sauce (page 41)

ADVANCE PREPARATION

Combine the shrimp, half an egg white, the sherry and a pinch of pepper. Mix well and refrigerate for 1 hour.

Combine the pork, the remaining egg white, sugar and cornstarch. Mix well and refrigerate for 1 hour.

PREPARING THE FILLING

Make a sauce with the cornstarch, sherry, soy sauce, fish sauce and sesame oil.

Heat 3 tablespoons of the peanut oil in a wok and fry the shrimp quickly, just until they start to turn opaque. Remove and drain in a sieve.

If necessary, add 1 tablespoon more oil to the wok, then fry the pork. Stir, breaking up the meat, until thoroughly cooked. Remove and drain with the shrimp.

Wipe the wok with a paper towel and add 2 tablespoons fresh oil. Quickly fry the mushrooms over high heat. Lower the heat and add the scallions, garlic, chile peppers and ginger. Stir briefly, and add the water chestnuts. Raise the heat and pour in the sauce. Bring to a boil, stirring constantly. Return the shrimp and pork to the wok; when well combined, remove from the heat and add the cabbage.

Mix thoroughly, adding the vinegar a tablespoon at a time. Toss the cabbage; it will decrease in volume as it is tossed with the hot ingredients. Turn the filling into a bowl, stir in the basil and let cool completely.

FINISHING THE SPRING ROLLS

If there is an accumulation of juices in the bowl containing the filling, press down on it and pour them off. (Excess juice will make the wrappers soggy.)

Place on your work surface a spring-roll skin with a corner pointing toward you. Moisten all the edges with a little water, then mound a portion of filling, centered, near that corner. Allow about 2 tablespoons filling for each roll. Partially wrap the spring roll, bringing up the corner of the dough to enclose the filling and giving it 2 turns. Then tuck in the 2 facing corners, envelope-fashion, and continue to roll the package, compactly, until sealed completely. Set aside on a dry baking sheet lined with wax paper and proceed with the next spring roll.

Fry the spring rolls as soon as possible after they have been wrapped.

Heat 3 or 4 cups of oil in a wok to 375°F. Preheat the oven to 200° to 250°F. and line a baking sheet with paper towels.

Without crowding, fry 3 to 5 spring rolls at a time. As they float to the surface and brown, turn them and, if necessary, press them down under the oil until evenly browned. Before they color too much, drain and transfer to the baking sheet. Keep warm in the oven.

(Continued)

TO SERVE

As soon as the frying is completed, arrange the spring rolls on a napkin or doily-lined platter and serve at once, accompanied by hot mustard and sauces for dipping.

An alternative arrangement, in the style of Thai cuisine, would be to decorate the serving platter with lettuce leaves, quarters of ripe tomato and a cucumber, scored and sliced on the diagonal. Scallion brushes would also make an attractive addition to the platter.

Indonesian Pork Balls with Coconut

Accompanied with a dipping sauce, these flavorful meatballs make a winning appetizer. For a change, make them slightly smaller and serve tucked into Boston lettuce leaves strewn with chopped fresh herbs. Pass Thai Spicy Herb Sauce to spoon over each package.

SERVES 8 AS AN APPETIZER

3 extra-large eggs
1¼ pounds ground pork
1 teaspoon sugar
2 cups grated coconut (page 81)
Grated zest of 1 lemon
4 whole scallions, finely chopped
Freshly ground pepper, preferably white
1 rounded tablespoon finely chopped
  fresh ginger

1 rounded teaspoon chili paste with
  garlic
1 rounded tablespoon ground coriander
About ½ cup chopped fresh basil leaves
Several tablespoons peanut oil for frying
Thai Spicy Herb Sauce (page 35)

ADVANCE PREPARATION

Combine the ingredients (except the oil and the sauce) in the order listed, starting with 1 egg, then adding another after the coconut and the third egg at the end. Mix well after each addition. Before cooking, refrigerate the mixture from 1 hour to overnight.

FINISHING THE MEATBALLS

Use your fingers to form the meat mixture into small balls, about the size of a walnut, or slightly smaller if serving in lettuce leaves.

Preheat the oven to 200°F. and line a baking sheet with paper towels. Heat just enough oil to coat the bottom of 1 or 2 large cast-iron skillets. Drop in the meatballs without crowding and fry over medium heat until nicely browned on all sides and cooked through. When they are cooked, transfer the meatballs to the baking sheet and keep warm until ready to serve. They do not need to be piping hot, but should be warm. If necessary, they can be reheated in a 350°F. oven.

Vietnamese Spring Rolls Wrapped in Rice Paper
ROULEAUX DE PRINTEMPS VIETNAMIENS

My husband and I first tasted these spring rolls in Sarlat, France. It was market day, cars were banned from the center of town, and it was transformed into a bustling, jostling free-for-all of fine foods. Among the stalls of perfect vegetables, cheeses, meats, fish, wine and what have you was a trailer with two young girls frying crisp spring rolls. What a refreshing change after a steady diet of the rich foods of Perigord!

Rice paper is extremely difficult to work with. Because it shatters easily, do not make the mistake of overwrapping the filling. Each wrapper should be a thin fragile shell. The egg in the filling will help hold it together, in contrast to the loose, crumbly filling you find in most spring and egg rolls.

This recipe makes a *lot* of filling. If you have filled all the spring rolls you need, freeze the leftover filling and use it for wontons. It is also good with the addition of a scant teaspoon of fiery Vietnamese chili garlic sauce.

MAKES ABOUT 20 SPRING ROLLS

FILLING

¾ pound ground pork
½ pound shrimp, peeled, deveined and finely chopped
1 extra-large egg
1 tablespoon fish sauce from Thailand
1 scant cup (½ ounce) dried Chinese mushrooms, soaked and finely chopped
7 or 8 scallions, finely chopped (about 1 cup)

4 large cloves garlic, minced
4 canned water chestnuts, chopped
Coarse salt
Freshly ground pepper
2 ounces rice noodles, soaked 15 minutes and coarsely chopped
¾ cup chopped fresh mint and coriander

Beer
20 sheets, or more (in case they break), rice paper (preferably Banh Trang brand), about 9 inches in diameter
Peanut oil for frying
Boston lettuce

Coarsely chopped fresh coriander, mint and scallions
Small wedges fresh ripe tomatoes *or* radishes
Fringed cucumber slices
Thai Spicy Herb Sauce (page 35)

Combine the pork, shrimp, egg, fish sauce, mushrooms, scallions, garlic, water chestnuts, a pinch of salt, the pepper, rice noodles and the mint and coriander. Mix thoroughly (this can be best done with your hands). Set aside.

Pour some beer into a shallow pan large enough to hold a sheet of rice paper—a pie or pizza pan will do. Working with one sheet of rice paper at a time, carefully submerge it in beer, just long enough to moisten it overall. Lay it flat on a work surface. When the rice paper becomes pliable, place several cylinder-shaped teaspoons of filling toward one end.

Make a full turn of the rice paper, enclosing the filling completely. Then tuck in the 2 facing sides, envelope-fashion, and continue to roll until complete. The beer should be sufficient to seal the rice paper. Continue with this operation until all the rolls are filled.

Preheat the oven to 200°F. Use several large cast-iron skillets for frying the spring rolls. Add about ½ inch oil to each one. The oil should be hot (about 325°F.), but not as hot as for deep-frying. The rolls need to fry long enough to cook the filling (about 20 minutes) without the rice-paper burning.

When the oil is hot, arrange the spring rolls in the skillets. Take care not to crowd, or they will stick together. Fry slowly, turning them on all sides until golden brown and very crisp. As they are done, drain on paper towels and keep warm in a low oven. If the rice paper begins to burn before the filling is fully cooked, transfer the spring rolls to a baking sheet and finish cooking them in a 350°F. oven.

TO SERVE

Arrange a large platter with individual leaves of Boston lettuce. Place a spring roll within each leaf and scatter fresh herbs over all. Add a garnish of tomato wedges and fringed cucumber slices. Serve at once. Pass Thai Spicy Herb Sauce separately.

Ham and Cheese Pastry with Chile Peppers

This is an untamed version of a French *gougère*—so far removed one would think it originated in the American Southwest. Only the method is recognizable.

Served warm, it makes a terrific appetizer. The small savory puffs are easily detached from the whole and can be eaten with the fingers.

SERVES 8 AS AN APPETIZER

8 tablespoons (1 stick) butter, cut into
   small pieces
Heaping ¼ teaspoon coarse salt
¼ teaspoon finely ground white pepper
Freshly grated nutmeg
1 cup flour
4 extra-large eggs
1 rounded teaspoon imported
   Dijon mustard
1 small clove garlic, minced

6 ounces Gruyère cheese, shredded
   (about 2 cups, tamped down slightly)
2 tablespoons seeded and minced fresh
   hot green or red chile peppers
3 ounces cooked ham, finely chopped
   (about ¾ cup)
1 egg yolk mixed with 1 tablespoon
   heavy cream for glaze
Watercress *or* fresh coriander leaves
   (optional)

Preheat the oven to 425°F. Line a baking sheet with parchment paper or grease it with butter and lightly dust with flour. In the center, trace a circle about 10½ inches in diameter to use as a guide.

Combine 1 cup water, the butter, salt, white pepper, and a generous grating of nutmeg in a small casserole. Bring to a boil. When the butter is melted, add the flour and beat the mixture with a wooden spoon until it leaves the sides of the pan.

Off heat, quickly add the eggs, one at a time, thoroughly incorporating each egg before adding the next. Continue to beat, adding the mustard, garlic, 1½ cups of the cheese, the chile peppers and ham. When the ingredients are well blended and the dough is smooth and glossy, use a teaspoon and fingers to form small balls, each the size of a large walnut. Following the guide, start arranging 20 balls in a circle, side by side, but *not* touching. Then make an inner circle, keeping each ball a little farther apart than in the outer circle. A third circle within the other two should finish the dough, leaving a space in the center. The balls in the third circle should be kept still farther apart than in the other two. When finished, there should be approximately 40 balls. Carefully brush each ball of dough with glaze, taking care not to blanket them by letting the glaze run together; this will prevent them from puffing individually and hinder their rising in general. Sprinkle with the remaining cheese.

Place in the oven and bake 15 minutes, then lower the heat to 375°F. and bake 15 minutes longer, or until nicely browned. Pierce each cheese puff with the point of a knife to release the steam (otherwise they will be soggy).

Return the pastry to the turned-off oven to dry. Open the oven door frequently to be sure the puffs do not continue to brown. Thirty to 45 minutes should be enough drying time.

Lift the entire pastry off the baking sheet and place it on a warm serving platter. If desired, fill the center with watercress or fresh coriander leaves.

Periwinkles and Lardons with Wine and Tomatoes

CARACOLES BAR ROCAS

Gathered at picnic tables in the open-air bar at the *playa* in Spain, we used to while away the early evening hours picking at *caracoles* (periwinkles). One never quite fills up on this dish, even when it is accompanied with a crusty loaf of bread to mop up the sauce. Serve the periwinkles steaming hot from a large shallow casserole, or in individual earthenware *cazuelas*.

SERVES 4 TO 6

2 pounds live periwinkles
Salt
5 ounces lean meaty bacon, in one piece
2 to 3 tablespoons olive oil
3 or 4 dried red chile peppers, broken
2 cups chopped onion
1 heaping tablespoon finely chopped garlic (about 4 large cloves)
1 small inner-stalk celery with leaves, finely chopped

1 small bay leaf
1 to 1½ cups dry white wine
2 cups Fresh Tomato Sauce (page 132) *or* 3 cups peeled and chopped ripe tomatoes
Freshly ground black pepper
½ to ¾ cup finely chopped fresh parsley
¼ cup coarsely chopped fresh oregano *or* basil leaves
Coarse salt (optional)

ADVANCE PREPARATION

Rinse the periwinkles and soak for several hours in a large volume of cold salted water. Keep changing the water until it remains clear when stirred.

Remove the bacon rind and cut it into thin slivers. Then cut the bacon into lardons, about ¼ inch x ½ inch. Place the rind and lardons into a pan of cold water and bring to a simmer. Blanch 1 minute, drain in a sieve and rinse under cold water. Pat dry with paper towels.

COOKING THE PERIWINKLES

Heat just enough olive oil to lightly coat the bottom of a heavy skillet or medium casserole. Add the chile peppers and, after a minute, the onion. Sauté over low heat until the onion begins to soften. Add the garlic, celery, and bay leaf. Cook until softened, taking care not to let the garlic brown.

Drain the periwinkles, add them to the skillet and pour in 1 cup of the wine. Bring to a brisk simmer and cook until the wine is reduced by about half. Add the tomato sauce or the tomatoes, lower the heat and simmer for 30 minutes. Stir frequently and adjust heat as necessary. (The heat should be high for fresh tomatoes and low for sauce.)

Sprinkle generously with freshly ground pepper; if the sauce is too thick, add more wine. Stir in half the fresh herbs and taste for salt. (Periwinkles are not salty, but, depending on the bacon, the sauce may need some.)

Lower the heat, cover the casserole and cook 1 hour or longer. Stir occasionally, and check that the sauce does not become too thick. Add more wine, if needed. At this point, the snails may be removed from the heat and set aside to be reheated later, or even the next day. Stir in the remaining herbs when ready to serve.

NOTE   The opening of the periwinkle shell is capped by a small thin disk—something like a large fish scale. If it is still in place after cooking, it should be discarded. (Each diner does this for himself.) Then, use a toothpick or, better yet, a small metal skewer, to secure the tiny periwinkle and retrieve it. Enjoying periwinkles makes for a long, drawn-out feast, a perfect time for lots of good conversation.

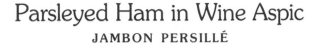
Parsleyed Ham in Wine Aspic
JAMBON PERSILLÉ

*J*ambon *persillé* with good crusty bread and butter and cornichons makes a wonderful appetizer or first course. Followed by a green salad or an omelet or both, it makes a fine light meal, especially welcome in summer.

Any cooked or ready-to-cook ham, with or without the bone, may be used for this dish, so long as it is not too salty. Often I set aside meat from a large ham that had originally served another purpose; therefore, it is simpler to give a boneless weight. There is no reason not to include the ham bone, or even a veal knuckle, to further strengthen the aspic.

Since *jambon persillé* will keep for a week, I usually make it in two molds to serve on separate occasions. The recipe can also be halved.

SERVES 12

STOCK

About 4 pounds boneless ham
2 quarts mild chicken stock
3 to 4 cups dry white wine
4 whole allspice
4 whole cloves
2 bay leaves
¼ cup freshly squeezed lemon juice
1 medium onion, sliced

4 cloves garlic, flattened and peeled
Several sprigs fresh thyme *or* 1 teaspoon dried thyme leaves
1 branch fresh tarragon *or* 1 teaspoon dried tarragon leaves
Parsley sprigs
½ teaspoon peppercorns

ASPIC

4 envelopes unflavored gelatin
1 cup cooled strained stock
3 egg whites
Crushed eggshells

2 cups finely chopped fresh parsley
2 tablespoons chopped fresh tarragon leaves *or* 1 tablespoon dried tarragon leaves, crumbled

2 to 3 tablespoons Madeira
1 tablespoon white wine vinegar (optional)

2 tablespoons white wine vinegar, preferably tarragon-flavored
2 cloves garlic, finely chopped
Watercress for garnish

Put two 6- to 8-cup bowls in the refrigerator to chill.

Place the ham in a large nonaluminum casserole and add the rest of the stock ingredients. Add just enough water to cover the meat. Bring to a boil, then reduce the heat to a simmer; cook, partially covered, for 3 hours or longer, depending on the ham. The meat should be almost falling apart. Let it cool completely in the stock.

Remove the ham and strain the stock into a clean casserole. About 8 to 10 cups liquid will be needed. If the stock has reduced too much, replenish it with white wine. If the broth is salty, add more wine or mild chicken stock. (Clarifying the aspic will also help.) Set aside 1 cup of broth to cool.

Allow 15 minutes to soften the gelatin over the cooled broth, then return it to the casserole. Beat the egg whites until frothy and add them, with the eggshells, to the stock. Bring to a boil, stirring frequently with a wire whisk. When foam rises and threatens to spill over, remove from the heat, stir once and let stand, undisturbed, for 10 minutes.

Saturate a clean dish towel with cold water and wring it out thoroughly; use it to line a fine sieve. Place the sieve over a large, deep bowl. Carefully pour the stock through the sieve; it must not touch the underside of the sieve. Do not touch it until the last drop has drained into the bowl. Remove sieve and stir in 2 tablespoons of Madeira. Taste the broth; if it seems bland, add 1 more tablespoon of Madeira and/or 1 tablespoon of vinegar.

Meanwhile, cut the ham into bite-size morsels. Mix with 1 cup of the parsley, the tarragon, vinegar and garlic. Set aside. (If preferable, this can be done much earlier.)

When the aspic has cooled, pour 1 cup of it into each of the chilled bowls. (Use glass bowls if not to be unmolded.) Stir ¼ cup parsley into each bowl and refrigerate until set.

Divide the ham between the bowls and pour over more aspic. Press down on the ham slightly to make it compact. Add enough aspic to almost, but not quite, submerge the ham, reserving 2 (or more) cups. Weight down each bowl with a plate and some light canned goods, and refrigerate about 30 minutes, or until set.

Remove the weights, stir remaining parsley into the rest of the aspic and pour it over the jellied ham. (If the aspic has begun to set, place the bowl in a basin of hot water.) Chill overnight or longer.

TO SERVE

Run a knife around the edge of the bowl, then dip it into a larger pan of hot water. Hold it there about 1 minute, then unmold onto a cold platter. Return it to the refrigerator to set the surface.

Add a garnish of watercress and accompany with good crusty bread, sweet butter, olives and cornichons.

Pheasant or Chicken Pâté with Fresh Herbs

For years, I made this pâté during the hunting season. Then I found that in summer it could be prepared quite successfully with chicken and fresh herbs from the garden. You will need a six-cup rectangular ovenproof terrine with a lid for this pâté.

Make any pâté at least twenty-four hours before serving.

SERVES 12 OR MORE

MARINADE

⅓ cup dry white wine
¼ cup cognac or brandy
2 medium bay leaves
⅓ to ½ cup chopped shallots
1 clove garlic, finely chopped
2 teaspoons fresh thyme leaves, stripped
    from their stems, *or* 1 teaspoon dried
    thyme

1 teaspoon chopped fresh tarragon
    leaves *or* ½ teaspoon dried tarragon
    leaves, crumbled
½ teaspoon coarse salt
¼ teaspoon white peppercorns, crushed

One 2-pound pheasant *or* one 3½-pound
    chicken
6 to 8 ounces pheasant or chicken livers
6 ounces cooked ham
¾ pound lean ground pork
1 large sweet Italian sausage, casing
    removed (about 7 ounces)
¼ pound lean salt pork, chopped as fine
    as possible (about 1 cup)
2 extra-large eggs, lightly beaten
1 teaspoon quatre-épices (see note)
Freshly grated nutmeg

Dash of cayenne
Freshly ground white pepper
½ teaspoon coarse salt
½ cup chopped shallots
12 to 14 ounces fatback, very thinly
    sliced
½ cup finely chopped fresh parsley
3 to 4 tablespoons chopped fresh chives
½ cup flour mixed with ¼ cup water for
    sealing the terrine
Lettuce leaves *or* watercress

ADVANCE PREPARATION

Combine the marinade ingredients in a shallow glass or earthenware bowl.

Bone the pheasant or chicken (use only the breast and thighs of a chicken) and cut the meat into long, thick strips.

Marinate the pheasant or chicken, the livers, and about 4 ounces of the ham, cut into long thin strips. Turn the meats in the marinade until saturated, then let stand from 3 hours to overnight, or longer, in the refrigerator.

While the meats marinate, combine the ground pork, sausage and salt pork. Add the eggs, spices, shallots and the remaining ham, chopped. Remove half the livers from the marinade, chop and add to the ground meats.

Pour off and save some of the marinade, leaving just enough to keep the meats moist. Add the marinade to the ground meat, mixing until well incorporated. Let stand several hours, or refrigerate overnight, until ready to assemble the terrine.

FINISHING THE PÂTÉ

Line the terrine with thin sheets of fatback, setting aside enough to cover the pâté. Carefully pour off all remaining marinade and combine it with the ground meats. Reserve the bay leaves.

Preheat the oven to 375°F. Make a bed of ground meats, about ½-inch thick, in the bottom of the terrine. Place strips of ham, in one even layer, down the length of the terrine. Then add a few whole livers and a few pieces of pheasant or chicken. Whenever the meats are added, sprinkle liberally with chopped parsley and chives, making sure they are well coated. Then add a few more strips of ham.

Spread more of the ground meat over the whole meats and repeat until all meats are used, ending with a layer of ground meat. (It may appear there is too much ground meat; however, when the terrine is cooked, weighted and cooled, the pâté will shrink and become compact. When it is unmolded, there will be an abundance of savory partially jellied meat juices.)

Place thin slices of fatback evenly over the meats, enclosing the pâté. Place the reserved bay leaves on top. Cover the terrine and seal the lid with a flour-and-water paste. Wrap the terrine in heavy-duty aluminum foil to catch the fat that will seep out toward the end of cooking. Place the terrine in a shallow roasting pan and add enough boiling water to reach about halfway up the sides. Bake 2 hours and 15 minutes, undisturbed. Remove from the oven and let cool completely in the water bath.

When cool, open the foil, break the seal and remove the lid. Wrap the terrine in fresh aluminum foil. Place a piece of wood cut to fit inside the rim of the terrine on the pâté, then place about 4 pounds of canned goods, evenly spaced, on top. If using a clean board, place it directly on the pâté. (Later, when the pâté is unmolded, it will adhere and can serve as a cutting board.) If a board is unavailable, lay cans on their sides on top of the foil.

If the pâté was cooked late in the day, let stand (with weights) overnight at room temperature. If the weather is quite warm, refrigerate overnight with the weights in place.

Chill the pâté 24 to 48 hours before serving.

(Continued)

TO SERVE

Unmold the pâté by running a knife around the sides of the terrine, then invert it onto a cutting board with a well to catch the juices. (If inverting onto the board used to weight down the pâté, place a baking sheet or platter underneath it.)

Cut the pâté into slices about ⅜ inch thick and arrange them on a chilled serving platter, bordered by delicate lettuce leaves or watercress. Spoon partially jellied juices collected from the terrine over all. Serve with cornichons, imported olives, good crusty bread and butter.

NOTE If quatre-épices (sometimes called spice parisienne) is unavailable, increase the amount of nutmeg and white pepper, and add a dash each of ground cloves, ginger and cinnamon.

Country Pâté with Pork Liver

SERVES 10

About 12 ounces lean salt pork, very
    thinly sliced
1 tablespoon butter
¾ cup coarsely chopped shallots
3 cloves garlic, peeled
1 pound pork liver, filament removed
    and cut into cubes
2 extra-large eggs
4 tablespoons cognac
2 large sage leaves, finely chopped, *or*
    1 teaspoon dried sage, crumbled
1 teaspoon chopped fresh tarragon *or*
    ½ teaspoon dried tarragon, crumbled
1 teaspoon fresh thyme leaves, rubbed
    from their stems, *or* ½ teaspoon
    dried thyme

¾ teaspoon freshly ground white pepper
Scant ⅛ teaspoon ground cloves
¼ teaspoon freshly grated nutmeg
½ teaspoon ground allspice
1½ teaspoons coarse salt
1 pound fresh ground pork butt
½ pound fatback, finely diced
2 tablespoons finely chopped fresh
    parsley
2 small bay leaves
½ cup flour mixed with ¼ cup water for
    sealing the terrine

Take 2 ounces of the salt pork and coarsely chop it. (There should be about ½ cup.) Place it in a small skillet with a little butter to keep it from sticking and, over low heat, render the fat without browning it. Add the shallots and cook only until softened. Set aside to cool.

Chop the garlic in a food processor, then add the liver and run the machine until the liver becomes almost liquid in consistency. Continuing to run the machine, add the eggs and 2 tablespoons of the cognac, followed by the rendered salt pork, shallots and fat from the skillet. Add the sage, tarragon, thyme, pepper, cloves, nutmeg, allspice and salt.

When well blended, turn the liver puree into a bowl and mix thoroughly with the ground pork butt. Add the diced fatback; when incorporated, stir in the parsley and remaining 2 tablespoons of cognac.

Preheat the oven to 350°F. If necessary, pound the slices of salt pork with a mallet to make them thin and malleable. Place a bay leaf at each end of an 8-cup terrine, about 9½ x 5½ inches. Line the terrine with the remaining slices of salt pork, placed side by side, across the bottom and up the sides. Be sure to leave an excess to cover the pâté after the terrine is filled. Mound the pâté evenly in the terrine, folding the slices of salt pork over to wrap it. Cover tightly with the lid, using a flour-and-water paste to seal it. If the terrine does not have a lid, cover with several layers of heavy-duty aluminum foil and secure it with string. Place the terrine in a slightly larger pan with enough boiling water to come halfway up the sides. Bake 2½ hours, undisturbed.

Remove the terrine from oven and let it stand in its water bath 1½ hours. When cool, remove from the bath and weight down the pâté with about 2½ pounds of canned goods, spaced evenly on top of a board or piece of heavy cardboard cut to fit the shape of the terrine. Let stand this way overnight in the refrigerator or at room temperature, depending on the weather. The next day, remove the weights, but allow the pâté to mellow in the refrigerator for another day before serving.

Serve from the terrine, or turn out onto a platter.

Terrine of Jellied Pork and Rabbit
TERRINE DE PORC ET LAPIN EN GELEÉ

The preparation of this old-fashioned terrine can be spaced out over several days.

SERVES 10 TO 12 AS AN APPETIZER

1 whole rabbit, about 4 pounds dressed, with heart, liver, kidneys, and fat reserved

1 fresh pork hock (pig's knuckle)

MARINADE

1 large bay leaf, broken

1 large bouquet fresh thyme and rosemary sprigs, tied together

2 small bouquets parsley sprigs, tied together

1 stalk celery with leaves, coarsely chopped

4 cups dry white wine, preferably Chablis

1 teaspoon black peppercorns, crushed with mortar and pestle

1 teaspoon fine salt

⅓ cup chopped shallot

4 large cloves garlic, flattened and peeled

STUFFING

1 pound lean pork, ground or in one piece

5 ounces bacon, with rind and in one piece

6 ounces ham, preferably in one piece

1 extra-large egg, lightly beaten

Freshly grated nutmeg

Freshly ground white pepper

½ teaspoon coarse salt

2 tablespoons cognac or brandy

1 veal knuckle bone, cut up

1½ tablespoons butter

¼ cup olive oil

¼ cup cognac or brandy

1 cup finely chopped fresh parsley

ADVANCE PREPARATION

A day ahead, arrange the rabbit with its heart, liver and kidneys and the pork hock in a large glass or ceramic bowl. Tuck a part of the bay leaf on each side of the rabbit and the bouquet of thyme and rosemary near the cavity. Add the parsley bouquets and scatter the celery and its leaves over all. Mix the white wine with the pepper, salt, shallot and garlic and pour over all. Adjust the rabbit so it is almost covered by wine. Marinate the rabbit and pork hock at a cool temperature for 24 hours, turning occasionally.

PREPARING THE STUFFING

If a home meat grinder is unavailable, buy the pork ground. Remove the rind from the bacon and reserve it, and mince the bacon, ham, marinated heart, liver and kidneys by hand. If you have a meat grinder, remove the bacon rind and reserve it, and run the pork, bacon, ham, marinated heart, liver, kidneys and any fat from around the kidneys through the meat grinder, using the fine blade.

Place the ground or minced meats in a bowl; add the egg, a generous grating of nutmeg, freshly ground pepper and salt. Mix well, then add the cognac and mix again until thoroughly combined. Set aside in the refrigerator.

Remove the rabbit from marinade and dry well with paper towels. Pack the pocket behind the rib cage with a portion of the stuffing; secure with skewers and string. Fill the rest of the cavity and close it tightly with more skewers and string. Tie the hind quarters and forelegs together to make the rabbit as compact as possible. Remove and dry the pork hock. Reserve the marinade.

COOKING

Place the pieces of veal knuckle bone in a saucepan and cover with cold water. Bring to a boil, reduce heat and simmer 1 minute. Drain and rinse the bones with cold water. Set aside.

Melt the butter in the olive oil over low heat in a large heavy casserole, about 12 to 13 inches in diameter. Just before the butter colors, add the rabbit, bacon rind and pork hock. Brown the rabbit on both sides, taking care not to mar the flesh when turning it. (Large wooden spoons or spatulas work very well for this.) Turn the hock also. When the rabbit has colored nicely, pour over the cognac and tilt the casserole to baste. After a minute, pour over the unstrained marinade. Add the veal knuckle bones, arranging them around the rabbit.

Bring to a boil, skim the surface, then lower the heat to a gentle simmer. Cover and cook about 3 to 3½ hours. Check frequently to be sure the liquid is not boiling. Carefully turn the rabbit, basting each time, and rearrange the bones and pork hock so they cook evenly.

When done, uncover the casserole and let the rabbit and hock cool in the liquid. Transfer them to a platter and cool completely.

(Continued)

Meanwhile, skim the fat from the cooking broth, then strain the broth through a fine sieve lined with several layers of cheesecloth, rinsed in cold water and wrung dry. If the broth jells before the terrine is assembled, reheat gently, just long enough for it to melt.

Remove the skewers from the rabbit and extract the stuffing in one or two pieces. Refrigerate the stuffing. Cut all the meat away from the carcass of the rabbit. Chop some of it coarsely, but leave bite-size pieces from the loin as is. Bone the pork hock, discarding the skin, and cut the meat into small morsels. Add them to the rabbit meat. When the stuffing is cold and firm, slice it. The slices will break into smaller pieces when the meats are combined. (Although fully cooked, the stuffing will be a rosy color because of the ham and bacon.) Mix the stuffing with the rabbit and add ¾ cup of the parsley.

FINISHING THE TERRINE

Ladle off enough strained broth to cover the bottom of an 8- to 9-cup terrine. Chill a few minutes until set. Arrange the meats in the terrine and pour over the rest of the broth. Weight down with a 1-pound weight placed on top of a board or piece of heavy cardboard cut to fit inside the rim of the terrine. When the meats have set, remove the weight. Sprinkle the pâté with the rest of the parsley. Refrigerate overnight.

TO SERVE

Serve directly from the terrine, or dip the terrine in hot water, run a knife around the sides and invert onto a cold platter. Return to the refrigerator long enough to set the surface of the aspic. Accompany the terrine with good crusty bread, butter, cornichons and olives.

Coarse Country Pâté with Duck, Pork, Green Peppercorns and Pistachios

PÂTÉ DE CANARD AU POIVRE VERT

This pâté is very versatile. You can increase one meat and use less of another; substitute veal for ham; add more duck or use game birds. Sausage can also be included. Make sure the amount of ground pork and the ratio of fat-to-meat is maintained. If you stint on fat, the pâté will be disappointing.

SERVES 12 OR MORE

MARINADE

⅓ cup cognac or brandy

1 teaspoon chopped fresh tarragon leaves *or* 1 scant teaspoon dried tarragon, steeped in the cognac or brandy

1 heaping teaspoon fresh thyme leaves, rubbed from their stems, *or* 1 level teaspoon dried thyme

2 heaping tablespoons chopped shallots

2 rounded teaspoons finely chopped garlic

¼ teaspoon coarse salt

Freshly ground white pepper

One 5-pound duck, with liver (about 1 pound meat when boned)

1 pound boneless pork, preferably from the loin

8 ounces fatty part of a smoked pork butt *or* ham

½ pound fatback

Slice of bread

1½ teaspoons coarse salt

Scant ⅛ teaspoon ground cloves

Scant ½ teaspoon ground allspice

2 extra-large eggs

2 tablespoons butter

1¼ to 1½ cups finely chopped onion

2 rounded teaspoons finely chopped garlic

2 tablespoons green peppercorns (packed in water), drained

⅓ cup blanched, peeled pistachio nuts

2 medium bay leaves

About 1 pound salt pork, very thinly sliced

½ cup flour mixed with ¼ cup water for sealing the terrine

ADVANCE PREPARATION

A day ahead, combine the marinade ingredients in a large bowl and bone the duck. Begin by cutting the meat away from the breast bone and work along the carcass to the legs. Leave all the skin and fat behind unless you are using Muscovy or Mallard ducks or substituting goose. The fat of Peking (Long Island) duck will not enhance this pâté. Pork fat is superior. Do not waste time on the wings; save them and the carcass (but not the fat) for the stockpot. Reserve the liver and heart, if there is one. Using a very sharp knife, carefully remove all sinews that merit attention, particularly from the legs.

(Continued)

There should be about 7 ounces of meat from the breast. Cut it into ¼-inch dice and drop the pieces into the marinade. Add the liver and heart to the marinade also. Refrigerate the flesh of the legs for grinding.

Cut half the boneless pork into ¼-inch dice and add to the marinade. Set aside the rest for grinding. Do the same with the smoked butt or ham.

FINISHING THE PÂTÉ

The next day, cut up the remaining duck legs, pork and ham and run them through a meat grinder, using the fine blade. Alternate them with fatback and the duck heart and liver, removed from the marinade. When finished, push a piece of bread through the grinder to catch and release any meats that may have lodged inside. As the bread comes out, discard it.

Mix the forcemeat in a bowl, adding the salt, cloves and allspice. Then add the eggs, one at a time, working them into the meat until fully incorporated. (The hands work best for this task.)

Melt the butter in a small skillet and sauté the onion and garlic over low heat. Cook until soft and translucent, taking care not to allow the garlic and onion to brown. Let cool. While the onion is cooling, combine the diced meats and marinade with the forcemeat. When well combined, add the peppercorns and pistachio nuts; continue to mix until the nuts are evenly distributed. Add the cooled onion, mixing thoroughly.

Preheat the oven to 350°F. Place the bay leaves on the bottom of an 8-cup terrine. Line the mold with thin slices of salt pork, pressing them against the bottom and sides. Reserve enough to cover the pâté. Mound the pâté evenly within the terrine and cover with slices of salt pork to enclose it completely. Cover and seal the edges of the lid with a flour-and-water paste. If there is no lid, use several thicknesses of heavy aluminum foil, secured tightly with string.

Set the terrine in a slightly larger pan and add enough boiling water to come halfway up the sides. Place it in the oven and bake 2½ hours, undisturbed. Turn off the oven and leave the pâté inside ½ hour longer.

Remove the terrine and its water bath from the oven and let it stand several hours until cooled completely. Remove the lid or foil and lay a board or other object slightly smaller than the rim of the terrine over the pâté. Weight down with about 4 pounds of canned goods or other weights and let stand overnight. If the kitchen is not cold, place the terrine (with weights) in the refrigerator.

The next day, remove the weights, but refrigerate the pâté at least another day before serving. Pâté improves with a few day's rest.

Country Pâté with Saddle of Rabbit
PÂTÉ DE LAPIN

If you cannot find a large enough rabbit, supplement the strips from the saddle and the ground forcemeat with either veal or more pork. The pâté will still be very good. Another alternative is to cut all the ingredients in half and make a smaller pâté, using a six-cup terrine and cooking it for two and a half hours.

Truffles may be included if the occasion warrants them. Let your pocketbook dictate the amount. They should be thinly sliced and added to the marinade. Later, intersperse the truffles with the strips of rabbit in the pâté.

This pâté does not pretend to be easy, but it is worth every bit of work involved.

SERVES 12 OR MORE

One large rabbit, about 4 to 5 pounds,
   dressed

MARINADE

1 cup dry white wine, preferably Chablis
¼ cup Madeira
1 large sprig fresh rosemary *or* parsley
Several sprigs fresh thyme *and/or* lemon
   thyme, leaves rubbed from the stems,
   or 1 teaspoon dried thyme
1 medium bay leaf

Freshly ground white pepper
¼ teaspoon coarse salt
¼ cup chopped shallots
2 large cloves garlic, finely chopped
2 tablespoons finely chopped fresh
   parsley

1 pound boneless pork shoulder
Enough slightly fatty salt pork *and/or*
   fatback to make ¾ pound when
   combined with the fat from the rabbit
Slice of bread
2 extra-large eggs

2 teaspoons salt
1 medium bay leaf
About 1 pound very thinly sliced fatback
½ cup flour mixed with ¼ cup water for
   sealing the terrine

ADVANCE PREPARATION

A day ahead, set aside the rabbit liver, then pull away all good fat from around the kidney and shoulder areas. Reserve the fat with the meats for grinding.

Use a good sharp boning knife to bone the rabbit. This is especially important when it comes to removing the sinews and membrane attached to most of the meat. Begin by removing the forelegs and hindquarters, then

(Continued)

separate the rib cage from the saddle (loin). Starting at the backbone, cut out the delicate fillets running along each side of the ribs; proceeding in the same manner, remove the larger segments that make up the saddle. Discard the "flaps," which are of no use in this recipe, and the forelegs, which are mostly muscle and contain little meat. When boning the hindquarters, first remove the hipbone, but leave the leg bone intact. Since most of the sinews emanate from the joint, it helps to work against it when cutting away the meat.

Combine the marinade ingredients, using a generous amount of freshly ground pepper. Place the rabbit liver and all but the smallest scraps of rabbit meat in the marinade and let stand overnight. (Set aside very small scraps with the pork for grinding.) Turn the meat in the marinade several times.

FINISHING THE PÂTÉ

The next day, remove the meats from the marinade. Remove the rosemary and bay leaf. Save only the bay leaf. Select about 12 ounces of the largest pieces of meat from the loin and cut them into long strips, about 4 to 6 strips from each piece from the saddle. The small thin strips from the rib cage can be left as is. Return all the strips to the marinade; then grind the rest of the meat, along with the liver, pork and the rabbit fat and salt pork or fatback, using the small blade of the meat grinder. When the last of the meats has been added to the grinder, push through a piece of bread. It will catch and release any good meat that may be trapped inside. When the bread comes through, discard it.

Preheat the oven to 350°F. Combine the meats and add the eggs, one at a time, and salt. Mix thoroughly. Then pour off ½ cup of marinade, taking as much of the shallots and parsley as possible. Add this to the ground meat and mix until thoroughly incorporated and no trace of liquid is present. (The hands really work best here.)

Place the bay leaf from the marinade and a second bay leaf at each end of an 8-cup terrine. Then neatly line the terrine with thin sheets of fatback, covering the bottom and sides completely. Reserve enough to cover the pâté after it is assembled.

Make a shallow bed of the ground meats in the bottom of the terrine and top it with strips of marinated rabbit, drained, arranged lengthwise. Add more of the ground meats and continue to fill the terrine, interspersing strips of rabbit with the ground meat at irregular intervals. Finish with a solid layer of ground meat.

Cover the pâté with enough fatback to enclose it completely, then cover the terrine. If using a lid, seal the edges with a flour-and-water paste. Otherwise, use several layers of heavy aluminum foil, secured tightly with string. Place the terrine in a larger pan and add enough boiling water to come halfway up the sides. Bake, undisturbed, for 3 hours.

Remove the terrine from the oven, but let it remain in its water bath for several hours, or until cooled completely. Then place a board or other object slightly smaller than the rim of the terrine over it and weight down the pâté with about 4 pounds of evenly distributed canned goods. Let stand overnight, weights in place. If the kitchen is warm, place the pâté (with weights) in the refrigerator. Remove the weights the next day.

All pâtés profit from several days' rest in the refrigerator. The rest will help to bring out their flavor.

Serve the pâté with cornichons, olives, a basket of good crusty bread and a block of cold butter.

PIG IN THE POT

Spanish Pork and Cabbage Soup

·

Hot Sour Soup

·

Spicy Chicken Stock

·

Fried Noodles

·

Fresh Fava and Green Bean Soup with Pasta

·

Thai Coconut Soup with Pork and Shrimp

·

Coconut Milk

·

Pork and Rice Soup with Vegetables and Bean Curd

·

Curried Split Pea Soup

·

Black Bean Soup

·

Pork Ball Soup with Lotus Root

·

Hearty Wonton Soup

·

Pork and Sausage Soup with Potatoes and Kale

·

Mallorcan Lentil Soup

Soups are an age-old source of nourishment and survival. A good soup is a reassuring late-night supper or mid-morning fuel on a blustery winter day. Soup warms the body, gladdens the heart and heals the spirit.

Many years ago, when I lived in Mallorca, I learned to make a number of hearty trencherman's soups: *cocido, caldo gallego,* lentil soup, and even a classic split pea soup that ignored the borders of Spain. Most of my recipes were gleaned from Catalina, a Spanish woman who was a very good cook.

Catalina, who lived with her husband, Jaime, and farmed the land where I was living, would put her soup together at dawn, adjust the wood fire to keep it simmering and go up into the mountains to do a good morning's work. Since the soup was prepared outdoors on a trivet (she preferred to keep her kitchen clean), I could watch her every step from my own kitchen window.

Returning at noon, she would pause in her garden to pick greens resembling our Swiss chard and add the glossy leaves to the long-simmering soup. Soon after, Jamie would arrive for the main meal of the day and, fortunately for me, there would often be a knock at my kitchen door, and I would be presented with a bowl of soup to try.

Later, when the sun was less intense, Catalina would return to the hills and work until dusk. Before going to bed, there would surely be another bowl of soup, this time a lighter one.

Spanish Pork and Cabbage Soup
COCIDO

There is a hearty welcoming quality to *cocido* that makes it a perfect cold-weather soup. Accompanied by good crusty bread, it constitutes a meal. There are elaborate versions of this soup, which place it more in the realm of a *bollito misto* or a *pot-au-feu,* but this one is less complicated and closer to its rustic origins. The recipe can successfully be halved.

SERVES 8

Olive oil
2 large onions, chopped
1 pound boneless pork, cut into
    1-inch cubes
Coarse salt
Freshly ground black pepper
1 whole head garlic, unpeeled, cloves
    not detached
2 bay leaves, broken
¾ cup chopped fresh parsley
2 cups peeled and chopped fresh plum
    tomatoes *or* chopped canned Italian
    plum tomatoes

⅔ cup dry white wine
2 quarts chicken stock or water
A pork bone (from the leg or shoulder) *or*
    1 fresh pork hock (pig's knuckle)
1½ to 2 cups dried chickpeas, soaked
    overnight in cold water to cover by
    several inches
½ medium cabbage, shredded and
    chopped (about 8 cups)
4 large new potatoes, peeled and cut into
    1-inch cubes (about 4 cups)

Heat enough oil to coat the bottom of a large soup kettle. Add the onions and cook over low heat until softened. Stir frequently. Push the onions aside, raise the heat and add the pork. Cook, turning the meat, until it loses its redness. Sprinkle with salt and freshly ground pepper and add the garlic, bay leaves, 2 tablespoons of the parsley, and the tomatoes. Cook a few minutes, then add the wine and bring to a boil. Add the rest of the parsley, the stock and pork bone or hock and return to a simmer.

Drain the chickpeas and add them with the cabbage. Bring to a boil, lower the heat to a simmer and cook, partially covered, about 2 hours, or until the beans are tender.

Add the potatoes and continue to cook over *very* low heat 2 hours longer. During this time, skim the fat from the surface of the broth. If preferable, extract the head of garlic before serving.

Serve the *cocido* in large soup plates.

Hot Sour Soup

The meats and vegetables in this soup can be increased or decreased, depending on what you have on hand.

SERVES 4 AS A MAIN COURSE OR 8 AS ONE OF SEVERAL COURSES

6 cups Spicy Chicken Stock (page 77)
1 clove garlic, minced
1 heaping tablespoon thinly slivered fresh ginger
1 scant cup (½ ounce) dried Chinese mushrooms, soaked, squeezed dry and cut into long slivers
½ small boneless chicken breast (about 6 ounces)
6 ounces lean boneless pork, in one piece, *and/or* 6 ounces cooked ham, smoked pork or sausage, cut into thin julienne strips

1 bamboo shoot, cut into thin slices, about ½ inch x 2 inches (about 3 to 4 ounces), *or* 3 Jerusalem artichokes, peeled and thinly sliced
4 tablespoons cornstarch
1 extra-large egg, lightly beaten

SPICE MIXTURE

3 tablespoons imported soy sauce
¼ teaspoon sugar
4 tablespoons strong rice, balsamic or cider vinegar

1 teaspoon freshly ground white pepper
Hot-pepper sauce to taste (optional)

A small handful of greens, coarsely chopped if necessary, choose among broccoli rape or mustard plant, snow peas, bok choy leaves, spinach, watercress, Swiss chard and escarole
2 cakes pressed bean curd (page 145), cut into large dice

1 tablespoon imported sesame oil
3 whole scallions, cut into ¼-inch pieces
Fresh coriander leaves
Fried Noodles (page 78)

Bring the stock to a boil; add the garlic, ginger and mushrooms. Lower the heat to a simmer. Cut the chicken and pork into long thin julienne strips and add to the soup. (This is easier to do if the meat is partially frozen.) After 20 to 30 minutes, when the meats are cooked, skim the surface and add the bamboo shoot or Jerusalem artichokes.

Dissolve the cornstarch in ¼ cup cold water (more, if necessary) and stir it into the soup over very low heat. Simmer, stirring constantly, until the broth is thickened.

Raise the heat and stir again to create an undulating movement. Then, without stirring, slowly and carefully pour the beaten egg evenly over the surface of the soup. (Do not stir: it will cloud the broth.) Cover and remove from the heat until the egg has set.

Over low heat, add the spice mixture, including hot-pepper sauce if desired. Taste for seasoning. Add the vegetables and bean curd. Cook only a few minutes to keep the vegetables slightly crisp. When ready to serve, stir in the sesame oil and scallions and garnish the soup with a few coriander leaves.

Accompany the soup with a large basket of crisp Fried Noodles.

Spicy Chicken Stock

If bones are not available, poach a chicken breast or even a whole chicken. The result will be a delicious stock as well as flavorful meat for a salad or other use.

MAKES 6 CUPS OR MORE

Chicken bones (necks, backs, wings,
    carcasses) *and*/*or* 1 large chicken
    breast
1 teaspoon coarse salt
½ teaspoon black peppercorns
4 large thick slices fresh ginger
2 or 3 small dried red chile peppers

1 onion, sliced
1 carrot, sliced
1 stalk celery with leaves
½ head garlic, unpeeled and cut in
    half crosswise
Several parsley sprigs and 1 bay leaf,
    tied together (bouquet garni)

Place all ingredients in a soup kettle or stockpot and add water to cover by at least 1 inch. Bring to a boil, skim the surface and lower the heat to a simmer. Cook the stock, uncovered, for several hours, or until the broth has reduced by several inches. Skim the fat from the surface and taste for seasoning. When satisfied with the flavor, strain the broth through a sieve into a bowl. Let cool, then pour the stock into storage containers and refrigerate or freeze until needed.

Fried Noodles

These noodles make a perfect garnish for Oriental soups. They are also a treat served with drinks before a meal.

They are so easy to make that once I stumbled on the method, I refused to settle for anything but homemade. The crispness of these noodles is unbeatable.

SERVES 6 TO 8

1 16-ounce package square wonton
  skins, fresh or frozen

Peanut or corn oil for deep-frying

If frozen, defrost the wonton skins. Take small portions, stacked together, and cut them into strips the size of egg noodles, about ⅜ inch wide. Spread them out loosely on your work surface.

Heat 3 to 4 cups oil to 375°F. Drop in the noodles, a handful at a time, and stir to separate. Turn the noodles in the oil as they puff and rise to the surface. Remove as soon as they are blistered and lightly colored. Do not allow the noodles to brown. Drain on paper towels.

Keep the noodles dry until ready to serve. A turned-off oven works very well for this. If storing overnight, protect the freshness of the noodles in airtight cookie tins.

Fresh Fava and Green Bean Soup with Pasta

The quantities of the ingredients in this hearty vegetable soup are flexible and may be determined by what is freshest in the market or thriving in the garden. When in season, cranberry beans may replace the fava beans.

SERVES 4

1 cup shelled fava beans (about 1½ to 2 pounds in the pods)

Salt

¼ pound large green beans or Romano beans, trimmed and cut into 1½-inch lengths (1 cup)

2 to 3 tablespoons olive oil

1 small onion, chopped

1 small carrot, thinly sliced

4 ripe plum tomatoes, peeled and diced (about 2 cups)

Freshly ground black pepper

About 1 cup diced cooked smoked pork butt or ham *or* thinly sliced sausage

About 6 cups chicken stock

1 cup small imported pasta shells

1 cup thinly sliced small zucchini

1 cup thinly sliced mushrooms (optional)

A handful fresh parsley sprigs, chopped, *or* parsley combined with other fresh herbs, such as basil, thyme, mint, oregano or marjoram

1 cup freshly grated Asiago or Parmesan cheese

Drop the fava beans into boiling salted water and cook 4 to 5 minutes. Drain, then slip off the outer skin. Set aside.

Drop the string beans into boiling salted water and cook 6 minutes. Drain and set aside.

Heat enough olive oil to coat the bottom of a 3- or 4-quart kettle. Add the onion and carrot and cook over low to medium heat until the onion has softened. Add the tomatoes, raise the heat, and cook until the consistency is saucelike. Add a generous grinding of pepper, followed by the meat. Pour in the chicken stock, stir and bring to a boil; add the pasta.

When the stock returns to a boil, reduce the heat to a simmer. Just before the pasta is done, add the fava beans, green beans and zucchini. If desired, sliced mushrooms can also be included. Do not overcook. If the soup is too thick, thin with a little more stock.

When ready to serve, stir in the chopped parsley, preferably combined with other fresh herbs, if available.

Pass a separate bowl of freshly grated cheese to add to the soup and accompany with good crusty bread.

Thai Coconut Soup with Pork and Shrimp

If the coconut milk is prepared in advance, this soup goes together fairly quickly. Both coconut milk and grated coconut freeze very well.

A wok is not necessary for making this soup, but I like to use it initially to stir-fry the ingredients, then transfer them to a casserole.

SERVES 6 AS A FIRST COURSE

½ pound medium shrimp, peeled, deveined and cut in half lengthwise
Finely ground white pepper
2 tablespoons dry sherry
About 6 tablespoons peanut oil
6 ounces pork, trimmed of all traces of fat and julienned (see note)
1 medium onion, thinly sliced
3 cloves garlic, cut into slivers
1½ tablespoons thinly slivered fresh ginger
2 fresh hot chile peppers, seeded and thinly sliced
2 tablespoons fish sauce from Thailand

¼ cup freshly squeezed lime juice
2 cups chicken stock *or* Spicy Chicken Stock (page 77)
2 cups Coconut Milk (page 81)
1 cup grated fresh coconut
½ cup coarsely chopped fresh coriander leaves
½ cup freshly shelled peas (optional)
2 whole scallions, thinly sliced
About ¼ pound fresh young spinach leaves, washed, drained and stems removed
4 large fresh basil leaves, shredded

Sprinkle the shrimp with pepper and marinate in the sherry for 1 hour. Pat dry with paper towels.

Heat 3 tablespoons of the oil in a wok and fry the shrimp briefly, only until they lose their translucency. Remove and set aside.

In the same oil, fry the pork until there is no trace of redness and it appears fully cooked. Before it becomes crisp, drain on paper towels, then transfer to a casserole.

Wipe the wok clean and add 3 tablespoons fresh oil. Over low heat, sauté the onion until soft and golden; add the garlic, ginger and hot peppers. Cook briefly, then add the fish sauce and lime juice. Bring to a simmer and pour in the chicken stock. Bring to a boil, then transfer to the casserole with the pork. Add the coconut milk, coconut and 2 tablespoons of the coriander leaves. Simmer 20 minutes, partially covered.

Just before serving, stir in the peas, if using, shrimp, scallions and spinach. As soon as the spinach wilts, add the remaining coriander and the basil.

Serve at once while the greens still have their fresh color.

NOTE   It is easier to julienne the meat if it is partially frozen.

Coconut Milk

It simplifies things to have coconut milk made in advance. I prefer to make a large quantity and freeze it in two-cup containers. When purchasing coconuts, shake them to be sure they are heavy with liquid.

MAKES ABOUT 6 CUPS

1 or 2 coconuts, weighing about 3
**   pounds**

Use a hammer and a clean screwdriver to puncture and penetrate the eyes of each coconut. Then turn them upside down in a sieve placed over a bowl to drain. Reserve the liquid; you should have about 1 cup.

Preheat the oven to 400°F. Roast the coconut for 15 minutes, then crack open the shell with a heavy cleaver and mallet (or use a hammer). Pry out the coconut meat, then peel off the thin brown skin. Remove any residue of shell from the meat and cut it up.

In several batches, grate the coconut in a food processor, using the steel blade, or in a blender. Measure the coconut meat: there should be about 6 cups. Set aside in a bowl.

In a saucepan, combine the reserved coconut liquid with as much water as you need to match the amount of grated coconut. Bring to a simmer, pour the coconut water over the grated coconut and let stand 15 minutes.

In several batches, return the grated coconut, with the liquid, to the food processor or blender (a blender is preferable for this step) and run the machine until thoroughly combined. When finished, let the coconut mixture steep 30 minutes.

Line a sieve with a double thickness of cheesecloth, rinsed and squeezed dry, and place it over a deep bowl. Turn the coconut into the sieve and let drain 1 hour. Press down on the coconut with a wooden spoon from time to time. Bring the edges of the cheesecloth together, twist and squeeze firmly to extract as much liquid as possible. Do this several times.

When finished, reserve the grated coconut for Thai Coconut Soup (page 80) or Indonesian Pork Balls with Coconut (page 53). Refrigerate or freeze the milk and the coconut until ready to use.

(Continued)

NOTE Some Oriental (particularly Southeast Asian) food stores stock canned coconut milk. I have found that, except for one that is made in the Philippines, they are much too sweet. There is a frozen product that is very good. It comes in a 1-pound block and is also made in the Philippines.

Any coconut milk that is not homemade should be strained before using to avoid a lumpy sauce.

Pork and Rice Soup with Vegetables and Bean Curd

SERVES 4

½ pound lean boneless loin of pork
¼ teaspoon finely ground white pepper
1 scant cup (½ ounce) dried Chinese
   mushrooms, soaked
3 to 4 tablespoons peanut oil
1 pound onions, thinly sliced
   (about 4 cups)
2 small dried red chile peppers
1 large clove garlic, finely chopped
   (1 heaping teaspoon)
1 tablespoon finely chopped fresh ginger
1 teaspoon ground coriander
5 cups strong Spicy Chicken Stock
   (page 77)

2 tablespoons medium-grain raw rice,
   rinsed
4 small leaves Chinese cabbage, from
   the heart
A handful watercress leaves, stems
   removed
1 cake pressed bean curd (page 145),
   cut into ½-inch dice
English or Chinese Mustard (page 41),
   optional
Thai Spicy Herb Sauce (page 35) or Soy
   Dipping Sauce (page 41), optional

Cut the pork into thin strips, ⅜ inch x 1½ inches. (This is easier to do if the meat is partially frozen.) Sprinkle with white pepper and set aside.

Squeeze the mushrooms dry and cut them into long slivers.

Heat 3 tablespoons of the oil in a large soup kettle and add the onions and chile peppers. Cook over low heat until the onions have softened, without letting them brown.

Push the onions to the side, add more oil, if necessary, and add the pork. Raise the heat slightly and cook, stirring, until all redness disappears and the meat is evenly colored. Add the mushrooms and cook a few minutes longer.

Combine the onions with the pork and mushrooms; add the garlic, ginger and coriander. Cook 1 or 2 minutes, stirring continuously. Pour in the stock and bring to a boil. Lower the heat, add the rice and simmer 10 minutes, uncovered.

Cut the leafy part of the cabbage away from the stem. Then cut the stems into 1-inch squares and the leaves into large shreds. Add the stems to the soup and simmer 5 minutes. Add the shredded cabbage leaves, watercress and bean curd; cook just until the bean curd is heated through.

Serve at once. Pass prepared mustard and Thai Spicy Herb Sauce or Soy Dipping Sauce for those who wish to add it to their soup.

Curried Split Pea Soup

I am addicted to the curried version of this classic. However, if your taste leans toward the traditional, see the variation at the end of the recipe.

Aside from the ham bone, if there are any other meats to be added—such as ham, smoked pork or sausage—leave them in one piece, then remove before pureeing the soup. Return them later, cut into small pieces.

SERVES 8

6 tablespoons butter
1 medium onion, chopped
1 leek, thinly sliced
1 carrot, chopped
1 stalk celery with leaves, chopped
½ head garlic, cloves flattened and peeled
2 bay leaves
1 heaping tablespoon good-quality curry powder
1 rounded teaspoon ground coriander

1 teaspoon ground cardamom
1 sprig fresh rosemary *or* ½ teaspoon crushed dried rosemary leaves
2 cups canned Italian plum tomatoes and their liquid
6 cups chicken stock
2 cups dried split peas, rinsed (1 pound)
1 ham bone with a little meat and gristle attached
Fresh coriander leaves
Yogurt (optional)

Melt the butter in a large soup pot and sauté the onion and leek over low heat until wilted. Add the carrot, celery, garlic and bay leaves; cover the pot and cook about 30 minutes, or until the vegetables have softened. Stir frequently. Add the curry powder, coriander, cardamom and rosemary. Cook, uncovered, stirring continuously, until the spices have dissolved into a paste. Add more butter, if needed.

Stir in the tomatoes, breaking them up. Raise the heat and bring to a boil. Add the chicken stock and return the soup to a brisk simmer. Add the split peas and ham bone. If the bone is not covered by liquid, add a little water. Reduce the heat to a very low simmer and cook for 4 hours, covered. Stir and turn the ham bone from time to time.

Remove the ham bone and pass the soup through a food mill into a clean casserole. Bring to a simmer and, if desirable, thin with more stock or water. Taste for seasoning.

Sprinkle each serving with a few coriander leaves and pass yogurt separately for those who wish to add a dollop to their soup.

VARIATION

.

Traditional Split Pea Soup

Follow the directions for Curried Split Pea Soup, omitting the curry powder, coriander and cardamom. If a green-pea color is preferable, omit the tomatoes as well. After the soup is pureed, return any meat, but not the ham bone. If the soup is too thick, thin with either cream, chicken stock or water. A basket of diced fried or toasted croutons is a must.

Black Bean Soup

Start this soup early on the day you plan to serve it or, better yet, in the early afternoon and let it stand overnight before finishing it the next day.

If there is any leftover cooked sausage, pork or ham in the refrigerator, by all means add it to the soup. My interpretation of this classic constitutes a meal in a soup plate.

SERVES 8 AS A MAIN COURSE

2 cups dried black turtle beans (1 pound)
2 smoked ham hocks (pig's knuckles)
8 to 10 ounces lean salt pork
1 or 2 tablespoons olive oil
2 medium onions, chopped
1 large carrot, finely chopped
1 leek, thinly sliced
1 large stalk celery, finely chopped
1 fresh long green chile pepper, seeded and chopped
5 cloves garlic, chopped (about ⅓ cup)
1 large bay leaf
3 small dried red chile peppers
1 tablespoon ground cumin
1 tablespoon ground coriander
1 teaspoon ground cardamom

GARNISHES

Chopped sweet onion
Sour cream

¼ teaspoon ground mace
2 cups peeled and chopped fresh plum tomatoes *or* chopped canned Italian plum tomatoes with their liquid
Freshly ground white pepper
Parsley sprigs, thyme and oregano, tied together (bouquet garni), *or* 1 teaspoon *each* dried thyme and oregano
Salt (optional)
1 or 2 tablespoons sherry vinegar (optional)
½ cup Madeira *or* dry sherry, to taste
Thin slices lemon or lime
Fresh coriander leaves

Tomato salsa or chopped fresh tomato

ADVANCE PREPARATION

Rinse and pick over the beans; soak overnight in cold water to cover by several inches.

COOKING THE SOUP

Drain the beans and place in a soup pot with 2 quarts cold water. Bring just to a boil and skim off the foam that rises to the surface. Lower the heat to the barest simmer and let cook while preparing the other ingredients.

Place the ham hocks in a pan with cold water to cover. Bring to a boil, reduce the heat to a simmer and cook 5 minutes. Drain the hocks and rinse with cold water; add them to the beans.

Remove the rind from the salt pork and add it to the beans. Cut the meat into medium to large dice and place in a large 7- or 8-quart casserole. Add 1 tablespoon of the olive oil and, over low heat, render the fat from the pork dice. Turn them frequently and fry until crisp and very lightly browned. Add a little more oil, if needed.

When the pork dice are finished, add the onions, carrot, leek, celery and fresh chile pepper. Cook over low heat for about 30 minutes, or until the vegetables have softened. Stir frequently and, if necessary, add a little more oil.

Add the garlic, bay leaf, and dried chile peppers. Cook briefly and stir in the cumin, coriander, cardamom and mace. Cook a few minutes, stirring constantly to prevent the spices from sticking. Add the tomatoes, a generous grinding of pepper, and the bouquet garni.

Raise the heat slightly and when the tomatoes are bubbling, add the ham hocks. Cook a few minutes longer and add the black beans with their liquid and the pork rind. Bring to a simmer, partially cover the casserole and cook at least 6 hours over very low heat. Stir frequently to make sure nothing sticks.

After about 2 hours, the soup should be very thick, but the beans will be far from ready. Add 1 cup boiling water to maintain a proper balance of liquid. After about 4 more hours, another cup of boiling water will probably be needed. Soon after this, I usually let the soup cool and rest overnight at room temperature. (If the kitchen is not cool enough, refrigerate the soup.) If there is enough time, it can be served the same day.

FINISHING THE SOUP

The next day, or before serving, another cup of boiling water will probably be needed. At this time, discard the bouquet garni and bay leaf and remove the hocks. Bone them, separating the meat into bite-size morsels. Discard the rind. Return the meat to the beans. The soup is now ready when you are.

Taste for seasoning. It is unlikely salt will be needed. Sometimes a dash of vinegar adds a nice spark to the flavor of the soup (it can be passed separately). My preference leans toward Madeira or sherry, enough to be discernable.

If serving the soup in individual bowls, add a thin slice of lemon or lime and scatter a few fresh coriander leaves over all. Pass the assorted garnishes separately.

This soup freezes very well.

Pork Ball Soup with Lotus Root

Served in large bowls, this soup easily constitutes a meal. For variation, use a little of the meatball mixture to stuff the holes of the sliced root, then poach it with the meatballs. After the meatballs are poached they are ready to serve, but you can also bake them. This leaves the meatballs firm and eliminates the risk of them coming apart in the soup. (The lotus root is not baked.)

Meatballs that have been finished in the oven are also delicious served warm, tucked into lettuce cups. They can be served as an appetizer or first course.

SERVES 6 TO 8 AS A MAIN COURSE

MEATBALL MIXTURE

1 tablespoon cornstarch
2 extra-large egg whites, beaten to
  a froth
½ teaspoon sugar
Scant ¼ teaspoon finely ground white
  pepper
¼ pound small or medium shrimp,
  peeled, deveined and finely chopped
  (½ to ⅔ cup)
1 tablespoon finely chopped fresh ginger

2 cloves garlic, finely chopped
½ pound ground pork
1 scant cup (½ ounce) dried Chinese
  mushrooms, soaked, squeezed dry
  and chopped
About 6 canned water chestnuts, finely
  chopped, or ⅓ cup finely chopped
  Jerusalem artichokes
1 tablespoon imported soy sauce
1 teaspoon imported sesame oil

SOUP

3 quarts Spicy Chicken Stock (page 77)
12 to 16 slices, ¼-inch thick, fresh lotus
  root, peeled
2 to 3 tablespoons imported sesame oil
  (optional)
¼ pound very small shrimp, peeled,
  deveined and sprinkled with a little
  dry sherry (optional)
1 cake firm pressed bean curd (page
  145), cut into ½-inch dice

1 cup matchstick-size pieces bamboo
  shoot
1 handful small snow peas, trimmed
3 whole scallions, thinly sliced
1 bunch watercress, tops only, or 1 large
  handful young spinach leaves, stems
  removed

GARNISHES

2 carrots, cut into fine julienne threads
  and crisped in ice water (see note)
1 new turnip, cut into fine julienne
  threads and crisped in ice water
  (see note)

Fried Noodles (page 78)

Mix the cornstarch and egg whites. When completely dissolved, add the sugar, pepper, shrimp, ginger, garlic, pork, mushrooms, water chestnuts, soy sauce and sesame oil, mixing well after each addition. Refrigerate until ready to cook.

Shortly before preparing the soup, wet your hands and form the meatballs, making each about the size of a small walnut. Have a bowl of cold water handy to moisten your fingers when needed.

COOKING AND FINISHING THE SOUP

The meatballs may be baked after they are poached. If you choose to bake them, preheat the oven to 350°F.

If not, heat the stock in a large saucepan or soup kettle. When it comes to a boil, add half the meatballs. When it returns to a boil, skim the surface and lower the heat slightly. After the meatballs bob to the surface, continue to simmer 10 minutes. Remove and set aside. Add the rest of the meatballs to the stock and when they have finished cooking, remove them and add the lotus root.

If you wish to bake the meatballs, grease a baking sheet with the sesame oil. Arrange the meatballs on it and bake 30 minutes, turning them after 15 minutes. While the meatballs are baking, keep the heat under the soup very low and skim the surface. When finished, return as many meatballs as needed to the soup. Any extra meatballs can be set aside to use at another time or frozen.

Raise the heat under the soup to a simmer and add the shrimp, if using. As soon as the shrimp starts to turn opaque, add the bean curd, bamboo shoot, snow peas, scallions and watercress or spinach.

When the watercress or spinach begins to soften, the soup is ready to serve. At the last moment, off heat, stir in the carrot and turnip.

Pass a basket of Fried Noodles to add to the soup separately.

NOTE   The julienne disk of a food processor works very well for this.

Hearty Wonton Soup

During the course of a week, small contributions gleaned from one meal and another lay the groundwork for this soup. As long as you have wontons—either freshly made or in the freezer—the selection of ingredients can be endless; choose more of some and omit others. Do not try to use them all. Since this soup is literally a meal in a bowl, serve it in the largest soup bowls or soup plates available.

SERVES 4 AS A MAIN COURSE

5 cups chicken stock *or* Spicy Chicken Stock (page 77)

2 tablespoons imported soy sauce

1 heaping tablespoon thinly slivered fresh ginger

2 large dried Chinese mushrooms, soaked and cut into long slivers, *or* 3 fresh mushrooms, thinly sliced

1 cup thin slices roast pork or ham, cut into long julienne strips (about 4 ounces)

¾ cup thinly sliced bamboo shoots

1½ cups buds broccoli rape, Chinese mustard plant or broccoli florets *and/ or* 1 heaping cup bok choy *or* Swiss chard leaves and stems *or* Chinese cabbage stems, cut into 1-inch pieces

1 cup diced cooked chicken breast (optional)

16 wontons (page 40)

4 whole scallions, thinly sliced

A small handful snow peas, trimmed and blanched 30 seconds in boiling water (about 2 ounces)

A small handful watercress leaves (optional)

Fried Noodles (page 78)

English or Chinese Mustard (page 41)

Soy Dipping Sauce (page 41)

Combine the stock, soy sauce, ginger and mushrooms. Bring to a simmer and cook 15 minutes. Add the pork or ham, the bamboo shoots, greens, chicken breast, if using, and the wontons; simmer until the greens are just tender. Stir in the scallions, snow peas, and watercress, if using, and cook 15 seconds longer.

Serve with a heaping basket of crisp Fried Noodles. Each person can add Mustard or Soy Dipping Sauce to their soup, or the Mustard and the Dipping Sauce can be served in individual dishes and the wontons can be dipped separately.

Pork and Sausage Soup with Potatoes and Kale

CALDO GALLEGO

This is a true trencherman's soup—a satisfying meal in a bowl.

SERVES 6 TO 8

1 cup dried white beans, such as baby limas, Great Northern, or navy (½ pound)

1 ham bone with a little meat attached

About ½ pound lean bacon, in one piece

2 fresh pork hocks (pig's knuckles)

1 stalk celery with leaves, 1 bay leaf and several parsley and thyme sprigs, tied together (bouquet garni)

1 carrot

1 medium onion, stuck with 2 cloves

8 cloves garlic, unpeeled

½ pound chorizo, kielbasa or other lightly smoked sausage, pricked with a skewer

2 to 3 tablespoons olive oil

1 large onion, chopped

1 leek, thinly sliced

1 rounded tablespoon chopped garlic

Several dried red chile peppers (optional)

4 cups meat or chicken stock, preferably homemade

1 pound new potatoes, peeled and cut into large dice (about 3 to 4 cups)

About ½ pound fresh kale, stems removed and leaves cut into large shreds (6 to 8 cups, pressed down)

ADVANCE PREPARATION

Soak the dried beans overnight in water to cover by several inches.

COOKING THE SOUP

Drain the beans and place them in a soup pot with the ham bone, bacon, hocks, bouquet garni, carrot, onion and garlic. Add enough cold water to barely cover the ingredients and bring to a boil. Skim the surface, lower the heat to a simmer and cook 1 hour. Remove and reserve the bacon, but leave in the ham bone and hocks. Add the sausage and cook about 30 minutes to release excess fat. Remove the sausage and set aside. Skim fat from the surface of the broth from time to time.

After about 2 hours, remove the ham bone and hocks and drain the beans in a sieve or colander, catching the broth in a bowl. Discard the onion and bouquet garni, except for the bay leaf. Reserve the carrot and squeeze out the sweet interiors of the garlic cloves, adding them to the beans. Wash the pot and return it to the stove.

(Continued)

Remove the rind from the bacon and cut it into thin strips. Cut the bacon into large dice, about ¼ inch x ¾ inch. Heat a little olive oil in the pot and, over low heat, render the fat from the diced bacon and rind. Push the bacon to the side of the casserole and add the chopped onion. When the onion begins to soften, add the leek and chopped garlic. If chorizo is not used and more spice is desired, sauté a few dried chile peppers with the onion. Return the bay leaf to the pot.

When the onion and leek have softened, pour in the stock and bring to a simmer. Return the hocks to the pot with any morsels of meat that can be salvaged from the ham bone. Discard the bone. Add the potatoes and the reserved carrot, diced. Return the beans and about 6 cups of the bean broth, skimmed thoroughly, to the pot. There should be enough to cover the ingredients. Cover the pot and barely simmer for about 1 hour or longer. Add more reserved cooking broth from the beans as needed.

When the meat begins to separate from the bones of the hocks, remove them. Cut or tear the meat from the hocks into bite-size morsels and return it to the soup. Discard the bones. (What to do with the rind is a matter of personal taste. In restaurants, it can usually be found in the soup, cut into small pieces. But since it is not all that digestible, you may prefer to discard it.)

Slice the sausage and peel off the casing if possible. Add the sausage to the soup and continue to simmer about 1 hour, or until almost ready to serve. Skim the surface frequently. Shortly before the soup is finished, stir in the kale and cook, covered, until tender.

This is a soup that can be set aside and reheated later; it improves after standing overnight.

Mallorcan Lentil Soup

Homemade chicken stock, or even water, can be used in this soup, but do not used canned chicken broth. In combination with the sausages, it will make the soup too salty.

Some people like to add a tablespoon or two of wine vinegar to this soup. I think the tomatoes contribute enough acidity, but it is an option to consider.

SERVES 6

1 spicy fresh sausage, such as a sweet or hot Italian sausage (about 6 to 8 ounces)

1 lightly smoked sausage *or* chorizo (about 4 ounces)

About 3 tablespoons olive oil

1 large onion, chopped (about 2 cups)

2 small carrots, finely diced (about ⅔ cup)

1 leek, chopped

1 small stalk celery with leaves

1 large bay leaf

6 to 8 large cloves garlic, chopped (about ⅓ cup)

1 cup chopped fresh ripe tomatoes (about ½ pound) *or* canned Italian plum tomatoes and their liquid

Freshly ground black pepper

2 tablespoons chopped fresh parsley

About 8 cups chicken stock *or* water

1 cup lentils, rinsed and drained in a sieve (½ pound)

¾ pound new potatoes, peeled and cut into small cubes (about 3 cups)

1 bunch fresh Swiss chard *or* spinach, stems removed and leaves coarsely shredded (about 6 cups loosely packed)

1 or 2 tablespoons red wine vinegar (optional)

Prick the sausages all over with a skewer and arrange in a skillet with just enough water to cover. Bring to a simmer and cook long enough to release excess fat from the sausages. Remove the smoked sausage from the skillet and set aside. Pour off about half the liquid remaining in the skillet, then continue to simmer the fresh sausage until all liquid evaporates and the meat browns in its own fat and juices. When nicely colored, remove and set aside with the smoked sausage. Slice the sausages before adding them to the soup.

Add 2 tablespoons of the olive oil to a soup pot and slowly sauté the onion, carrots and leek. If needed, add a little more oil. When the vegetables begin to soften, add the celery and bay leaf and, when the vegetables have all softened, add the garlic. Cook together, stirring, for 1 minute, then add the tomatoes and a generous grinding of pepper. Raise the heat and cook, stirring, until the tomatoes are incorporated into the vegetables.

Add the parsley, 6 cups chicken stock or water, the sliced sausages and lentils. Over low heat, bring the soup to a simmer, then skim the surface and add the potatoes. Partially cover the soup pot and cook several hours, adjusting the heat to keep the soup simmering gently. As the lentils absorb the liquid, more water or stock may be needed. Taste for salt and seasoning before adding more stock. Water may be preferable.

When the potatoes are tender to the touch of a fork, add the leafy greens. Continue to simmer, partially covered, until the greens are wilted.

At this point, the soup is ready to serve. It can be set aside or refrigerated overnight and reheated. Add the vinegar, if using, just before serving.

PIG AND GREENS AND OTHER GOOD THINGS

Sausage, Potato and Tomato Salad

·

Green and Yellow Squash Salad with Sausage

·

Cold Noodles with Pork and Cucumber in Sesame Sauce

·

Salad of Pork Hocks with Mustard Vinaigrette

·

Beaujolais Chicory Salad with Bacon

·

Warm Chicory Salad with Assorted Sausages

Lentil Salad

·

Thai Grilled Pork Salad with Lettuce and Herbs

·

Asparagus Wrapped in Ham with Walnut Vinaigrette

·

Oriental Pork Salad with Walnuts

·

Red Cabbage Salad with Bacon and Vinegar Dressing

·

Smoked Pork Salad with Vegetables à la Grecque

A salad can be many things—from a salute to spring to salvation on a sweltering summer evening. Thai Grilled Pork Salad, heady with fresh mint and basil just picked from summer's garden, provides a reinvigorating repast when the temperature hovers around 90 degrees. A salad composed of lardons, croutons and hard-boiled egg on a bed of frizzy white chicory can be served as a first course to awaken and delight the taste buds or a luncheon dish when opting for something light and refreshing. An earthy Lyonnaise platter of sausages, vegetables and lettuces is a festive meal in itself and makes a welcome luncheon or supper dish in fall and winter.

Sausage, Potato and Tomato Salad

SALADE PAYSANNE

This substantial summer salad is a meal in itself. It is excellent made with warm kielbasa or some similar cooked or lightly smoked sausage, as well as ham or smoked pork butt. Sausage should be sliced, but if other meats are used, cut them into thick julienne strips.

SERVES 4

¾ pound kielbasa

VINAIGRETTE SAUCE

1 heaping teaspoon imported coarse-grained mustard
3 tablespoons red wine or sherry vinegar
6 to 7 tablespoons olive oil
Coarse salt (optional)

Crisp lettuce leaves, such as Romaine or chicory
1 sweet red or white onion, thinly sliced
1 sweet red bell pepper, cut into thin strips (optional)

1 pound new potatoes

Freshly ground black pepper
1 tablespoon coarsely chopped fresh tarragon or basil leaves, cut into shreds
2 tablespoons chopped fresh parsley

2 or 3 medium vine-ripened tomatoes, cut into small wedges
2 hard-boiled eggs, sliced
3 tablespoons tiny niçoise olives
4 to 6 radishes, thinly sliced

About 1 hour before serving, poach the sausage and steam the potatoes. Remove the casing and slice the sausage ¼ inch thick. Peel and slice the potatoes ¼ inch thick as well. They should be warm when the salad is made.

Make the vinaigrette by blending the mustard with the vinegar, then slowly adding olive oil to form a smooth emulsion. Stir in salt to taste (depending on the saltiness of the sausage) and freshly ground pepper; taste for seasoning. Add half the fresh tarragon or basil and parsley.

Line a shallow bowl or platter with lettuce leaves. Set aside.

Combine the sausage and potatoes in a bowl with the onion, bell pepper, tomatoes, hard-boiled eggs, olives and radishes. Pour the vinaigrette over the salad and toss carefully until well mixed.

Arrange the salad in the center of the lettuce-lined bowl and sprinkle the remaining tarragon or basil and parsley over all. Serve while the sausage and potatoes are still slightly warm.

Green and Yellow Squash Salad with Sausage

SERVES 6

3 small bright green zucchini (about 5
    ounces each)
3 small yellow crookneck squash (about
    5 ounces each)
Salt
3 large cloves garlic, unpeeled
Olive oil
2 cups large dice slightly stale French or
    Italian bread
¼ teaspoon coarse salt

1 teaspoon ground cumin
4 tablespoons sherry vinegar
2 fresh long green chile peppers, seeded
    and thinly sliced
About 2 ounces cooked sweet sausage,
    sliced, *or* smoked or cured sausage,
    such as kielbasa
2 tablespoons chopped fresh parsley
Fresh coriander leaves (optional)

Using a vegetable peeler, make ¼-inch stripes down the length of each zucchini. Do the same with the yellow squash. Then cut both into ¼- to ⅜-inch rounds. Discard the stem and blossom ends. Drop into boiling salted water and cook 4 minutes. Drain and plunge into ice water. When cool, drain well in a colander.

Place the unpeeled garlic in a 10-inch skillet with enough olive oil to coat the bottom generously. Sauté the garlic about 10 minutes over medium to low heat, turning frequently, until slightly softened. Add the bread, adjust the heat, and toss until the cubes are golden brown on all sides. Remove from the heat.

Remove the garlic and press the soft pulp into a small bowl. Discard the skins. Add the coarse salt and cumin; stir in ¼ cup olive oil, blending the garlic paste into a smooth puree. Mix in the vinegar, a little at a time. Taste for seasoning. The dressing should be sharp, but a little more oil may be desirable.

Place the squash in a serving bowl and pour over the vinaigrette dressing. Add the chile peppers and sausage and toss together. Just before serving, add the parsley and croutons. If desired, sprinkle the salad with whole fresh coriander leaves.

Cold Noodles with Pork and Cucumber in Sesame Sauce

Cold Poached Pork Butt (page 175) is excellent in this salad. All the salad ingredients except the cucumbers should be at room temperature, or it will be difficult to combine the noodles with the sauce.

Except for the final addition of sauce and garnish, this salad can be made several hours before serving. Do not add the crisp cucumber sticks, though, until ready to bring the salad to the table; if you must refrigerate the salad, be sure to let it return to room temperature before serving.

SERVES 6

2 medium cucumbers, cut lengthwise, seeded and cut into small sticks, about 2 inches long
Coarse salt

SAUCE

1 or 2 cloves garlic, peeled
1 inch fresh ginger, sliced
4 tablespoons tahini *or* Oriental sesame paste
1 tablespoon imported sesame oil
2 teaspoons light brown sugar
2 tablespoons dark or black soy sauce

7 scallions, thinly sliced, white and green parts separated
2 cups diced cooked pork

1 pound thin Oriental egg noodles, fresh or frozen
2 tablespoons peanut oil
1 tablespoon imported sesame oil

1 tablespoon balsamic vinegar
1 slightly rounded tablespoon Korean hot bean mash
½ cup, or more, greaseless cooled cooking broth from Poached Pork Butt (page 175) *or* Spicy Chicken Stock (page 77) *or* tea

Vietnamese chili garlic sauce *(túóng ót tói Viet-nam)*, optional
A large handful fresh coriander leaves

Place the cucumber sticks in a bowl and sprinkle well with salt. Refrigerate 1 hour or longer.

Drop the noodles into a large volume of boiling salted water with 1 tablespoon peanut oil added. Cook only a few minutes, testing the strands frequently. When done, drain in a colander and rinse with cold water. Add the remaining tablespoon of peanut oil and use your hands or 2 forks to toss the noodles. Transfer them to a bowl and mix with sesame oil, then set aside. Toss again from time to time. If they tend to stick together, add a little more oil.

Place the sauce ingredients in a food processor or blender, one at a time, running the machine after each addition. Keep the sauce thin or it will be difficult to coat the noodles evenly and combine them with the pork. Add the broth or tea a little at a time. If needed, add more broth later. Taste for seasoning. The sauce should be very spicy. Let stand at room temperature until ready to combine the salad.

Rinse the cucumbers in cold water, then drain and pat dry in a towel. Return them to the refrigerator until ready to serve.

TO SERVE

Use chopsticks or your hands to combine the noodles with half the white part of the scallions and half the diced pork. Top with the rest of the white part of the scallions, the remaining pork, the cucumber sticks, and half the green part of the scallions.

Pour over all but about a quarter of the sauce and mix together, using chopsticks, or large forks, until the ingredients appear evenly distributed.

Thin the remaining sauce with more broth or tea, if necessary, and spoon it over the noodles. Add little dabs of bright red Vietnamese sauce here and there. The accent will be more than just color! Scatter the rest of the chopped scallion tops over all and add a garnish of coriander leaves.

Bring to the table, then toss again when ready to serve.

Salad of Pork Hocks with Mustard Vinaigrette

This salad makes a light and refreshing meal on a sweltering summer evening. In winter, served in small portions, it makes a good first course; however, out-of-season tomatoes should probably be omitted from the garnish.

A large amount of vinaigrette will be needed for this salad, and it should be a little more acerbic than usual. After the necessary amount has been mixed with the pork, add enough olive oil to the remainder of the vinaigrette to make a smooth, agreeable sauce for the rest of the salad.

SERVES 3 OR 4

2 large fresh pork hocks (pig's knuckles), about 2 to 2½ pounds
Spicy wine broth for poaching pork (page 175)

Chicken bones

VINAIGRETTE

1 heaping tablespoon imported Dijon mustard *(extra-forte)*
About ¼ cup red wine vinegar

A good pinch of coarse salt
Freshly ground black pepper
About ½ cup olive oil

3 heaping tablespoons chopped fresh parsley, coriander or marjoram
Olive oil
About 6 cups combined lettuces, such as frisée, mâche, arugula, hearts of Boston or Bibb
2 medium vine-ripened tomatoes, cut into wedges

2 hard-boiled eggs, quartered
Coarse salt
Freshly ground black pepper
½ cup small black Gaeta olives
1 tablespoon small capers (optional)

ADVANCE PREPARATION

Early in the day, place the hocks in a large kettle or casserole and add enough broth to cover them completely. Add a few chicken bones for extra flavor. Bring to a simmer, skim the surface and regulate the heat to keep the liquid at a brisk simmer. Cook the hocks about 3 hours, covered or uncovered, until the meat begins to separate easily from the bones. If the liquid reduces noticeably, add enough water to keep the level almost covering the meat. As the hocks cook, turn them and skim the surface of the broth occasionally. When they are done, remove them from the liquid and set aside on a plate to cool.

MAKING THE SALAD

When the hocks are almost cool, prepare the vinaigrette. Stir the mustard, vinegar, salt, pepper and olive oil together, tasting to be sure the flavor is strong enough not to become lost in the meat.

Bone the cooled hocks and cut the meat into medium dice. I discard the skin and fat, but this is a matter of personal taste. Pour over about half the vinaigrette and mix until well combined; taste for seasoning. Add a little more vinaigrette if needed. When satisfied, add 2 tablespoons of whichever herb you prefer, toss and set aside.

Stir enough olive oil into the remaining vinaigrette to make a mild and less acidic dressing. Set aside.

TO SERVE

Make a bed of lettuce on a chilled serving platter. Spread the lettuce out to cover the platter. Make a border of tomato wedges, interspersed with quarters of hard-boiled egg. Sprinkle the tomatoes very lightly with coarse salt and freshly ground pepper. Scatter olives around the platter, then spoon the mild vinaigrette over all.

Mound the pork in the center of the lettuces, leaving a small display of lettuce leaves all around it. If desired, garnish the meat with a few capers.

Sprinkle the remaining herbs over all and serve.

NOTE   In summer freshly picked green beans, cooked just until tender, make a nice addition to this platter.

Beaujolais Chicory Salad with Bacon
SALADE DE BEAUJOLAIS

Even within the region of Beaujolais, its place of origin, this salad varies from one home to the next. Salt pork, fresh belly or bacon, hard-boiled egg and croutons are *always* included. But I have also enjoyed it with diced roast pork and even fried chicken livers. Usually the meats are warm, if not actually hot. Only the lettuce should be crisp and cold.

The best lettuce for this salad is frisée or the pale yellow heart of chicory, but escarole can also be used with a few sprigs of peppery arugula.

Some prefer the vinaigrette to be mild, not to mask the flavor of the ingredients, but others (myself included) find a strong, tart, mustardy vinaigrette particularly well suited. In any event, taste the sauce, tempering it to your liking, and be sure to include a little walnut oil with the olive oil.

SERVES 4

1 clove garlic, peeled
Olive oil
2 cups large dice slightly stale French or Italian bread
5 to 6 ounces lean salt pork, fresh belly *or* bacon, in one piece
About 6 to 8 cups frisée, chicory or other lettuce

2 hard-boiled eggs, still slightly warm from cooking
About 5 chicken livers (optional)
Coarse salt (optional)
Freshly ground black pepper
Vinaigrette Sauce (page 98)
1 rounded tablespoon freshly chopped chives

Rub a large cast-iron skillet with the garlic. Add just enough olive oil to liberally coat the bottom. Heat the oil and add the cubes of bread. Over low heat, sauté the bread, turning the cubes frequently until golden brown on all sides. Remove from the pan and set aside. Give the skillet a quick wipe with paper towels.

Remove the rind from the salt pork, fresh belly or bacon and cut the meat into small lardons, about ¼ inch x 1 inch. Add 1 or 2 tablespoons fresh oil to the skillet, just enough to keep the meat from sticking. Fry the lardons over low heat, turning them frequently, until slightly crisp and lightly browned on all sides. Remove and drain on paper towels. If cooking chicken livers, keep the fat in the pan.

Tear the lettuce into bite-size pieces and place in a large salad bowl. Chill in the refrigerator until ready to serve.

Shell the eggs. Press the yolks with about half the whites through a coarse sieve. Chop the rest of the whites into small pieces.

Shortly before serving, remove any filament from the chicken livers. Sprinkle lightly with salt and liberally with pepper. Heat the fat remaining from the lardons and when hot, quickly fry the livers. Brown them nicely on all sides, while keeping the interior a rosy pink. When finished, cut them into small pieces.

TO SERVE

Sprinkle the lettuce with about half the hard-boiled eggs, both sieved and chopped. Add the croutons, lardons, and chicken livers. If desired, sprinkle the salad with freshly ground pepper, then add the rest of the hard-boiled eggs and spoon over the vinaigrette. Toss briefly, add the chives and toss just until the ingredients are evenly distributed. Serve at once.

Warm Chicory Salad with Assorted Sausages
SALADE LYONNAISE

This salad, with its warm meats, hard-boiled eggs and crisp lettuce is similar to the Beaujolais Chicory Salad on pages 104–105. This is a specialty from the same region and is often called Salade Lyonnaise, pinpointing its origin. (It is a favorite of the wine growers and is also referred to as Salade Vigneronne.) Salade de Beaujolais is composed of fewer ingredients, usually tossed together; Salade Lyonnaise is presented as more of an assembly, the assorted ingredients remain easy to recognize and are often presented on a large platter. The variety of ingredients, particularly the kinds of sausages and the proportion of each, are quite flexible and make this a salad that stimulates the imagination.

A large number of servings is feasible if several platters are used. However, the rustic nature of the salad makes it more appropriate for a family meal, kept on a smaller scale and using whatever ingredients are on hand.

The vinaigrette should be assertive and several kinds of mustard should be passed.

This salad definitely constitutes a meal.

SERVES 4 TO 6

(Continued)

About 6 to 8 cups assorted lettuce, such as chicory, red leaf, escarole, mâche, arugula, radicchio or romaine

2 to 3 pounds assorted warm cooked sausages (see note)

3 to 4 hard-boiled eggs, cut into halves, quarters or slices

3 to 4 medium *or* 8 to 12 whole baby warm cooked beets, peeled and cut into small wedges

1 to 1½ pounds warm cooked new potatoes, peeled or unpeeled, whole or cut into quarters, depending on size

Cooked baby turnips, wedges of fennel hearts, green beans, Romano beans or asparagus (optional)

1 bunch radishes, whole or fan-cut

2 to 3 tablespoons freshly chopped chives and parsley, chervil or dill

Vinaigrette Sauce (page 98)

Make a bed of lettuce on a large platter or shallow wide-rimmed bowl. Chill until ready to complete the salad.

Cut the sausages into large thick slices (on a diagonal if sausages are small) and place them in the center of the lettuce. Then add the hard-boiled eggs, interspersing them with the sausage or tucking them into the lettuce leaves. Distribute the beets and potatoes around the edge of the platter, along with whatever other cooked vegetables you are using and the bright accent of the radishes. Sprinkle freshly chopped herbs over all.

If necessary, double the recipe for the vinaigrette, then taste for seasoning. A mustardy tang should be noticeable.

When ready to serve, spoon the vinaigrette evenly over the salad. If the salad is tossed, try to include a little of everything in each serving.

NOTE Bockwurst, weisswurst or any other white sausage is preferable, but such other varieties as garlic sausage, lightly smoked sausage, beerwurst, bratwurst or kielbasa can be included.

Lentil Salad

SALADE DE LENTILLES

Save the cooking liquid when you prepare the lentils, and if there is any leftover salad, it can be transformed into lentil soup.

For a more substantial salad, poach a small lightly smoked sausage with the lentils, then slice it and add it to the salad. Leftover diced ham could also be used.

SERVES 8

2 cups lentils, rinsed, picked over and drained (1 pound)
One 5- to 7-ounce piece lean bacon, cut into small lardons, about ¼ inch x ½ inch
1 medium onion, stuck with 2 cloves

1 carrot
1 stalk celery with leaves, several sprigs fresh parsley, 1 bay leaf and several sprigs fresh thyme, tied together (bouquet garni)
7 whole scallions, thinly sliced

VINAIGRETTE

1 rounded teaspoon imported Dijon mustard
4 tablespoons red wine vinegar

½ cup olive oil
Freshly ground pepper
Coarse salt to taste

½ cup chopped fresh parsley
2 tablespoons chopped fresh mint leaves (optional)
Romaine lettuce leaves, taken from the heart

Ripe plum tomatoes, quartered, *or* radishes, sliced (optional)
2 hard-boiled eggs, quartered (optional)

Put the lentils, bacon, onion, carrot and bouquet garni together in a soup pot. Add enough water to cover by 1 inch. Bring to a simmer, uncovered, and cook over low heat for about 35 minutes, or until the lentils are just tender. Do not allow to boil.

Drain the lentils and bacon, but reserve the broth for other uses. Discard the bouquet garni, onion and carrot. Mix the lentils and bacon with the scallions.

Combine the mustard, vinegar, olive oil, pepper and coarse salt. Just before serving, add the vinaigrette to the lentils. Combine the chopped fresh herbs and toss about three-quarters of them with the lentils. Reserve the rest.

Line a wide-rimmed bowl or deep platter with crisp lettuce leaves. Mound the salad in the center and, if desired, surround with tomatoes or radishes alternating with quarters of egg. Sprinkle with the remaining herbs and serve the salad warm or at room temperature.

Thai Grilled Pork Salad with Lettuce and Herbs

What makes a recipe especially memorable is sometimes no more than a chain of circumstances falling neatly into place, such as when an abundance of seasonally limited ingredients appear together in the garden or the market. In my case, every annual in the garden was either bolting or diminishing, and it fazed me not at all to ruthlessly snip off fading coriander and spindly mint along with a profusion of hearty basil. Vine-ripened tomatoes and cool cucumbers were pure heaven, their salad days already numbered. An Italian nurseryman produced a small basket of fresh hot peppers—tiny red devils—literally untouchable, and limes in the market were a relative steal.

The weather may be less than perfect, but this salad is in total harmony with even the worst heat wave, especially the kind that makes a chilled soup or crisp salad the only conceivable meal to arouse an appetite.

The meat should be grilled using any marinade in this book, except the very thick one for spareribs. I prefer to grill extra-thick boneless center-cut chops, allowing one per person, but a whole roast—which will take longer to cook and to slice—can also be used.

Good crusty bread is the perfect accompaniment, just what is needed to take advantage of a delicious residue of sauce and juices.

SERVES 4

1 large head romaine or other lettuce, leaves washed, dried and torn into bite-size pieces

1 large or 2 small unwaxed cucumbers, skin scored with a fork and thinly sliced

7 whole scallions, cut into ¼-inch segments

2 large vine-ripened tomatoes, cut into small wedges

½ cup fresh mint leaves

½ cup fresh basil leaves

½ cup fresh coriander leaves

SAUCE

⅓ cup fish sauce from Thailand

½ cup strong greaseless beef stock

½ cup freshly squeezed lime juice

½ teaspoon sugar

1 tablespoon finely chopped garlic

1½ to 2 pounds thick boneless center-cut pork chops

1 rounded tablespoon finely chopped fresh ginger

1 tiny fresh hot red chile pepper, minced, *or* scant ½ teaspoon cayenne

If using a charcoal grill, light the fire. It will take about 45 minutes for the charcoal to burn down to glowing coals with a dusting of white ash. Preheat a gas grill 15 minutes in advance of cooking.

Combine the lettuce, cucumbers, scallions and tomatoes in a large salad bowl. Combine the mint, basil and coriander; coarsely chop them and add half to the salad. Finely chop the remaining herbs and reserve to add to the sauce. Toss the salad briefly to distribute the ingredients evenly. Refrigerate until ready to serve.

Combine the sauce ingredients, one at a time, stirring after each addition. Add the reserved herbs and set aside.

Grill the pork chops about 30 minutes, turning frequently so the meat cooks evenly and they do not burn. When the chops are done, let stand 10 minutes so the juices settle in the meat. Then cut the meat into thin slices. If very large, cut the slices in half again.

Remove the salad from the refrigerator. Arrange half the meat over all, then pour over about two-thirds of the sauce and toss briefly. Arrange the rest of the meat over the salad. Then spoon the remaining sauce evenly over all and bring the salad to the table. Finish combining it when ready to serve. The meat should be slightly warm and the lettuce crisp and cool.

Pass a large basket of good crusty bread.

Asparagus Wrapped in Ham with Walnut Vinaigrette

This makes a festive appetizer and would also serve nicely as a light meal or luncheon dish, accompanied by a basket of good crusty bread and butter. Young leeks can replace the asparagus.

SERVES 4 AS A FIRST COURSE OR 6 TO 8 AS AN APPETIZER

**16 to 20 fat asparagus stalks *or* bundles
    of thin asparagus**

Salt

VINAIGRETTE

**1 rounded teaspoon imported
    Dijon mustard**
**2 tablespoons freshly squeezed lemon
    juice**
1 tablespoon sherry vinegar

Freshly ground pepper
A pinch of coarse salt
3 tablespoons imported walnut oil
4 tablespoons olive oil

2 or 3 ripe plum tomatoes
**About 10 large thin slices cooked ham
    or prosciutto**
Several large Belgian endives
**Red leaf lettuce, Boston, Bibb or butter
    lettuce (optional)**
2 hard-boiled eggs, quartered

1½ tablespoons freshly chopped chives
**½ cup broken or coarsely chopped
    walnuts**
**Small black niçoise olives, packed in
    water, drained (optional)**
**Raw mushroom salad (see note),
    optional**

Break off the bottom of each stalk of asparagus where it snaps most easily. Avoiding the delicate tip, peel large spears with a vegetable peeler. Cook the asparagus, tied in small bundles, in boiling salted water until just tender, about 7 to 10 minutes depending on size. Refresh them in ice water to stop the cooking, then drain and set aside.

Make the vinaigrette by combining the mustard, lemon juice, vinegar, pepper, salt, walnut and olive oils, one at a time, stirring to form a smooth sauce. Cut the tomatoes into small wedges and use a few tablespoons of the vinaigrette to marinate them.

Cut the ham or prosciutto into strips, roughly 1 to 1½ inches x 8 inches.

Arrange 16 to 20 of the large exterior leaves of the endives in a sunburst pattern on a round platter (save the smaller leaves for another use). If desired, fill in the platter with contrasting leaves of other lettuces.

Dip each stalk of asparagus in vinaigrette, then wind a strip of ham around it, working in a spiral from the base and leaving the tip exposed. Place each asparagus in an endive leaf, circling the platter.

Arrange quartered eggs around the edge of the platter, tucking them in between the endive leaves. Remove the tomato wedges from their marinade and mound them in the center of the platter or radiate them in a pattern outward from the center.

Sprinkle the salad with chives, then strew walnuts over all. If desired, add niçoise olives to the border. Mix the tomato marinade with the rest of the vinaigrette and spoon it evenly over all and serve.

NOTE   I frequently prepare a simple salad of thinly sliced mushrooms in a lemon and fresh herb vinaigrette and mound this in the center of the platter. The taste and texture of the mushrooms mingle nicely with that of the asparagus and walnuts.

Oriental Pork Salad with Walnuts

I like to serve this salad—especially on a warm summer's night—family style. The family gathers around the table and, armed with chopsticks, they demolish the contents of the platter. Marinated in dressing, the pork has an uncanny resemblance to duck in taste and texture, but it is much less fatty and easier to prepare.

SERVES 3 AS A MAIN COURSE OR 6 AS AN APPETIZER

1 pound cold Poached Pork Butt (page 175) *or* cold barbecued pork butt

SALAD DRESSING

1 tablespoon imported Dijon mustard, preferably *extra-forte*
About ¼ teaspoon freshly ground white pepper
Pinch of coarse salt
1 tablespoon bottled pomegranate juice
¼ cup freshly squeezed lime juice
1 tablespoon fish sauce from Thailand
1 tablespoon sherry vinegar

½ teaspoon crushed dried red chili peppers
1 rounded teaspoon Vietnamese chili garlic sauce *(túóng ót tói Viet-nam) or* more dried chiles, to taste
1 teaspoon finely chopped garlic
1 tablespoon finely chopped fresh ginger
2 tablespoons imported walnut oil
3 to 4 tablespoons extra-virgin olive oil

½ cup finely chopped celery heart with leaves
3 large scallions, thinly sliced
½ cup chopped fresh mint leaves
½ cup chopped fresh basil leaves

¼ cup coarsely chopped fresh coriander leaves
½ cup broken toasted walnuts
Boston or butter lettuce leaves, preferably from the heart

GARNISHES

Vine-ripened tomato, cut in wedges
Well-iced raw turnip, thinly sliced
Cooked young green beans *or* asparagus

Iced cucumber sticks
Iced fan-cut radishes

About 1½ hours before serving, cut the pork into slices ⅛ to ¼ inch thick. Then cut into ½-inch strips, removing any traces of fat and letting the pieces break where they may. Drop the pork into a large bowl.

In a small round-bottomed bowl, combine the mustard, pepper, salt, pomegranate juice, lime juice, fish sauce, vinegar, chile peppers, chili garlic sauce, garlic and ginger to make the salad dressing, stirring after each addition. Add the walnut and olive oils, 1 tablespoon at a time, mixing thoroughly to form a smooth sauce.

Pour ¼ cup of the dressing over the pork and toss briefly. Then pour ¼ cup more dressing evenly over all, but do not toss. Set aside until ready to finish the salad.

Shortly before serving, add the celery and scallions to the pork with about half the mint, basil and coriander. Toss together, then strew walnuts over all.

To finish the salad, pour over the remaining dressing (if tomatoes are to be part of the garnish, dip them in and out of the sauce, then set aside). Add the rest of the herbs and mix until well combined. Once combined, the salad can wait 1 hour before serving. If you are not serving immediately, add the walnuts only when ready to arrange the salad on the platter.

Mound the pork on a platter on top of a bed of small lettuce leaves. If desired, add some or all of the garnishes, scattered at intervals around the edge of the platter.

NOTE   This salad can be enjoyed with forks or chopsticks, but some people may prefer to use the lettuce leaves as scoops, wrapping the salad in them.

Red Cabbage Salad with Bacon and Vinegar Dressing

Do not make this salad too far in advance. It should stand briefly so the cabbage will take on the flavor of the vinaigrette, but after an hour the tang of the vinegar will dissipate, and worse, the cabbage will lose its crisp texture.

SERVES 6 TO 8

One small red cabbage (about 1½ pounds)
4 to 6 ounces lean bacon, in one piece
4 tablespoons olive oil
¼ cup red wine vinegar *or* sherry vinegar
1 rounded teaspoon imported Dijon mustard

Freshly ground white or black pepper
Coarse salt (optional)
2 scallions, thinly sliced
2 tablespoons chopped fresh parsley

Quarter the cabbage and cut out the core. Shred the cabbage, discarding all hard white areas. Place in a large bowl and set aside.

Remove the bacon rind and discard; cut the bacon into lardons, about ¼ inch x ¾ inch. Put them in a skillet with 1 tablespoon of the olive oil and fry until crisp over medium to low heat. Remove and set aside.

Pour off all but about 2 tablespoons of fat from the skillet. Add the vinegar and boil down until reduced by half. Stir in the mustard. Off heat, add enough olive oil (about 3 tablespoons), a little at a time, to form a smooth sauce. Add freshly ground pepper and taste for seasoning. Salt may be needed. The sauce should be sharp.

Pour the vinaigrette sauce over the cabbage and strew lardons over all. Toss until the lardons are evenly distributed and the cabbage is well coated with sauce. Let stand briefly, tossing several times.

When ready to serve, taste again for seasoning. Add the scallions and parsley. Toss again. The salad will have settled and can probably be turned into a smaller bowl.

Smoked Pork Salad with Vegetables à la Grecque

This salad is more of a concept than a structured recipe. It is derived from a first course I ordered a number of years ago at a small London restaurant whose name I have since forgotten. It was billed as "Smoked Suckling Pig Salad." The suckling pig was served warm, with the slices of meat and small riblets surrounded by a variety of vegetables cooked in the familiar wine and lemon court bouillon known as à la grecque.

Smoked suckling pig is not the most readily available meat, so I have looked for substitutions. The simplest and most economical is a good-quality *lean* smoked pork butt. The meat should be served while still warm.

For the vegetables, I prefer the combination of cauliflower, carrots, mushrooms and tiny white boiling onions. In season, small turnip *bâtons* or fennel wedges, simmered in the same court bouillon, make a nice addition. Sometimes, I mix coarsely chopped coriander leaves with the vegetables just before serving. And, on occasion, I have included a small amount of crisp-cooked green beans. The lemon juice in the marinade will discolor the green beans, but they still taste good. Green beans should be the last ingredient added to the court bouillon. Raise the heat to a brisk simmer and cook them about three to four minutes, depending on size. Though this recipe must be prepared in advance, if the vegetables have been refrigerated, make sure the dish is brought back to room temperature before serving.

SERVES 8

(Continued)

2 smoked pork butts, 1¾ to 2 pounds each (see note)

COURT BOUILLON

1 cup dry white wine
1¾ cups water
½ cup freshly squeezed lemon juice
½ cup olive oil
4 large cloves garlic, flattened and peeled
1 small stalk celery with leaves
1 large or several small bay leaves, broken

1 sprig fresh rosemary, if available
1 stalk fresh fennel with leaves, if available
1 teaspoon cumin seeds
2 teaspoons coriander seeds
½ teaspoon white peppercorns
1 or 2 small dried red chile peppers
1 teaspoon fenugreek seeds

12 small boiling onions, peeled, *or* scallions
1½ pounds carrots, peeled and cut into ¼-inch-thick sticks
2 small fennel hearts, cut into wedges (optional)
¾ to 1 pound turnips, peeled and cut into ¼-inch-thick sticks (optional)
1 pound mushrooms, stems trimmed evenly and quartered if large

1 small cauliflower, divided into small florets
½ pound green beans, ends trimmed (optional)
Coarse salt to taste
1 clove garlic, minced
Small green French olives (*picholine du gard*), or Spanish *alcapardo* olives
Fresh coriander leaves (optional)

Cook the pork butts as directed for Boiled Dinner with Smoked Pork Butt (pages 176–177). Combine the ingredients for the court bouillon in a non-aluminum saucepan. Bring to a boil, lower the heat and simmer, covered, for 10 minutes.

Add the onions and simmer, covered, for 5 minutes, or until just tender, but still firm enough to hold their shape. Remove with a slotted spoon.

Add the carrots and cook, covered, 5 to 7 minutes. Keep them slightly crisp. If fennel and turnips are to be included, cook them after removing the carrots. Simmer the fennel 10 to 15 minutes and the turnips for 5 minutes.

After removing the carrots, raise the heat and add the mushrooms. Boil the mushrooms 2 minutes, uncovered. Turn them in the liquid as they float to the surface, then lower the heat while removing them.

Cook the cauliflower at a brisk simmer, covered, about 5 minutes. Remove from the casserole while the florets are still crisp.

When all the vegetables have been cooked, bring the court bouillon to a rapid boil. At this time, the bowl or plate containing the mushrooms will have accumulated quite a bit of juice. Carefully pour it back into the court bouillon.

Boil down the court bouillon until reduced by half. Add the salt and taste for tartness. If the flavor of lemon does not assert itself, reduce further. Off heat, add the minced garlic to the court bouillon and let stand a few minutes. Meanwhile, gather the vegetables together in a bowl and strain the court bouillon over them.

Turn the vegetables frequently, until cooled, tilting the bowl and spooning the marinade over them. Refrigerate overnight or leave at room temperature for 24 hours, tossing occasionally.

To serve, arrange the succulent slices of meat in the center of large individual plates. Surround them with the vegetables; scatter a few olives and sprinkle a little freshly chopped coriander over all. Freshly prepared horseradish sauce or hot mustard are good accompaniments.

NOTE Other possible choices would be a moist smoked loin of pork, roasted and carved into individual chops, or thin precut smoked pork chops, simmered in a mild stock to which a little wine has been added (½ cup dry white wine to every 2 cups chicken stock).

PIG
ON THE
HEARTH

Spicy Marinades for Barbecued Pork

·

Grilled Pork, Chinese Style

·

Barbecued Spareribs with Cooked Marinade

·

Quick Uncooked Marinade for Spareribs

·

Grilled Double Pork Chops with Mustard Marinade

·

Applesauce

·

Pork Chops in Fresh Tomato Sauce

·

Fresh Tomato Sauce

·

Grilled Pork Slices in Herbal Infusion

·

Shish Kebab of Boneless Pork and Chicken Thighs

·

Indonesian Pork Satay with Peanut Sauce

·

Pork Satay with Bean Mash and Citrus Marinade

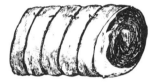

There is something about the lure of the barbecue that kindles nostalgia. At our house fresh local cider with juicy caramelized sausages, hot from the grill, has been a favorite breakfast for countless Sundays in autumn. I still vividly recall spareribs that in our youth we barbecued in the dark on a beach in Big Sur; pigs roasted over fruitwood embers under the shade of olive trees in sunny Mallorca; and the ongoing easy meals of pork chops cooked over smoldering coals at dusk, bringing to a close a day on the lake.

Being able to barbecue makes almost any occasion more festive and more relaxed. Cooking on the grill is both a pleasurable way to cook for one and an ideal way to feed a crowd.

BARBECUING

When planning to grill over a charcoal fire, you should arrange and light the charcoal about 35 to 45 minutes in advance of cooking. The flames need time to burn down before the fire is ready, transforming the charcoal into hot glowing orange coals with a dusting of white ash. More ash will accumulate the longer the coals burn, making the fire even and the heat consistent. The risk of the coals flaring up and burning the meat will be diminished, as will the presence of any chemical aroma from the briquettes. (This taste can be imparted to the food.)

When a low fire and long, slow cooking are required, use more charcoal and spread the coals out as soon as the fire is established. The burning embers of a good fire should retain their heat for at least one hour after they are ready for grilling. If a much longer grilling time is needed, add a few additional briquettes from time to time, keeping them on the periphery of the fire until they have a measurable amount of ash. They may then be added to the coals directly under the food being grilled.

Preheat a gas grill fifteen minutes with the hood down (if there is one) and the temperature control set to high. After the grill has preheated, adjust the heat according to your needs.

A pork roast will need to cook anywhere from forty-five minutes to about one hour over medium heat with the hood down. The meat should be basted and turned every ten to fifteen minutes. If the grill does not have a hood, cook slightly longer and raise the heat, if needed. If unsure whether the meat is done, insert a thermometer into the thickest part of the roast. The American Meat Institute recommends 170°F., but I feel this is overkill. Trichinae are killed at 140°F.; to be absolutely safe, I would suggest a temperature between 150° and 160°F. The meat itself will vary within, more so when cooked on a barbecue grill than in the oven.

After barbecuing, a pork roast will profit by standing for fifteen to thirty minutes before carving. Cover with heavy aluminum foil to keep it warm. In warm weather, it can stand even longer. This rest will allow the juices to settle evenly in the meat, making it moister and increasing its tenderness.

All barbecued pork roasts are just as delicious served at room temperature as hot (a great convenience) and most are equally good served cold. This makes pork the ideal meat to consider for a party.

Spicy Marinades for Barbecued Pork

Use any of these marinades for boneless pork butt, pork loin roast or chops. A standard boneless pork butt usually weighs between two and two and a half pounds; the size of a roast or number of chops is variable.

These thin marinades are different from the thick barbecue sauces used for spareribs and Chinese-style barbecued pork. The quantities are variable; most marinades benefit from a creative touch.

Combine all ingredients and marinate the pork at least three hours, preferably overnight, turning it occasionally. If preparing a whole piece of meat, it is helpful to puncture it with a skewer, dotting it evenly on all sides, to better absorb the marinade. (I find a lean boneless pork butt ideal for this treatment.)

When ready to barbecue the pork, combine all excess marinade in a bowl and stir in a little oil. Use this for a basting sauce. If the amount is inadequate, combine as much oil and lime juice, in equal parts, as you need to finish grilling the meat. A lean loin roast, permeated with the flavor of any one of these marinades, will be very good cold.

MARINADE I

MAKES ENOUGH FOR 1 PORK BUTT

1 tablespoon fish sauce from Thailand
2 tablespoons bottled Mexican green
    sauce (see note) *or* homemade
    Mexican Green Tomato Sauce
    (page 267)
2 tablespoons mild imported soy sauce
1 teaspoon sugar
⅓ cup freshly squeezed lime juice

1 tablespoon balsamic vinegar
2 cloves garlic, finely chopped
    (1 scant tablespoon)
1 tablespoon finely chopped fresh ginger
2 tablespoons Korean hot sauce with
    bean mash and sesame seeds
2 tablespoons imported sesame oil

NOTE Mexican green sauce is any variety of green salsa containing green tomatoes, hot green chiles, onion, coriander and spices.

MARINADE II

MAKES ENOUGH FOR 1 PORK BUTT

2 rounded teaspoons Chinese chili paste
    with garlic *or* chili paste with
    black beans

1 tablespoon chili sauce *or* ketchup
    (optional)

2 teaspoons sugar

1 rounded tablespoon imported
    coarse-grained mustard

⅓ cup freshly squeezed lime juice

2 tablespoons imported soy sauce

1 tablespoon chopped fresh ginger

2 tablespoons finely chopped fresh
    mint leaves

2 tablespoons imported sesame oil

MARINADE III

MAKES ENOUGH FOR 2 PORK BUTTS

½ cup dry red wine

2 tablespoons Korean hot sauce with
    bean mash, with or without
    sesame seeds

2 tablespoons imported soy sauce

¼ cup freshly squeezed lemon juice

⅓ cup freshly squeezed lime juice

1 tablespoon red wine vinegar or
    cider vinegar

1 teaspoon sugar

1 rounded teaspoon imported
    coarse-grained mustard

2 large cloves garlic, finely chopped
    (about 1 tablespoon)

1 tablespoon finely chopped fresh ginger

1 tablespoon imported sesame oil

Grilled Pork, Chinese Style

Although this method of cooking pork is not the same as that of Chinatown grocery stores, I find the results are very close in both appearance and taste. This is a good way to prepare a large quantity of pork for a party. It is good served at room temperature or even cold and also lends itself nicely to stir-frying with vegetables.

The initial cooking is done in the oven and needs no attention. The only concern is later, when the meat should be basted frequently to insure a rich glaze on all sides.

SERVES 6

One 3-pound boneless loin of pork, well trimmed, *or* lean boneless pork butt (see note)

MARINADE

5 large cloves garlic, finely chopped
1½ tablespoons finely chopped fresh ginger
1 fresh hot green chile pepper, seeded and finely chopped
½ cup finely chopped onion

¼ cup freshly squeezed lime juice
¼ cup Hoisin sauce
1 tablespoon ketchup *or* chili sauce
¼ cup imported soy sauce
¼ cup dark Jamaican rum

English or Chinese Mustard (page 41)

ADVANCE PREPARATION

Make shallow punctures with a skewer all over the pork, to help it better absorb the marinade. Combine all the marinade ingredients in a bowl. Place the meat on several thicknesses of heavy-duty aluminum foil and spoon over enough marinade to coat generously on all sides. Reserve any excess marinade. Bring up the edges of the foil and crimp them to seal the meat tightly. Refrigerate overnight.

COOKING THE PORK

Preheat the oven to 350°F. Remove the pork from the refrigerator 1 or 2 hours before cooking, but do not unwrap. Place the foil package in a shallow baking pan to prevent spills.

Roast the pork, still wrapped in foil, for 1½ hours undisturbed. During the last hour, prepare a fire for finishing the meat. It will need to cook about 1 hour over hot smoldering coals. (A gas grill should be set to a medium temperature after preheating and lowered, if necessary.)

After 1½ hours in the oven, unwrap the pork and pour the marinade and juices into a saucepan. Add any reserved marinade and bring to a boil. Cook about 3 minutes, or until slightly reduced and thickened.

Transfer the pork to the grill and cook 1 hour. Turn the meat and baste frequently with the cooked marinade. When done, place the pork on a carving board and let stand 15 minutes before slicing.

Accompany the meat with a small dish of hot mustard.

NOTE   A boneless pork butt weighs 2¼ to 2½ pounds. The meat will not be as lean as the loin, but its juiciness will be a trade-off. A butt will serve 4; cook 2 to serve 8.

Barbecued Spareribs with Cooked Marinade

This cooked marinade is well worth the little extra time it takes to cook and cool it. If you are in a real rush to get the ribs on the grill, use the Quick Uncooked Marinade (page 127) instead.

SERVES 6 TO 8

COOKED MARINADE

2 tablespoons olive oil
1 cup finely chopped onion
¼ cup red wine vinegar
½ teaspoon powdered mustard
½ teaspoon paprika
¼ cup imported soy sauce
2 tablespoons Worcestershire sauce
2 tablespoons Pickapeppa sauce

2 racks spareribs, each in one piece
Olive oil (optional)

¼ cup brown sugar, firmly packed
½ tablespoon finely chopped fresh ginger
1 bay leaf
1 large clove garlic, flattened and
　finely chopped
2 cups bottled chili sauce
½ cup combined lime and lemon juice

Lemon juice (optional)

ADVANCE PREPARATION

Heat the oil in a 2-quart saucepan over medium heat. Add the onion and sauté until soft and golden but not browned. Then add the vinegar, mustard, paprika, soy sauce, Worcestershire sauce, Pickapeppa sauce, brown sugar, ginger, bay leaf, garlic, chili sauce and citrus juice; bring to a boil. Lower the heat to a simmer and cook for 20 minutes, stirring occasionally. Let the sauce cool before using it.

Spread the ribs out, flesh side up, on 1 or 2 large baking sheets. Coat them lavishly with sauce. Using the point of a small sharp knife, pierce the flesh between each rib in several places to allow the sauce to penetrate the meat. (For now, do not waste the sauce on the bony underside of the ribs.) Let the ribs marinate several hours at room temperature or overnight in the refrigerator.

GRILLING THE RIBS

Prepare the coals, allowing enough charcoal for a lengthy cooking over a well-tempered fire. If using a gas grill, regulate the heat to medium.

Scrape excess marinade into a bowl for basting, then arrange the ribs on the grill, flesh side up. Cook the ribs about 1 hour and 15 minutes, in all. Turn and baste every 15 minutes (or more often if dripping juices cause the coals to flare). After they have been turned once, the bony underside can be basted from time to time. If the sauce is used up, continue to baste with olive oil mixed with lemon juice.

When the ribs are cooked, cut the racks into single ribs and serve on a carving board or a large platter. Plenty of paper napkins are in order!

Quick Uncooked Marinade for Spareribs

The soy sauce contributes a dark rich color, which makes pork spareribs look especially inviting.

MAKES ABOUT 2 CUPS

2 rounded tablespoons imported coarse-
  grained mustard
1 cup bottled chili sauce
¼ cup dark or black imported soy sauce
¼ cup freshly squeezed lemon juice

½ cup freshly squeezed lime juice
1 tablespoon balsamic vinegar
¼ cup ketchup, depending on sweetness
  of the chili sauce

Combine all the ingredients in a small bowl.

NOTE   Except for the mustard, chili sauce and soy sauce, the amount of the ingredients is flexible. The flavor should be tangy with a noticeable acidity and not too sweet.

Grilled Double Pork Chops
with Mustard Marinade

SERVES 4 TO 6

MARINADE

2 rounded tablespoons imported
    coarse-grained mustard
2 tablespoons mild imported soy sauce
2 level tablespoons ketchup

⅓ cup freshly squeezed lime juice
1 tablespoon imported sesame oil
1 tablespoon chopped fresh ginger

4 to 6 double-thick center-cut pork
    chops, bone in (about 12 ounces each)
Olive oil (optional)
Freshly squeezed lime juice (optional)

Fresh coriander leaves
Warm Applesauce (page 129), optional
Corn on the cob (optional)

Combine the mustard, soy sauce, ketchup, lime juice, sesame oil and ginger for the marinade, stirring after each addition. Spoon over just enough marinade to coat the chops, then turn them and coat the other side. Let marinate several hours. Turn the chops once or twice, coating with a little more marinade, if needed. Reserve some marinade.

Prepare a charcoal fire or preheat a gas grill. A grill with a hood is preferable. When ready, the live coals should be a glowing orange and topped with a fine white ash. After preheating a gas grill, set the temperature control to medium-high. Brush the grill rack with a little oil, then arrange the chops side by side. Pour the excess marinade back into the bowl with the reserve.

Cook the chops about 40 minutes, with the barbecue hood down. Turn them and baste with marinade every 10 to 15 minutes, depending on how rapidly they color. Do not allow them to burn. If the quantity of marinade is insufficient, finish by brushing the chops with a mixture of 2 parts olive oil to 1 part lime juice. (If uncertain as to doneness, check by cutting into the flesh of the largest chop near the bone. The meat should be white.) When done, arrange the chops on a hot platter and scatter fresh coriander leaves around them.

Serve the chops accompanied by a bowl of warm Applesauce, if desired, and fresh corn on the cob in season.

Applesauce

It is hard to go wrong making applesauce. Simply the fact that it is homemade is a step in the right direction. If possible, make the applesauce shortly before serving, so it is still warm when brought to the table. I prefer to use tart Granny Smith apples and they often manage to retain some of their shape. For a change of pace, combine sliced underripe pears or ripe quince with the apples. (Quince will need more sugar and a longer cooking time.)

MAKES ABOUT 3 CUPS

1½ pounds tart apples, peeled and sliced
2 tablespoons butter
3 tablespoons orange or lemon
   marmalade
Grated zest of 1 orange *or* 1 large lemon

¼ cup freshly squeezed lime juice
⅓ cup freshly squeezed orange juice
½ cup crystallized ginger, cut into slivers
2 or 3 tablespoons brandy (optional)

Combine all the ingredients in a heavy saucepan. Bring to a boil, then reduce the heat slightly and cook, uncovered, until most of the juices have been absorbed, about 45 minutes. Stir frequently.

When finished, the applesauce should have the rich glossy hue of a marvelous confiture—which, in a sense, it is.

NOTE Taste the sauce. The crystallized ginger and the marmalade may contribute enough sugar, but if the applesauce is not sweet enough, stir in 1 tablespoon brown sugar or raw sugar and cook until it is dissolved.

Pork Chops in Fresh Tomato Sauce
COSTOLETTE DI MAIALE ALLA PIZZAIOLA

Simple, unadorned buttered pasta and a bowl of freshly grated cheese are an ideal accompaniment for these Italian-style pork chops.
SERVES 4

Herbal infusion (page 133)
4 thick well-trimmed, center-cut pork
 chops, bone in (about 12 ounces each)
2 cups Fresh Tomato Sauce, thickened
 (page 132)

1 tablespoon chopped garlic
3 tablespoons chopped fresh hot red
 cherry peppers
1 rounded tablespoon chopped fresh
 parsley *or* basil leaves

ADVANCE PREPARATION

Prepare the Herbal infusion and marinate the chops in it for at least 1 hour, preferably longer. Turn and baste the chops occasionally.

GRILLING THE CHOPS

Start a charcoal fire about 45 minutes in advance of cooking, or preheat a gas grill for 15 minutes.

Grill the chops over glowing hot coals with a thin topping of white ash or regulate the heat from medium to high on a preheated gas grill. Turn the chops frequently until fully cooked without letting them char (this would mar the sauce). Switch them around on the grill if the juices cause the coals to flare. Allow about 40 minutes cooking time. When they appear done, remove them and check each one by making a small incision near the bone. If the flesh is pink, return the chops to the grill or cook the chops longer in the tomato sauce.

FINISHING THE CHOPS

Prepare the Fresh Tomato Sauce. Have it simmering in a skillet or shallow casserole just large enough to contain the chops in one layer. Transfer the chops to the skillet and sprinkle with the chopped garlic and cherry peppers; spoon the sauce over them. Simmer over low heat for about 10 minutes. Tilt the skillet and spoon the sauce over the chops so the meat juices permeate the sauce and the garlic and cherry peppers are well combined.

Sprinkle with chopped parsley or basil and serve each chop with a generous dollop of sauce.

NOTE   The chops may also be fried. Sear them on each side in a skillet coated with a little olive oil. Lower the heat and cook, covered, turning them frequently and basting with pan juices. Cook slowly until done, about 45 minutes.

Fresh Tomato Sauce

The herbs in this sauce must be fresh, even if you are limited to parsley. If you have an herb garden or a resourceful greengrocer, make basil a priority and also include thyme, oregano, marjoram, savory and mint. If available, add tarragon and chervil, but in smaller amounts than the other herbs. Decrease the amount of parsley in favor of variety.

MAKES ABOUT 8 CUPS

About 10 pounds firm, ripe vine-ripened
 tomatoes
Olive oil
4 cloves garlic, crushed slightly and
 peeled
¼ teaspoon coarsely ground white
 peppercorns

¼ teaspoon coarse salt
1 rounded tablespoon finely chopped
 garlic
About ¾ cup chopped fresh herbs

Peel and core the tomatoes, then cut them into large wedges and scrape out the seeds. Spread the tomato segments on paper towels to absorb some of the juice.

Liberally coat the bottom of a large heavy stockpot with olive oil. Add the whole cloves of garlic and fry over low to medium heat until they are golden and faintly crisp. Allow 15 to 20 minutes for this and make sure they do not burn. Press down hard on the garlic, mashing it, then discard.

Heat the garlic-flavored oil until almost smoking. Add the segments of tomato, pepper and salt. Raise the heat and when the tomatoes are bubbling, add half the chopped garlic and lower the heat to a simmer. Cook, uncovered, stirring frequently to be sure the tomatoes do not stick to the bottom of the pan. If any excess olive oil appears on the surface, skim it off.

Stir half the herbs into the sauce. When the sauce has reduced by about a third, stir in the remaining garlic and herbs and remove from the heat.

Allow the sauce to cool completely, then ladle it into storage containers and freeze until ready to use.

NOTE   If the sauce needs to be thickened, add ¼ teaspoon sugar and 1 scant teaspoon tomato paste to 2 cups of sauce. Cook over medium to low heat, stirring frequently, until very thick.

Grilled Pork Slices in Herbal Infusion

This unusually simple recipe has little need for exact measurements. Success depends on the fresh herbs. Allow two slices of pork per person.
SERVES 4

½ cup extra-virgin olive oil
⅓ cup freshly squeezed lemon juice
A small bouquet fresh rosemary
A small bouquet sprigs fresh thyme
Freshly ground white pepper

About 1¾ pounds boneless center-cut pork, sliced ¼ inch thick
Imported Dijon mustard, preferably *extra-forte*

ADVANCE PREPARATION

Pour the olive oil into a shallow dish large enough to hold the slices of pork in one layer. Thin the oil with lemon juice, stirring with a fork to blend. Strip the leaves from the stems of the herbs. There should be about ½ cup all together. Chop them and add to the oil. There should be enough herbal essence to turn the marinade green. Stir, pressing down on the herbs with a fork.

Add a generous grinding of pepper, then the pork slices. Turn them in the marinade, one at a time, to make sure they are saturated with herbs. Let stand at least 1 hour, preferably longer. Turn the pork and baste it with marinade several times.

GRILLING THE PORK

Make a charcoal fire or preheat a gas grill. The coals should be very hot. If the fire is not adjustable, be sure there is a space over the coals where the heat is less intense.

Arrange the slices of pork on the grill over the hottest part of the fire and sear them on each side. Before the meat chars beyond normal grid marks, lower the heat or transfer the pork to a more moderate part of the fire. Turn the slices frequently, slathering them with herbs each time they are turned. Cook only until the pork is done (about 10 minutes should be long enough). Do not allow the meat to char, or the flavor of the herbs will be lost.

Pass hot mustard for those who like it with their meat.

NOTE Grilled vegetables, brushed with fresh herbal infusion (not the one in which the pork was marinated), make a good accompaniment. Good choices include eggplant slices, zucchini (cut lengthwise), leeks, red and yellow peppers, fresh shiitake mushrooms and sweet Vidalia onions in season.

Shish Kebab of Boneless Pork and Chicken Thighs

Cut the meat from the chicken thighs larger than the cubes of pork. This will insure that when both meats are cooked through the chicken will not be dried out. If each thigh is divided into two pieces, the size should be about right.

SERVES 6

1¾ to 2 pounds lean boneless pork butt, cut into 1¼-inch cubes

8 to 10 small chicken thighs, boned and halved

Spicy Marinade for Barbecued Pork (choose one on pages 122–123)

4 medium onions, quartered and layers separated

4 large sweet red or green peppers, cut into 1½-inch squares

ADVANCE PREPARATION

Marinate the pork and chicken several hours or overnight, turning the meats in the marinade from time to time.

Thread the pork and chicken on separate skewers, alternating the meat with pieces of onion and peppers.

GRILLING THE SHISH KEBAB

Grill the meats over low coals. Baste frequently with the marinade and turn the skewers every 10 minutes; 45 minutes should be sufficient cooking time. By threading the chicken and pork on separate skewers, one can be removed before the other.

NOTE   If necessary, this shish kebab can also be cooked indoors under the broiler. With the protection and insulation of the oven, the meats will probably be done a little sooner than on an outdoor grill.

Indonesian Pork Satay with Peanut Sauce

Satays are usually served as one of a number of dishes. Often other satays, such as chicken or shrimp, will be included. A satay also makes a nice appetizer.

SERVES 8

MARINADE

1 cup roasted unsalted peanuts
2 tablespoons ground coriander
2 tablespoons brown sugar
2 tablespoons crushed dried red chile peppers
Grated zest of 1 lemon
2 tablespoons freshly squeezed lemon juice
1½ to 2 tablespoons finely chopped fresh ginger

4 to 5 cloves garlic, finely chopped
1 small to medium onion, finely chopped
3 tablespoons imported soy sauce
3 tablespoons freshly squeezed lime juice
1 cup Coconut Milk (page 81) *or* frozen or canned *unsweetened* coconut milk
Freshly squeezed orange juice

2 pounds lean boneless pork, cut into 1-inch cubes

1 cup chicken stock

ADVANCE PREPARATION

Grind the peanuts in a food processor or blender. Add the rest of the marinade ingredients, except the orange juice, blending until smooth. If the marinade is too thick, thin with a little orange juice. Coat the pork generously with sauce and marinate in the refrigerator for 4 hours or overnight.

Soak bamboo satay skewers for 1 hour before using.

GRILLING THE SATAYS

Preheat a gas grill 15 minutes before cooking or start a charcoal fire 45 minutes to 1 hour in advance. The coals should be hot glowing embers with a topping of fine white ash.

Thread the pieces of pork on the skewers. Collect the excess sauce and bring it to a boil. Add chicken stock and simmer briefly. Use this sauce to baste the pork as it cooks and to pass separately at the table.

(Continued)

Grill the meat about 30 minutes or until done over the low coals. Adjust the temperature of a gas grill to medium; lower it further, if necessary. Baste the satays from time to time and turn the skewers frequently to keep the sauce from burning.

NOTE   If necessary, the pork can also be cooked in a 475°F. oven for about 30 minutes. Be sure to place aluminum foil under the meat, as the sauce and juices burn easily and will stick to the baking sheet.

Pork Satay with Bean Mash and Citrus Marinade

This satay has a thin marinade redolent of citrus and herbs. Accompany it with Thai Spicy Herb Sauce for dipping. The satay will serve six as an appetizer, but could also be served in the company of other satays as a main course.

SERVES 6

MARINADE

2 heaping tablespoons Korean hot bean mash
1 tablespoon fish sauce from Thailand
1 tablespoon mild imported soy sauce
⅓ cup freshly squeezed lime juice
⅓ cup freshly squeezed orange juice

1½ pounds lean boneless pork, cut into ¾-inch cubes

1 heaping tablespoon finely chopped garlic
1 heaping tablespoon finely chopped fresh ginger
½ cup chopped fresh mint and basil leaves

GARNISH

Fringed sliced cucumbers
Fan-cut radishes

Scallion brushes
Thai Spicy Herb Sauce (page 35)

ADVANCE PREPARATION

Combine the marinade ingredients in a bowl, stirring to dissolve the bean mash. Marinate the pork at least several hours or overnight.

Soak bamboo satay skewers for 1 hour before using.

GRILLING THE SATAYS

Preheat a gas grill 15 minutes before you are ready to cook or start a charcoal fire 45 minutes in advance. The coals should be orange and glowing with a topping of fine white ash.

Thread the meat on skewers and grill for about 30 minutes, or until done. Adjust the temperature control of a gas grill, lowering or raising the heat as necessary. Baste frequently with the marinade while cooking and turn the skewers often.

Garnish the satays with fringed sliced cucumbers, fan-cut radishes and scallion brushes.

PIG IN A WOK

Fresh Pork Slices with Shiitake Mushrooms, Tomato and Bok Choy

·

Eggplant, Family Style

·

Hot and Spicy Bean Curd with Ground Pork and Peas

·

Green Pork with Asparagus, Lime and Herbs

·

Spicy-Tangy Pork with Green Beans

·

Stir-Fried Spinach

·

Spicy Pork Strips in Black Bean Sauce with Spinach

·

Sesame Pork with Green Sauce

·

Thai Pork with Green Curry

·

Catfish with Pork Strips and Vietnamese Sauce

·

Chinese Clams with Pork and Black Bean Sauce

·

Sea Scallops with Mushrooms and Salt Pork

·

Crab with Pork and Black Bean Sauce

·

Spicy Shrimp with Ham and Coconut Milk

This gathering of recipes is a reflection of China and Southeast Asia and the reliance there on pork. In these countries, many bordered by the sea, the word meat is simply another way of saying pork. In many recipes, even though the featured ingredient might be green beans, eggplant, bean curd, crab or clams, the dish would not attain its full worth without being bolstered by pork to make it more interesting and more substantial.

Fresh Pork Slices with Shiitake Mushrooms, Tomato and Bok Choy

SERVES 4

MARINADE

2 extra-large egg whites
2 tablespoons cornstarch

2 teaspoons chili paste with garlic
1 tablespoon dry sherry

1½ pounds lean pork butt
1¾ cups (1 ounce) dried shiitake
    mushrooms *or* ¼ pound fresh shiitake
    mushrooms

SAUCE

½ cup chicken stock
1 teaspoon chili paste with garlic
1 rounded tablespoon Korean hot sauce
    with bean mash and sesame seeds
¼ teaspoon sugar
2 tablespoons freshly squeezed lime juice

1 tablespoon bottled Mexican green
    sauce (see note) *or* homemade
    Mexican Green Tomato Sauce (page
    267)
2 large cloves garlic, chopped
2 tablespoons long slivers fresh ginger

About 3 cups peanut or corn oil for frying
1 large onion, cut into small wedges,
    layers separated
1 large red or green bell pepper, cut into
    1-inch squares
1 small bunch bok choy, cut into 1-inch
    segments, leafy part separated

7 scallions, cut into ¼-inch slices, white
    and green parts separated
2 large ripe plum tomatoes, peeled and
    cut into long thin strips
½ cup fresh coriander leaves

ADVANCE PREPARATION

In a bowl large enough to contain the pork, beat the egg whites to a froth. Blend in the cornstarch and when smooth, stir in the chili paste and the sherry.

    Cut the pork into thin slices, then cut each in half lengthwise. (This is easier to do if the meat is partially frozen.) Add the pork slices to the marinade and stir until well coated. Let marinate at least 1 hour, turning the slices from time to time.

(Continued)

If using dried mushrooms, soak them in lukewarm water until softened, then squeeze dry and cut the caps into long slivers. Cut fresh mushrooms into long slivers just before cooking.

Combine the sauce ingredients in a bowl and mix in half the garlic and ginger.

COOKING

Heat 2 to 3 cups of oil in a wok and when almost smoking, add a small portion of pork slices. When crisp and fully cooked, remove and drain in a sieve, then transfer to a platter lined with paper towels. Continue until all the pork has been cooked.

Pour off the oil, wipe the wok and add 2 tablespoons fresh oil. When searing hot, add the onion, followed by the bell pepper. Stir until black blister spots appear on the vegetables, then add the thicker segments of bok choy stems and stir briefly. Remove the vegetables from the wok while they are still crisp.

Add the mushrooms and a little more oil, if needed. Stir-fry until they begin to curl. Add the remaining garlic and ginger. Stir briefly and add the white part of the scallions. A moment later add the tomatoes. The dense flesh of plum tomatoes will release few juices. As soon as the wok appears dry, pour in the sauce and bring to a boil. (At this time cooking may be halted temporarily.)

Boil the sauce rapidly and add the leafier segments of bok choy. Stir briefly. Return the pork to the wok, turning the slices in the sauce until well coated and heated through. At the last moment, return the rest of the vegetables and stir to combine.

Transfer the pork and vegetables to a warmed serving platter and sprinkle with the green part of the scallions and fresh coriander leaves. Serve at once.

NOTE Mexican green sauce is any variety of green salsa containing green tomatoes, hot green chiles, onion, coriander and spices.

Eggplant, Family Style

I sometimes imbed a wok in a charcoal fire and find that the smoke from the coals contributes nicely to the flavor of the eggplant.

In season, hot red cherry peppers may replace the green chiles.

SERVES 4

2 small eggplants (about ¾ pound each)
Coarse salt
½ pound lean pork, coarsely ground (see note)

½ cup strong dark beef stock
1 rounded tablespoon Korean hot sauce with bean mash (without sesame seeds)
1 teaspoon sugar
1 tablespoon balsamic or cider vinegar
2 tablespoons mild imported soy sauce
7 scallions, cut into pea-size pieces, white and green parts separated

1 teaspoon cornstarch
1 tablespoon mild imported soy sauce
About 2 cups peanut or corn oil for frying

5 large cloves garlic, peeled and thinly sliced
1½ tablespoons long slivers fresh ginger
4 or more fresh hot green chile peppers, seeded and thinly sliced
2 teaspoons imported sesame oil
Fresh coriander leaves for garnish

ADVANCE PREPARATION

Trim the stems and cut the eggplants into slices 1¼ inches thick. Then cut each slice in half, or into large quarters, depending on size. Sprinkle the pieces well with coarse salt and toss together in a colander. Let drain 1 to 2 hours, turning the eggplant from time to time.

Using a fork, blend the pork with the cornstarch and soy sauce. Let marinate 1 hour or longer.

COOKING

Pat the eggplant dry with paper towels, removing most of the salt. Heat 1½ to 2 cups of the oil in a wok and when very hot, fry the eggplant pieces, a few at a time. When well browned on all sides, remove and drain in a sieve or colander, catching the oil in a bowl. Transfer to paper towels to dry.

Pour off all but a few tablespoons of the oil used to cook the eggplant. Add the pork mixture, stirring constantly to break up the meat. Fry until completely cooked and lightly browned, then remove and drain on paper towels.

(Continued)

Combine the stock, bean mash, sugar, vinegar and soy sauce in a bowl.

Add 1 or 2 tablespoons fresh oil to the wok. Add the white part of the scallions with half the garlic and all the ginger and hot peppers. Stir-fry for 1 minute. Add the sauce mixture and bring to a rapid boil. Return the pork and eggplant to the wok and add the green part of the scallions and remaining garlic.

When well combined, stir in the sesame oil and turn out onto a warmed serving platter. Scatter with coriander leaves and serve at once.

NOTE   If you prefer, partially freeze the meat and mince it by hand with a Chinese cleaver.

Hot and Spicy Bean Curd with Ground Pork and Peas

This dish can be made without the peas, in which case Stir-Fried Spinach (page 149) would make a very good accompaniment.

SERVES 4

3 to 4 cakes pressed bean curd (see note), cut into 1-inch dice

SAUCE

2 tablespoons Korean hot sauce with bean mash (without sesame seeds)

1 tablespoon mild imported soy sauce

3 tablespoons peanut oil

5 cloves garlic, flattened, peeled and cut into slivers

2 tablespoons slivers fresh ginger

2 or more fresh hot green chile peppers, seeded and thinly sliced *or* canned jalapeño peppers

¼ teaspoon cayenne

½ teaspoon sugar

1 teaspoon cider or balsamic vinegar

6 to 8 ounces lean ground pork

½ cup chicken stock

3 or 4 whole scallions, cut into ¼-inch pieces

1 teaspoon cornstarch

1 cup shelled fresh peas

1 teaspoon imported sesame oil

ADVANCE PREPARATION

If pressed bean curd is not obtainable, press regular bean curd as directed below.

COOKING

Combine the bean mash, soy sauce, cayenne, sugar and vinegar in a bowl to make a sauce.

Heat the oil in a wok. Add the garlic, ginger and chile peppers. Just as the garlic begins to color, add the pork, stirring to break it up. When the pork is fully cooked, pour over the sauce mixture. Cook briefly, then stir in the bean curd. Mix only until combined, then reduce the heat to low. Add the chicken stock and scallions and bring to a simmer.

Mix the cornstarch with 1 teaspoon cold water, stirring until dissolved. Add to the sauce and continue to stir until thickened. Add the peas and stir in the sesame oil. Serve at once.

NOTE   Pressed bean curd can be cut neatly and will not break up when stirred into soups and sauces. If your grocer does not stock it, press it yourself, allowing several hours for satisfactory results.

Fold 1 sheet of paper towel into quarters and center it on a deep plate. Place drained bean curd on top. Fold a second sheet of paper towel, cover the bean curd with it and weight down evenly with a small flat plate. Place an object weighing about 1 pound on the plate to increase pressure.

Let stand several hours. Change the paper towels twice, or whenever saturated with water. Refrigerate the pressed bean curd until ready to use. (If bean curd is kept longer than 2 days, it should be submerged in cold water.)

Green Pork with Asparagus, Lime and Herbs

Abundant with fresh herbs and served over crisp lettuce, this dish makes a refreshing meal on a warm summer evening.

Serve it with rice or a good crusty loaf of French or Italian bread to mop up the juices.

SERVES 4

1½ pounds lean boneless pork

MARINADE

½ teaspoon sugar
3 tablespoons freshly squeezed lime juice
1 tablespoon imported soy sauce

1 pound thin asparagus stalks
2 cups peanut oil

SAUCE

½ cup chicken stock
1 rounded tablespoon Korean hot sauce with bean mash and sesame seeds *or* 1 rounded teaspoon chili paste with garlic
¼ cup freshly squeezed lime juice
½ teaspoon sugar
2 tablespoons fish sauce from Thailand

1 scant cup (½ ounce) dried shiitake mushrooms, soaked, squeezed dry and cut into thick strips *or* fresh shiitake mushrooms
8 scallions, some of the green stems set aside, the rest cut into 1-inch pieces
4 fresh long green chile peppers, seeded and cut on the diagonal into 1-inch pieces

1 tablespoon dry sherry
1 teaspoon crushed dried red chile peppers

½ head crisp romaine lettuce, cut into large shreds

2 tablespoons mild imported soy sauce
1 tablespoon dry sherry
2 teaspoons finely chopped garlic
1 tablespoon finely chopped fresh ginger
2 rounded tablespoons chopped fresh herbs, such as coriander, basil and mint (see note)

1 tablespoon slivers fresh ginger
1 tablespoon slivers garlic
¾ cup combined chopped fresh coriander, basil, mint and the reserved green part of the scallions
8 small fan-cut radishes *or* 4 large radishes, thinly sliced

ADVANCE PREPARATION

Cut the pork into large matchsticks. (This is easier if the meat is partially frozen.) Mix together the sugar, lime juice, soy sauce, sherry and chile peppers to make the marinade. Combine the pork with the marinade, mixing well. Let stand 1 hour or longer, turning the meat from time to time.

Snap off the woody end of the asparagus stalks where they break most easily, then cut the stalks on a sharp diagonal into 1½-inch lengths. Soak briefly in ice water, then drain and dry thoroughly before frying.

COOKING

Heat the oil in a wok and, when very hot, fry the asparagus all at once. Remove it from the oil almost immediately so they remain firm. Drain in a sieve placed over a bowl to catch the residue of oil. When drained, transfer to a plate lined with paper towels.

Using the same oil as for frying the asparagus, fry the pork in small batches, draining it in the sieve. When all the pork is cooked, discard the oil in the wok.

Before proceeding, arrange the lettuce in the center of a large serving platter. Combine the sauce ingredients in a bowl.

In the wok, heat 2 or 3 tablespoons of fresh oil, or use the residue of oil collected from the pork. Add mushrooms to the wok, followed by the scallions, green chile peppers, ginger and garlic. Stir together until the garlic and ginger are lightly colored, then return the pork to the wok and mix until well combined.

Pour in the sauce mixture and raise the heat to high. Bring to a boil and cook until the pork is piping hot. Off heat, immediately stir in the asparagus and about two-thirds of the herb mixture.

Mound the pork and vegetables on top of the lettuce and spoon over any remaining sauce. Scatter the remaining herbs over all, then surround the platter with a bright border of radishes.

NOTE   If you are taking advantage of the spring asparagus crop, some herbs may not be ready yet in the garden. If they cannot be found at a greengrocer's or a nursery, increase the scallion tops. Do not substitute dried herbs.

Spicy-Tangy Pork with Green Beans

This recipe is notable for two reasons: first, it is prepared more quickly than most Oriental recipes; and second, there is no garlic or ginger in the recipe. Fresh hot peppers are the key ingredient for spice and flavor. I use fresh hot red cherry peppers when available; otherwise, long hot green chiles, cut to match the string beans, provide excellent results. Make do with whatever is obtainable, so long as the peppers are *not* canned.

SERVES 2

¾ pound boneless pork
Coarse salt
Coarsely ground white pepper
6 to 8 ounces green beans

6 to 8 long green hot chile peppers *or*
    5 hot red cherry peppers
1 cup fresh coriander leaves

SAUCE

¼ cup imported soy sauce
2 tablespoons dry sherry

1 scant tablespoon imported sesame oil
2 tablespoons mild rice vinegar

Scant ¼ cup peanut oil
Scant 2 teaspoons cornstarch, dissolved
   in 1 tablespoon cold water

Cut the pork into long, thin matchsticks. (This is easier if the meat is partially frozen.) Sprinkle lightly with coarse salt and freshly ground pepper. Set aside. Trim the ends of the beans and work them through a bean slicer (see note). There should be about 2 cups. Remove the seeds and veins from the peppers and cut them into long thin strips. If using long green chiles, cut them to match the beans. Coarsely chop half the coriander leaves.

    Combine the soy sauce, sherry, sesame oil and vinegar in a bowl to make the sauce.

    Heat the oil in a wok and when hot, add the pork all at once. Stir-fry the strips until all redness disappears. Just before the meat is fully cooked, add peppers to the wok. Stir together until the pork begins to take on color, then pour over the sauce mixture and bring to a boil.

Add the beans and continue to stir until the pork is completely cooked. (This should take no time at all.) Stirring constantly, thicken the sauce with the cornstarch dissolved in cold water. The sauce will reduce to a glaze. Add the chopped coriander leaves.

Immediately turn the pork out onto a warmed serving platter and scatter the remaining whole coriander leaves over all. Serve at once.

NOTE Most vegetable peelers have a bean slicer in the end of the handle. If not, cut each bean into 3 slices lengthwise.

Stir-Fried Spinach

This method also works well for watercress, broccoli rape, Swiss chard, escarole, beet tops and other greens.
SERVES 4

1½ pounds fresh young spinach leaves

SAUCE

1 tablespoon dry sherry
1 tablespoon imported soy sauce

Scant ¼ teaspoon sugar
1 teaspoon imported sesame oil

2 tablespoons peanut oil
1 clove garlic, finely chopped

Coarse salt

Wash the spinach well in several changes of water. Strip off the coarser stems and taste a small curly leaf from the heart to check for sand. Drain well in a colander, tossing the leaves from time to time.

Combine the sherry, soy sauce, sugar and sesame oil in a bowl; set aside.

Heat the oil in a wok; add the spinach, garlic and a pinch of salt. Stir continuously over high heat until the leaves begin to wilt. Then pour over the sauce mixture and continue to stir-fry until the spinach is tender, but still bright and succulent. Push the spinach to the side of the wok and boil down the residue of marinade and juice, then stir briefly to recombine. Serve at once.

Spicy Pork Strips in Black Bean Sauce with Spinach

The Vietnamese chile products (manufactured in the United States) listed in this recipe are *very* hot. Any used in the marinade will dissipate upon frying, but those used in the sauce will not. If you're sensitive, substitute a less intense chile product. The black bean addition should be a mild sauce *not* chili paste with black beans.

The pork can be cooked in a large cast-iron skillet. I prefer to cook it in a wok, then keep it warm in a skillet while preparing the spinach—which takes almost no time at all. To serve, arrange the pork and spinach side by side on a large platter. This is a dry pork dish. Although there is a sauce of sorts, the pork strips absorb most of it.

SERVES 4

1½ pounds boneless pork from the loin
   ***or* pork hips (see note)**

MARINADE

1 level tablespoon Vietnamese pepper
   saté *(tia chieu sa-té) or* Vietnamese
   chili garlic sauce *(túóng ót tói*
   Viet-nam)

8 large scallions

1 tablespoon Chinese black bean sauce
¼ cup freshly squeezed lime juice
1 tablespoon dry sherry
1 tablespoon cornstarch

SAUCE

1 tablespoon Chinese black bean sauce
1 teaspoon Vietnamese chili garlic sauce
   (túóng ót tói Viet-nam)
¼ cup freshly squeezed lime juice

¼ teaspoon sugar
1 tablespoon imported soy sauce
2 tablespoons water

About 1 cup peanut or corn oil for frying
1 tablespoon slivers garlic
2 heaping tablespoons large slivers
   fresh ginger
About 1¾ cups (1 ounce) dried shiitake
   mushrooms, soaked, squeezed dry
   and cut into large slices

3 long thin mild green chile peppers,
   seeded and cut into 1½-inch pieces
½ cup combined chopped fresh
   coriander and mint leaves
Stir-Fried Spinach (page 149)
Hot rice

ADVANCE PREPARATION

Cut the pork into long slices, as thin as possible. (This is easier if the meat is partially frozen.) Cut each slice into long strips. Combine the marinade ingredients, stirring until the cornstarch is dissolved. Add the pork strips and using 2 forks or your hands, stir until each piece of meat is well coated. Let the pork marinate about 2 hours, tossing occasionally.

Trim the scallions and cut into ¾-inch pieces. Chop half the green parts; set aside.

Combine the sauce ingredients in a small bowl; set aside.

COOKING

Preheat the oven to 450°F. Heat about 1 cup of peanut oil in a wok. When hot, fry the pork in small batches. When fully cooked, drain and transfer to a large cast-iron skillet lined with paper towels. When all the pork has been fried, remove the paper towels and place the skillet in the hot oven. Proceed immediately with cooking the rest of the ingredients. (The pork should not remain in the hot oven longer than 5 minutes.)

Pour off the oil and add 2 tablespoons fresh oil to the wok. Then stir-fry the garlic, ginger and the scallion pieces. After a moment, add the mushrooms. Cook briefly and add the mild chile peppers, stirring just to combine. Pour in the sauce mixture and bring to a boil. Turn off the oven and return the pork to the wok with half the fresh coriander and mint leaves. Stir over high heat until the sauce thickens. (This should go quickly so the chile peppers remain crisp and brightly colored.)

Return the pork to the skillet so the wok can be used to cook the spinach. Place the skillet in the turned-off oven to keep warm. (If the oven is still very hot, keep the door ajar to let some of the heat escape.) Rinse and wipe the wok before preparing the spinach.

TO SERVE

The moment the spinach is ready, arrange it toward one end of a large warmed serving platter. Then place the pork at the other end. Mix the reserved chopped scallion tops with the remaining coriander and mint and sprinkle over the pork. Serve at once with bowls of hot rice.

NOTE   A pork hip is the connecting meat between the loin and the ham.

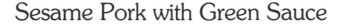

Sesame Pork with Green Sauce

SERVES 3 TO 4

MARINADE

1 extra-large egg white, beaten to a
   froth
1 tablespoon cornstarch
1 rounded tablespoon toasted sesame
   seeds, crushed slightly
2 tablespoons freshly squeezed lime juice
1 rounded teaspoon chile paste with
   garlic

1 tablespoon bottled Mexican green
   sauce (see note) *or* homemade
   Mexican Green Tomato Sauce
   (page 267)
1 large clove garlic, finely chopped
   (about 2 teaspoons)
1½ tablespoons finely chopped fresh
   ginger

1½ to 2 pounds lean boneless pork

SAUCE

¾ cup strong beef stock
2 tablespoons bottled Mexican green
   sauce *or* homemade Mexican Green
   Tomato Sauce

1 tablespoon mild imported soy sauce
2 tablespoons freshly squeezed lime juice

2 to 3 cups peanut or corn oil for frying
1 medium onion, thinly sliced
1 sweet red bell pepper, cut into long
   thin strips
1 to 3 fresh hot green chile peppers,
   seeded and thinly sliced
3 cloves garlic, cut into long slivers
1½ tablespoons long slivers fresh ginger

4 scallions, sliced, white and green parts
   separated
½ cup thinly sliced canned water
   chestnuts
3 to 4 ounces fresh snow peas, trimmed
½ cup coarsely chopped fresh
   coriander leaves
Hot rice

ADVANCE PREPARATION

Combine the marinade ingredients in a bowl, one at a time, mixing well after
each addition. Cut the pork into strips, about the thickness of a green bean
and 2 inches long. (This is easier if the meat is partially frozen.) Put the pork
strips in the marinade and toss until thoroughly coated. Refrigerate at least 4
hours or overnight. Stir occasionally.

COOKING

Combine the stock, 2 tablespoons Mexican green sauce, soy sauce and lime
juice in a bowl for sauce; set aside.

Heat the oil in a wok, reserving 2 tablespoons. When hot, fry the pork
strips in small batches until fully cooked. Remove the pork with a slotted

spoon and drain in a sieve. Transfer the pork to a warm platter lined with paper towels. Pour off the oil and, if any sesame seeds have adhered to the wok, wipe them off with a paper towel.

Add 2 tablespoons fresh oil to the wok. Over medium to high heat, fry the onion until slightly softened. Add the red and green peppers and after a moment, the garlic, ginger and white part of the scallion. Stir-fry briefly, then return pork to the pan.

Stir until the meat is hot. Push it to the side of the wok and pour in the sauce mixture. Bring to a boil and reduce slightly. Combine the pork with the sauce; add the water chestnuts and snow peas. Mix together and add the scallion tops and coriander leaves. Stir until just combined.

Turn out onto a warmed platter and serve at once. Accompany the pork with bowls of hot rice.

NOTE   Mexican green sauce is any variety of green salsa containing green tomatoes, hot green chiles, onion, coriander and spices.

Thai Pork with Green Curry

This curry is not for the timid. Coconut milk tempers the hot peppers as it unites the diverse flavors. Beware, however, this still ranks among the fieriest —as well as most delicious—curries I have had the pleasure of eating.
SERVES 4 TO 5

1¾ cups Coconut Milk (page 81) *or* frozen or canned *unsweetened* coconut milk
3 whole cardamom pods
2 cloves

GREEN CURRY PASTE

4 tiny fresh hot red chile peppers *or* tiny green serrano chiles, stems removed
2 large shallots
8 large cloves garlic
2-inch piece thick fresh ginger

4 tablespoons peanut oil
3 large fresh long green chile peppers, seeded and cut into fair-size pieces
¼ cup (packed) coarsely chopped fresh mint leaves

1 star anise
1-inch piece cinnamon stick
2 pounds boneless loin of pork, partially frozen for easier slicing

3 fresh long green chile peppers, seeded
1 tablespoon hot curry powder
1 tablespoon fish sauce from Thailand
3 tablespoons freshly squeezed lime juice

1 cup (packed) coarsely chopped fresh basil leaves
2 cups (loosely packed) fresh whole coriander leaves
Hot rice

Combine the coconut milk and whole spices in a small saucepan. Over low heat, bring just to a simmer. Set aside, off heat, to steep.

Slice the pork as thin as possible. (This is easier if the meat is partially frozen.) Trim the meat of all fat and cut each slice in half. Set aside.

Prepare the green curry paste in a food processor or blender. Remove the stems from the tiny hot peppers, but not the seeds. Place them in the workbowl and process until coarsely chopped. Cut the shallots, garlic, ginger and green chiles into small pieces and drop them into the workbowl; process until very finely chopped. Add the curry powder and mix again. Add the fish sauce, 1 tablespoon water and lime juice, mixing briefly after each addition. Transfer the paste to a small bowl and set aside.

Heat the peanut oil in a wok; when almost smoking, add the pork all at once. Stir to separate the pieces of meat. When the pork loses all trace of rosiness, add the curry paste.

Stir the pork until combined with the paste. Just before it begins to stick to the wok, pour in the coconut milk with the spices. Bring to a boil, lower the heat to a simmer, cover and cook 10 minutes.

Uncover the wok, add the green chiles and simmer 5 minutes, stirring occasionally. Add the herbs, all at once. Let them remain on the surface for 1 minute, undisturbed, then mix them with the pork. As soon as the herbs are well combined, serve the curry turned out onto a deep warmed platter.

Accompany the curry with more than the usual amount of rice. There will be more than enough sauce.

Catfish with Pork Strips and Vietnamese Sauce

Farm-raised catfish is frequently available in supermarkets as well as fish markets.

SERVES 4 TO 5

10 ounces boneless loin of pork
¼ cup freshly squeezed lime juice
1 teaspoon Vietnamese pepper saté
    (tia chieu sa-té) or 1 tablespoon
    Vietnamese chili garlic sauce
    (túóng ót tói Viet-nam)

1 teaspoon cornstarch
2 teaspoons dry sherry (optional)

SAUCE

⅓ cup, or more, Spicy Chicken Stock
    (page 77)
2 tablespoons fish sauce from Thailand
1 tablespoon balsamic vinegar

¼ teaspoon sugar
1 tablespoon Vietnamese chili garlic
    sauce (túóng ót tói Viet-nam)

1½ pounds catfish fillets
Coarse salt
Freshly ground white pepper
Cornstarch
About 3 cups peanut or corn oil for frying
8 cloves garlic, chopped (about 3
    tablespoons)
3 tablespoons chopped fresh ginger

7 scallions, cut into 1½-inch pieces
1 small inner-stalk celery, chopped
3 long thin chile peppers, seeded and
    cut into 1-inch pieces
1 cup chopped fresh ripe tomatoes or
    canned Italian plum tomatoes
Fresh coriander leaves
Hot rice

(Continued)

ADVANCE PREPARATION

Slice the pork and cut it into very thin strips. (This is easier if the meat is partially frozen.) Place the strips in a bowl and combine with the lime juice, pepper saté and cornstarch. If the mixture needs moistening, add a little sherry.

Combine the sauce ingredients in a small bowl; set aside.

COOKING

Preheat the oven to 200°F. Divide the catfish fillets into slightly larger than bite-size pieces, about 1 inch x 2½ to 3 inches. Sprinkle the fish with salt and freshly ground pepper, then dredge in sifted cornstarch.

Heat several cups of oil in a wok to 375°F. and fry about 5 pieces of catfish at a time. When crisp and lightly browned, lift out with a slotted spoon and drain on paper towels. Keep the catfish warm in a low oven. Pour off the oil and use paper towels to wipe away any residue of cornstarch left in the wok.

Heat 2 tablespoons fresh oil in the wok and, stirring constantly, fry the pork strips about 3 or 4 minutes, or until thoroughly cooked. Remove and set aside.

Add 2 to 3 tablespoons more oil to the wok and briefly stir-fry the garlic, ginger, scallions and celery; add the chile peppers and cook a moment longer. Return the pork strips, stirring until combined. Remove and set aside.

Add the tomatoes to the wok and cook down slightly. Pour in the sauce mixture and cook briefly. Return the pork to the wok and combine with the sauce. Add the catfish in batches, taking care that the pieces are well coated with sauce. (The cornstarch adhering to the fried catfish will act as a thickener.) If the sauce is too thick, thin with a little more stock.

As soon as the catfish is hot, turn it out onto a warmed platter and spoon the sauce over it. Add a garnish of fresh coriander leaves and serve at once. Accompany the dish with bowls of hot rice.

Chinese Clams with Pork and Black Bean Sauce

One dozen clams per person is an ample portion, but it is unwieldy to cook more than three dozen in a wok. No need to worry. The hearty sauce, accompanied by bowls of hot rice, will make a satisfying meal for four.

SERVES 4

3 dozen of the smallest littleneck clams
   obtainable

SAUCE

1 teaspoon sugar
1 cup chicken stock
1 tablespoon mild imported soy sauce

2 tablespoons peanut oil
2 tablespoons chopped garlic
2 tablespoons long slivers fresh ginger
4 to 6 fresh hot red cherry peppers,
   seeded and chopped
7 scallions, sliced, white and green parts
   separated

1 tablespoon dried salted black beans
6 tablespoons dry sherry

2 rounded teaspoons hot chili paste
   with garlic

6 ounces pork, ground once
A handful fresh coriander leaves,
   coarsely chopped
1 tablespoon cornstarch, dissolved in 1
   tablespoon cold water
1 teaspoon imported sesame oil

ADVANCE PREPARATION

Wash the clams well, scrubbing them with a brush. Soak them in cold salted water for several hours, changing it periodically.

Soak the beans in 2 tablespoons of the sherry. After 1 hour, squeeze out the sherry and coarsely chop the beans. Return them to the bowl with the remaining sherry.

Combine the sugar, chicken stock, soy sauce and chili paste in a bowl.

COOKING

Heat the oil in a large wok and stir-fry half the garlic, ginger and peppers with all of the white and light green part of the scallions. When softened, add the pork and stir constantly to break up the meat. Cook about 5 minutes, or until the pork loses all rosiness and appears fully cooked.

Add the clams and stir to combine with the pork. Pour over the black beans with sherry and mix until the beans are well distributed.

Pour in the sauce mixture and bring to a boil. Stir, reduce the heat to a vigorous simmer, cover and cook about 10 minutes, or until the clam shells begin to open slightly.

(Continued)

Mix the coriander leaves with the green part of the scallions and divide into 2 piles.

Add the remaining garlic, ginger and peppers. When the clams are fully opened, stir in the cornstarch mixture and add the sesame oil. When the sauce begins to thicken, add half the scallion tops and coriander leaves.

TO SERVE

Serve immediately, transferring the clams to a warmed deep serving dish; pour over the sauce and sprinkle the remaining coriander and scallion tops over all.

Spoon the clams and sauce into soup bowls rather than plates and be sure to have plenty of hot rice to accompany them. Small individual rice bowls are ideal for this. Have a dish handy for the discarded clam shells.

Sea Scallops with Mushrooms and Salt Pork

SERVES 4

SAUCE

¾ cup strong beef stock
1 tablespoon balsamic vinegar
1 teaspoon sugar
1 heaping teaspoon chili paste with
 black beans

2 tablespoons imported soy sauce
1 tablespoon dry sherry

1¼ pounds sea scallops
3 tablespoons freshly squeezed lemon
 juice
About 1 cup cornstarch, sifted with ¼
 teaspoon finely ground pepper
About 3 cups peanut or corn oil for frying
½ pound very large fresh mushrooms,
 quartered, or smaller mushrooms, left
 whole
5 ounces lean salt pork or bacon, in one
 piece, cut into small dice
3 or 4 small yellow onions (about ¾
 pound), quartered, layers separated
1 red or green bell pepper, cut into
 ½-inch squares
1 small celery stalk, cut into ½-inch
 pieces (optional)

7 scallions, cut into ¼-inch pieces, white
 and green parts separated
1 rounded tablespoon long slivers garlic
1 rounded tablespoon long slivers
 fresh ginger
Thinly sliced fresh hot chile peppers,
 to taste
1½ cups broccoli florets or 1 handful
 snow peas, trimmed and blanched
 30 seconds (optional)
2 teaspoons cornstarch, dissolved in
 1 tablespoon cold water
A handful fresh coriander leaves
A small handful fresh basil leaves,
 shredded (optional)

Combine the sauce ingredients in a bowl; set aside.

Rinse the scallops in a bowl of cold water acidulated with lemon juice. If large, divide them in half with the grain, or, if very large, into quarters. Drain the scallops in a sieve, then pat dry with paper towels. Dredge in cornstarch and set aside.

When ready to cook, heat the oil in a wok to deep-fry temperature (375°F.). Dust the mushrooms with cornstarch, then fry in small batches until lightly browned. Remove with a slotted spoon and drain in a sieve; transfer to a baking sheet lined with paper towels.

Roll the scallops in cornstarch one more time, shaking off excess. Fry quickly in small batches, only until browned. Remove, drain and transfer to paper towels. Keep warm in a low oven.

When finished frying, pour off all the oil, and wipe the cornstarch residue from the bottom of the wok. Add the salt pork or bacon. Cook over low heat, tossing frequently, until the fat is rendered and meat is crisp. Remove the pork from the wok and set aside.

Add the onions, bell pepper and celery all at once. Raise the heat and stir-fry, searing them until black spots appear. There should be hardly any oil in the wok so the vegetables char slightly and remain crisp.

Remove the vegetables and add 1 or 2 tablespoons of fresh oil. Add the white part of the scallions, the garlic, ginger, fresh chiles, and if you like, broccoli florets. (If using snow peas, add them with the scallops toward the end of cooking.) Lower the heat and stir briefly, adding a little more oil, if necessary.

Pour in the sauce mixture and bring to a boil. Lower the heat and add the cornstarch dissolved in cold water. When the sauce has thickened, return the sea scallops, mushrooms, salt pork and vegetables to the wok. Stir until coated with sauce. Add the green part of the scallions. Cook, stirring, just until piping hot.

Turn the scallops and vegetables out onto a warmed serving platter and sprinkle with fresh coriander leaves. In season, combine coriander with fresh basil.

Crab with Pork and Black Bean Sauce

I first tasted this dish in a Chinese restaurant on Staten Island. The restaurant was almost two hours away from home but always worth the trip just for this particular dish. Blue-claw crabs, native to the East Coast, were used in the recipe; however, a year or so later, I enjoyed almost the same dish in northern California, made with Dungeness crab. Occasionally, I have found live Dungeness crabs in East Coast fish markets and so have been able to prepare this dish with both kinds of crab.

SERVES 2 AS A MAIN DISH OR 4 WITH OTHER DISHES

1 rounded tablespoon salted black beans
4 tablespoons dry sherry
Coarse salt

SAUCE

About 1½ cups chicken stock
1 teaspoon sugar
1 rounded teaspoon chili paste with
   black beans
2 tablespoons mild imported soy sauce

About 3 tablespoons peanut oil
1 teaspoon crushed dried red chile
   peppers
3 large cloves garlic, chopped
2 tablespoons large slivers fresh ginger
8 large scallions, cut into pea-size pieces,
   white and green parts separated
1 red bell pepper, cut into long thin strips
6 ounces pork, ground once

1 to 1½ dozen large blue-claw crabs (big
   jimmies or females with roe) *or* 2
   large Dungeness crabs, preferably live
   (1½ to 2 pounds each)

2 teaspoons sherry vinegar
1 heaping teaspoon chopped garlic
1 tablespoon large slivers ginger
1 tablespoon ketchup

1 tablespoon cornstarch, dissolved in
   1 tablespoon cold water
1 extra-large egg or 2 smaller eggs, well
   beaten with a fork
1 teaspoon imported sesame oil
A handful fresh coriander leaves,
   coarsely chopped (optional)
Hot rice

ADVANCE PREPARATION

Soak the black beans several hours in 2 tablespoons of the sherry. Squeeze the beans dry, discard the salty sherry, and soak in 2 tablespoons fresh sherry until ready to cook.

   In advance, but not too long before planning to serve, bring a large pot of salted water to a roaring boil. Use tongs to drop the live crabs into the water. Cook blue-claw crabs in batches without fully cooking them; 3 to 5 minutes is enough time. Lift out the crabs and let cool slightly while adding the next batch. Continue until all of the crabs have been partially cooked. Dungeness crabs should be fully cooked; boil them 40 to 45 minutes.

While the crabs are still hot, proceed to clean and dismember them. Lift the tab on the underside and pull open the "apron." Continue this action while grasping the main shell and applying pressure to snap it away from the body. Then remove the stomach sac, located between the eyes, and break the body in half. Pull away and discard the gills (false spongy fingers attached to the underside) and break off all the legs and pincers. These are not to be part of the dish; however, if the claws are of reasonable size, the meat will be quite succulent. Put them aside for a snack when the hard work is finished. Break the bodies of Dungeness crabs in half or if very large, divide into quarters. Either crack the claws and legs and use them in this dish or eat them separately.

Combine the sauce ingredients in a bowl; set aside.

COOKING

Heat the oil in a wok and swirl it around the pan. Adjust the heat to medium and add the diced chile pepper, garlic, ginger, the white part of the scallions and the bell pepper. Stir-fry until the bell pepper softens slightly. Before the garlic and ginger take on too much color, add the pork. Raise the heat and cook the pork, stirring constantly to break it up.

When the pork is fully cooked, add the crabs and the black beans with the sherry to the wok. Stir together until well combined, then pour over the sauce mixture. Lower the heat and simmer 15 minutes, covered, for blue-claw crabs. Fully cooked Dungeness crabs only need to simmer 5 minutes. Stir from time to time.

Dissolve the cornstarch in the water and stir it into the sauce. If the sauce should thicken too much, thin with a little more chicken stock. After a moment, slowly and evenly pour the beaten egg over and around the crab. Without stirring, cover the wok and cook, undisturbed, for 2 minutes, or until the egg begins to set. Remove the lid and carefully blend in the sesame oil and half the scallion tops. Cover and cook about 30 seconds longer

(Continued)

TO SERVE

Transfer the crabs and sauce to a warmed deep platter. Scatter the remaining scallion tops over all, followed by the coriander leaves, if desired.

Serve bowls of hot rice as an accompaniment and be sure to have a large dish nearby to collect the empty shells. Except for eating the rice, this meal is a job for the fingers. Some find crab picks make the work easier, but most prefer just to suck the meat out of the shells. Needless to say, there should be plenty of napkins. Be sure to make a lot of rice. It is delicious topped with the sauce and the crab will not be all that filling.

Spicy Shrimp with Ham and Coconut Milk

This Asian-inspired dish is as delicious as it is spicy and, best of all, takes almost no time to prepare.

SERVES 4

SAUCE

¾ to 1 cup Spicy Chicken Stock
  (page 77)
1 tablespoon fish sauce from Thailand
2 teaspoons hot curry powder

¼ cup freshly squeezed lime juice
1 tablespoon Vietnamese chili garlic
  sauce (tuong ot toi Viet-nam)

About 4 tablespoons peanut oil
1 rounded tablespoon chopped
  fresh ginger
7 scallions, cut into pea-size pieces,
  white and green parts separated
1½ pounds extra-large shrimp (about 20
  to the pound), peeled and deveined
1 rounded tablespoon long slivers
  fresh ginger

¾ cup cooked ham or smoked pork butt,
  cut into small dice
¼ cup canned crushed Italian plum
  tomatoes
¾ cup combined chopped fresh
  coriander, basil and mint leaves
1 cup Coconut Milk (page 81)

Combine the sauce ingredients in a bowl; set aside.

Heat 3 tablespoons of the oil in a wok. Add the chopped ginger and white part of the scallions with about half the green part. Stir briefly to coat with oil, then add the shrimp. Over high heat, stir-fry the shrimp until they begin to turn opaque and curl slightly. Remove all ingredients from the wok *before* the shrimp and scallions are fully cooked.

Add the remaining tablespoon of oil and add the slivers of ginger. After a moment, add the ham and stir together briefly. Adjust the heat so the ham does not burn, then add the crushed tomatoes. Stir together until the tomatoes have thickened. Pour in the sauce mixture. If the sauce becomes too thick, thin slightly with additional chicken stock.

Add half the chopped herbs to the sauce and return the shrimp with the scallions and chopped ginger. Add the remaining green part of the scallions to the wok and cook, stirring, until the shrimp appears firm and opaque. Pour over the coconut milk, raise the heat, and cook until bubbling hot. If the sauce is too thick, add a little more stock. Stir in all but a tablespoon of the remaining herbs and turn out onto a warmed serving platter. Strew the rest of the herbs over all. Serve at once, accompanied with bowls of hot rice.

THE RUSTIC PIG

Pork Chops with Cabbage and Madeira Sauce

·

Pork Chops with a Crust of Onions

·

Grilled Pig's Feet and Knuckles with Mustard and Bread Crumbs

·

Mélange of Meats, Sausage, Vegetables, Beans and Cabbage

·

Poached Pork Butt

·

Boiled Dinner with Smoked Pork Butt

·

Fresh Horseradish Sauce

·

Italian Green Sauce

Pork and Sausages with Sauerkraut

·

Andouillette Maconnaise

·

Veal Breast Stuffed with Pork, Ham, Swiss Chard and Mushrooms

·

Veal and Ham Rolls with Mozzarella and Fresh Tomato Sauce

·

Spaghetti Baked in Parchment with Mushrooms, Pancetta and Tomatoes

·

Pasta with Meat Filling

·

Béchamel Sauce

·

Pork Chili

·

Chili-Raisin Sauce

·

Pork with Eggplant and Vegetables

·

Romano Beans with Potatoes and Bacon

·

Stuffed New Potatoes from Spain

ustic food is honest, earthy and restorative. It brings a vision to senses aroused by fragrant aromas—the vapor of a steaming *choucroute* fogging the windows on a raw day in Alsace, or the smell of bacon frying that will bring me back to my mother's kitchen. There are no surprises; anticipation is rewarded. This food delivers!

The cooking is ageless; it often appears as a one-dish meal—a boiled dinner, robust pasta, hearty stuffed meats and vegetables, chili, long-simmering casseroles. Some recipes rely on cured ham and sausage, staples throughout history. For the most part, these dishes make good use of the less esteemed and more economical parts of the pig, those ideal for grinding, sausage-making and long, slow cooking; even the pig's feet and hocks get special treatment.

Pork Chops with Cabbage and Madeira Sauce
CÔTES DE PORC AUX CHOUX ET SAUCE MADÈRE

Once in provincial France, carefully cooked slices of pork belly and a Savoy cabbage beautiful enough to paint comprised a meal at a friend's home. Since then, I have sometimes added game birds to my interpretation of that dish, always maintaining a generous ration of pork belly. As game became less and less available, I started using pork chops, which lend themselves perfectly to this way of cooking.

Find a butcher (usually German) who sells truly lean fresh or salted pork belly. This is unsmoked bacon and an honest piece of meat, not fat for flavoring. If it is unobtainable, a slab of *very* lean bacon, blanched, can be substituted.

The pork chops should be thick and well trimmed. Smoked pork chops could also be used or a combination of both. Buttered egg noodles, celery root puree or mashed potatoes make a good accompaniment.

SERVES 4 TO 6

1 medium Savoy cabbage (about 3 to 4 pounds)
Salt
6 to 8 ounces very lean fresh or salted pork belly, in one piece
About 2 tablespoons butter
4 or 6 center-cut pork chops, bone in, 1¼ to 1½ inches thick (about 12 ounces each)
Freshly ground white pepper
1 large onion, thinly sliced
2 large carrots, peeled and thinly sliced

4 cloves garlic, flattened and peeled
1 large bay leaf
1 branch fresh tarragon *or* 1 teaspoon dried tarragon leaves, crumbled
2 sprigs fresh thyme *or* ½ teaspoon dried thyme
3 tablespoons chopped fresh parsley
¾ cup dry white wine
1 cup strong chicken or veal stock
2 tablespoons Madeira
1 teaspoon arrowroot (optional)
Chopped fresh parsley

Quarter the cabbage and drop it into a large pot of rapidly boiling salted water and cook 10 minutes. Drain well in a colander. Cut out the core and press the leaves to remove water.

Cut the pork belly into 2 x 3-inch slices, about ⅜ inch thick. Blanching is optional.

Over low heat, melt the butter in a large ovenproof casserole and add the pork belly. Cook very slowly, for about 30 minutes, turning the meat frequently until it is lightly browned and faintly crisp. Remove and set aside.

Raise the heat to medium and arrange the pork chops in the casserole. Sprinkle with freshly ground pepper and sear them on both sides to seal their juices. Add a little more butter, if necessary. When nicely browned, remove and set aside.

Add the onion, carrots, garlic and bay leaf to the casserole and, if needed, more butter. Lower the heat and cook, stirring frequently, until the onion begins to soften. (If you wish, cover the casserole to speed up this operation.) Add the tarragon, thyme and parsley. When the onion has softened completely, add the cabbage and return the pork belly. Stir together, uncovered, only until the cabbage is coated with the casserole juices.

Preheat the oven to 350°F. Add the wine to the casserole and raise the heat. Bring to a boil and cook until slightly reduced, then add the stock. Return to a boil, lower the heat to a simmer and arrange the chops on top of the cabbage. Baste well, cover and place in the lower part of the oven. Cook 45 to 50 minutes, basting chops with the casserole juices every 15 minutes.

When the chops are done, remove and cover to keep warm. Also remove the cabbage, pork belly and vegetables. Press down on the cabbage to release all broth possible. If using fresh herbs, discard the twigs. Arrange the drained cabbage and pork belly on a hot platter and scatter the carrots over all. Lay the pork chops on top, then place in the turned-off oven to stay warm.

FINISHING THE SAUCE

Boil down the broth until reduced to about 1 cup. Skim any traces of fat from the surface. Add the Madeira and lower the heat to a simmer. If a thicker sauce is preferred, mix arrowroot with 1 tablespoon cold water. Off heat, stir it into the broth, then cook 2 minutes over low heat, stirring constantly.

Before serving, return any juices accumulated from the cabbage to the sauce. Cook 1 or 2 minutes, then spoon half the sauce over the pork chops and cabbage. Pass the rest of the sauce separately in a hot sauceboat.

Sprinkle the platter generously with chopped fresh parsley and serve at once.

Pork Chops with a Crust of Onions
CÔTES DE PORC FOYOT

The recipe for this dish can be traced back to one of Paris's great restaurants —famous from its inception in the late nineteenth century until it closed in the 1930s. The restaurant retained the name of Foyot, the former chef to Louis Philippe who opened it, through the tenure of four other great chefs.

The restaurant's veal chop and its components of onions, wine, cheese and bread crumbs was renowned. I have adapted these signature ingredients to pork, which I prefer.

SERVES 4

4 large center-cut pork chops, bone in
    (about 10 ounces each)
Coarse salt
Freshly ground white pepper
5½ tablespoons butter
2 teaspoons chopped fresh tarragon *or* 1
    teaspoon dried tarragon leaves

4 cups chopped onions (about 4 onions)
Fresh or dried thyme
⅔ cup dry white wine
⅔ cup chicken stock
⅔ cup fine fresh homemade bread
    crumbs
⅔ cup freshly grated Parmesan cheese

Preheat the oven to 400°F.

Sprinkle the chops with salt and freshly ground pepper. Over medium-high heat, melt 2½ tablespoons of the butter in a skillet just large enough to hold the chops in one layer. Place the chops in the pan and as they begin to brown, adjust the heat and turn them frequently to be sure they do not stick or burn. When they are well browned, remove them from the skillet and sprinkle with the tarragon. Cover to keep warm.

Add 1 tablespoon more butter to the fat remaining in the skillet; add the onions. Cook over low heat, stirring frequently, for about 30 minutes or until soft and golden.

Spread two-thirds of the onions over the bottom of a shallow casserole and arrange the chops, tarragon-sprinkled side down, on top of them. Sprinkle lightly with thyme and cover with the remaining onions.

Pour the wine into the skillet and bring to a boil. Add the chicken stock and return to a boil; cook until the liquid is reduced to about ⅔ cup. Pour this evenly over the chops.

Combine the bread crumbs with the cheese. Cover the onions and chops with the mixture. Melt the remaining 2 tablespoons of butter and drizzle it over the bread crumbs. Bake 30 minutes.

Grilled Pig's Feet and Knuckles with Mustard and Bread Crumbs

PIEDS DE PORC ET JAMBONNEAU SAINTE-MENEHOULD

The French village of Sainte-Menehould is to pig's feet what Dijon is to mustard. Its classic way of preparing this dish requires the pig's feet to be cooked for 48 hours so they can be eaten bones and all. This really doesn't work here. However, it *is* important that the pig's feet have a long, slow simmering, cooked over the lowest heat, at least overnight and as long as 36 hours.

Sometimes you can purchase pig's feet with the hocks (also called pig's knuckles) attached. If not, include an equal number of pig's hocks so you won't leave the table hungry. The meaty hocks are delicious prepared this way and, to my taste, much better than the feet!

With this meal I would suggest a white bean or Lentil Salad (page 107) or even mashed potatoes. However the standard accompaniment of the region would be French fries—true bistro fare.

SERVES 4

4 pig's feet
4 pig's hocks (pig's knuckles)
1 large or 2 small leeks, sliced
2 carrots, sliced
2 medium to large onions, stuck with 3 cloves each
3 cups dry white wine, preferably Chablis
½ cup white wine vinegar
4 cups good strong meat stock *or* chicken stock
1 head garlic, unpeeled and cut in half
Sprigs of parsley and thyme and 2 bay leaves, tied together (bouquet garni)
1 large stalk celery with leaves, cut into small pieces
½ teaspoon black peppercorns
1 teaspoon coarse salt
About ½ cup imported Dijon mustard
About 4 tablespoons olive oil
2 or 3 tablespoons melted butter
About 2 cups very fine dry bread crumbs

PREPARATION OF THE FEET

In the United States, a good butcher will probably sell pig's feet that are ready to cook. If this is not the case, scrub the feet with a stiff brush and drop them into a pot of cold water. Bring to a boil, simmer 5 minutes and drain. Shave the feet if necessary, then split them between the toes, but not so far as to cut them completely in half.

(Continued)

To keep the feet from falling apart during cooking, make a splint for each foot using half a chopstick, then bind tightly with cheesecloth, wrapping each completely and securing with string. Wrap the hocks also, although a splint is unnecessary.

COOKING

Make a bed of leeks and carrots in a large casserole (about 12 inches in diameter). Arrange the pig's feet and hocks on top, then wedge in the onions. If they are unwieldly, cut them in half, crosswise. Pour in the wine, vinegar and stock. Add the garlic, bouquet garni, celery, peppercorns and salt and just enough water to keep the feet and hocks covered by liquid.

Bring the wine and stock to a boil and lower the heat to the barest simmer. Partially cover the casserole and cook the pig's feet and hocks for as long as possible, 8 hours at the very least. Skim the surface occasionally and add more water as needed to maintain the proper level of liquid. When finished cooking, let the feet and hocks cool in the broth for about 2 hours.

Remove the feet and hocks and cut the string securing the cheesecloth. Very carefully unwrap them while holding the meat together. The meat will tend to fall apart easily and a few small bones will surely slip out. This is okay so long as the larger bones that form the structure of the feet remain in place. Lay each piece on a baking sheet to cool completely. As they cool, the meat will hold its shape. Meanwhile, skim and strain the cooking liquid and pour 1 cup of it into a soup plate. Save the rest of the stock for other uses (see note).

Lightly coat each foot and hock with mustard and dip each into the cooled broth. If everything is cold, the broth will adhere slightly, leaving a glossy finish. Place the pieces on a baking sheet lined with wax paper and chill completely in the refrigerator.

GRILLING

When ready to grill, preheat the broiler. The rack should be as far from the heating element as possible or the heat turned low. Otherwise, roast the pig's feet in a 450°F. oven rather than risk burning the bread crumbs.

Stir the olive oil into the melted butter and brush it over each foot and hock. Roll them in the bread crumbs to coat and arrange them on a baking sheet. Place under the broiler just long enough for the bread crumbs to turn golden brown on all sides. Serve at once with good French mustard.

NOTE This broth can be used in most recipes where a strong meat stock is required, especially one in which the stock will eventually become a sauce.

Mélange of Meats, Sausage, Vegetables, Beans and Cabbage

POTÉE

There are endless variations to this stew. For example, a *potée* can be made with lentils instead of dried beans, or without either. Always included, though, are cabbage and some kind of pork product. I often add a veal shank to enhance the broth. (If you do not include a shank, be sure to increase the number of sausages.) Sometimes the broth is strained and degreased, then served as a first course over croutons while the meats and vegetables are kept warm. For the main course, drained beans (or lentils) are placed in a mound in the center of a very large platter; then the meats are sliced and arranged with the vegetables, surrounding and partially overlapping the beans. The mélange is then basted with juices and a handful of chopped fresh herbs is strewn over all. Thick crouton slices are passed separately.

An assortment of mustards should accompany the *potée*. Other accompaniments might include an Italian Green Sauce (page 178) or a strong mustardy vinaigrette sauce.

SERVES 6 TO 8

One small Savoy cabbage, quartered
   (about 2 pounds)
Salt
1 pound lean meaty bacon, in one piece,
   or 1 pound lean meaty salt pork
2 tablespoons olive oil
1 cup chopped onion
3 large carrots, peeled and cut into
   2-inch pieces
½ pound small young turnips, peeled and
   left whole or quartered
1½ cups peeled and chopped fresh ripe
   tomatoes and their juices *or* canned
   Italian plum tomatoes
1 pound, or less, imported *flageolets or*
   small dried white beans, soaked
   overnight and drained before cooking
1 whole veal shank, cut into 2 or 3 pieces
   and tied (optional)
Several fresh pork hocks (pig's knuckles)

Freshly ground pepper
Sprigs parsley and thyme, 1 large bay
   leaf and 1 stalk celery with leaves,
   tied together (bouquet garni)
1 small whole onion, stuck with 2 cloves
1 head unpeeled garlic, preferably new,
   left whole, with excess papery skin
   removed
¾ to 1 pound small new potatoes, left
   whole
2 to 3 small lightly smoked sausages,
   pricked with a skewer
¾ to 1 pound kielbasa *or* a similar
   sausage
2 to 3 bockwurst *or* weisswurst, pricked
   with a skewer
6 to 8 young leeks, tied in small bunches
2 to 3 tablespoons coarsely chopped
   fresh parsley, chervil or basil
Thick croutons

(Continued)

Leaving the core in place, drop the quarters of cabbage into a large pot of boiling salted water. Cook 5 minutes, then drain. Set aside.

Remove the rind from the bacon or salt pork, but save it. Cut the meat into thick slices, about 1½ x 2 inches. Place them, with the rind, in a saucepan and add cold water to cover. Bring to a simmer and cook 5 minutes. Drain and refresh with cold water. Drain again, separate the rind and set aside.

Coat the bottom of a large pot with the olive oil. Over low heat, add blanched bacon or salt pork and without letting it become overly crisp, render as much fat as possible. Turn the slices frequently, then remove and set aside.

Add the chopped onion and cook until softened. Add the carrot pieces and cook briefly, stirring to coat. Add the turnips and turn them in the fat until coated. Add the tomatoes, stir and raise the heat slightly. Add the beans and mix to combine.

Add the veal and hocks, the bacon or salt pork and the rind, burying them in the beans. Sprinkle liberally with freshly ground pepper and add enough water to barely cover. Bring to a boil and skim the surface. Reduce the heat to a low simmer. Bury the bouquet garni, whole onion and garlic in the beans. Cover and cook 1 hour and 45 minutes, maintaining the liquid at a low simmer. Skim the surface occasionally, removing as much fat as possible.

After 1 hour and 45 minutes, arrange the quarters of cabbage, core down, on top of the meat. Baste, cover and cook about 30 minutes. Then add the potatoes and the kinds of sausages that will benefit from a long cooking (add bockwurst or other delicate sausages last).

Cook about 1 hour, or until the potatoes are tender when pierced with the tip of a knife. Shortly before serving, add the bockwurst and leeks. Cook about 15 to 20 minutes, taking care that the leeks do not overcook.

When ready to serve, strain off the broth and save. Discard the pork rind, whole onion and bouquet garni. If desired, squeeze the soft sweet garlic cloves out of their skins and add them to the beans. Mound the beans in the center of a very large platter. Slice the meats and arrange them, with the marrow bones and vegetables, around the platter, slightly covering the beans. Baste with juices and strew the herbs over all. Pass the croutons separately.

NOTE   Later in the week, extra meats and sausage can be reheated in the reserved broth. Serve them in Warm Chicory Salad (page 105). The broth is excellent and can be reheated with pasta and beans to make a hearty Mediterranean-style soup, best served with croutons and freshly grated cheese.

Poached Pork Butt

A long, slow simmering in aromatic broth produces a succulent piece of meat. Tender enough to break apart with a fork, it can be used in any of the recipes calling for cooked pork. This includes soups, salads, enchiladas and a variety of other dishes. The meat is especially good cold. When the cooking is finished, the flavorful broth will also come in handy.

Poached pork is delicious to eat as is. Slice it and serve warm or cold with Italian Green Sauce, a sauce rémoulade or ravigote or simply mustard. Lentil Salad or a white bean salad would be a good accompaniment.

SERVES 4 TO 5

1 large onion, thinly sliced
1 carrot, sliced
1 lean boneless fresh pork butt (2 to 2½ pounds)
Chicken necks and backs *or* roasted pork bones (optional)
2 cups dry white wine (optional)
1 teaspoon coarse salt
1 inch fresh ginger, sliced
½ teaspoon black peppercorns
3 small dried red chile peppers
1 whole clove

1 star anise (optional)
1 small head garlic, unpeeled and cut in half crosswise
1 rounded teaspoon coriander seed
1 rounded teaspoon cumin seed
1 celery stalk, 1 bay leaf and sprigs fresh thyme, parsley and rosemary, tied together (bouquet garni)
Italian Green Sauce (page 178), mustard or other sauces (optional)
Lentil Salad (page 107), optional

Make a bed of onion and carrot slices in a medium pot. Place the pork butt on top and add a few chicken bones or roasted pork bones, if available, to enrich the stock. Add enough wine and water to cover the meat. Add the rest of the ingredients, except the sauces.

Bring to a boil and skim the surface. Lower the heat to a simmer, partially cover and simmer for about 3 hours, or until the meat is tender enough to be pierced easily with a cooking fork. Skim the surface occasionally and turn the pork, spooning the onions over it. As the stock reduces and the pork is only partially covered by liquid, spoon the onions and broth over it at frequent intervals.

If not serving the pork hot and if time allows, let the meat cool in the broth before serving at room temperature or cold.

After the pork has been removed, strain the broth and remove all traces of fat. Use it in place of Spicy Chicken Stock in Asian dishes.

Boiled Dinner with Smoked Pork Butt

A succulent smoked pork butt does not need to cook quite as long as this recipe suggests. The intention here is to give the vegetables a long, slow simmering in the briny aromatic broth.

SERVES 4 OR MORE

1 boneless smoked pork butt for every 4 to 6 persons (2¼ to 2½ pounds each)
Sprigs of parsley and thyme and 1 stalk celery, tied together (bouquet garni)
3 bay leaves
2 medium onions, stuck with 3 cloves each

1 teaspoon white peppercorns
1 teaspoon mustard seed
1 teaspoon celery seed
1 whole head garlic, unpeeled and cut in half crosswise

VEGETABLES (WITH APPROXIMATE COOKING TIMES)

Savoy or green cabbage, quartered (1½ hours)
Carrots, preferably large and long (1 hour)
Large new potatoes, cut in half (45 minutes)
Small whole turnips (30 minutes)
Celery root, cut into large *bâtonnets*, about ¾ inch x 3 inches (25 minutes)

Small whole onions (25 minutes)
Small leeks, tied together (20 minutes)
Whole parsnips (20 minutes)
Banana squash, butternut squash, pumpkin or other hard squash, cut into 1½- to 2-inch chunks (15 to 20 minutes)
Celery hearts, tied together (15 minutes)
Beets, cooked separately (see note)

Butter
2 to 3 heaping tablespoons chopped fresh parsley

Assorted mustards
Fresh Horseradish Sauce (page 177)

Place the meat in a large casserole or stockpot and cover by several inches with cold water. (Do not add salt.) Add all the herbs and spices and the garlic and bring to a boil, uncovered. Reduce the heat to a gentle simmer, partially cover the casserole and cook for 1 hour before adding any vegetables. Plan to simmer the meat about 3 hours, though 2 hours will be sufficient.

Using the cooking guide for vegetables, begin to add your choices. Timing will vary, depending on the size of each vegetable. Check for doneness from time to time, testing the vegetables gently with the tines of a fork.

TO SERVE

Keep the vegetables warm in the briny liquid while carving the meat. If preparing this dish for a large number of people, serve the meat on its carving board or on a hot platter and arrange the vegetables separately on another hot platter.

Dot the vegetables with a little butter and sprinkle the chopped parsley over all. Have a block of sweet butter handy for those who want to add more to their vegetables, plus an assortment of mustards and fresh horseradish sauce to go with the meat.

NOTE   Cook whole beets (ahead of time, if you wish) in enough salted water to cover. The cooking time will depend on size, but they are done if tender when pierced with a fork. Leave them in their cooking water until just before serving. Then, peel, slice and warm them, covered, in a little butter over low heat.

Fresh Horseradish Sauce

The longer this sauce stands, the hotter it gets. After several days, you might want to cool it by stirring in a little more sour cream.

MAKES 2 CUPS

1 horseradish root, about 8 ounces (the size of a very large carrot)
1 cup thick sour cream
1 tablespoon freshly squeezed lemon juice

¼ teaspoon coarse salt, or to taste
Chopped fresh dill *or* chives

Peel the horseradish and grate it by hand, using the fine shredding (not cheese-grating) plate of a grater. If desired, refine the grated horseradish further, using a food processor or blender. You should have 1 cup.

Stir in the sour cream, lemon juice, and salt and mix well. Refrigerate until ready to serve.

A few tablespoons of chopped fresh dill or chives make a nice addition to this sauce.

Italian Green Sauce
SALSA VERDE

MAKES 2 CUPS

1 tablespoon fresh homemade bread crumbs
1 teaspoon tarragon-flavored white wine vinegar
1 clove garlic, finely chopped
6 flat anchovies, chopped

½ cup finely chopped fresh parsley
1 rounded tablespoon capers, drained and finely chopped
1 hard-boiled extra-large egg
½ cup olive oil
Salt (optional)

Using a mortar and pestle or a round-bottomed ceramic bowl and wooden spoon, combine the bread crumbs, vinegar and garlic. Grind to a paste. Add the anchovies, parsley and capers, grinding to incorporate each addition thoroughly. Add the hard-boiled egg yolk, mashing it with the other ingredients. Chop the egg white very fine and mix it into the paste.

Add the olive oil in a slow steady stream, stirring constantly. The sauce will be thick but thinner than mayonnaise. Set aside at room temperature for 2 hours before serving.

Pork and Sausages with Sauerkraut
CHOUCROUTE GARNIE

The meats for this Alsatian specialty are flexible and I vary them with each cooking. The addition of a generous slab of lean blanched pork belly would be in keeping with the best *choucroutes* of Alsace. Knockwurst or hot dogs of good quality can also be included, but my own preference is for more unusual sausages. On occasion, I have also enjoyed *choucroutes* where several of the sausages were grilled separately, then combined with the rest of the meats just before serving.

My problem in making this dish is choosing the sausages. Knowing my own favorites and those of others, I *always* make too much! When using a large selection of small sausages for the *choucroute,* do not count one sausage per person. Instead, divide the wursts at the table (provide an extra knife and fork for this purpose), with everyone joining in to try a piece of each.

Choucroute is good reheated, either in a slow oven or over low heat. Though not necessary, I sometimes find it preferable to start the sauerkraut the day before and take the recipe as far as browning and adding the pork chops; then I let it stand overnight. On the second day, I reheat the *choucroute* and add the sausages. (There is no reason why the sausages that require a longer cooking could not be added on the first day also.)

SERVES 6 TO 8

About 3½ to 4 pounds fresh sauerkraut
8 to 12 ounces very thinly sliced lean salt pork *or* bacon, preferably salt pork
1 or 2 onions, depending on size, stuck with 2 cloves each
2 smoked ham hocks (pig's knuckles)
About 1½ pounds meaty salt pork, in one piece, *or* fresh belly, cut into several large pieces and blanched 5 minutes (optional)
1 small tart apple, peeled, cored and finely chopped
Several large sprigs fresh thyme *or* 1 teaspoon dried thyme
2 large bay leaves, broken
4 large cloves garlic, finely chopped
15 juniper berries, crushed slightly
30 white peppercorns
2 cups dry white wine, preferably an Alsatian Riesling
2 cups strong chicken or veal stock
2 tablespoons rendered goose, chicken or bacon fat *or* butter

1 to 1½ cups finely chopped onion
1 small boneless smoked pork butt (see note)
4 to 6 small boneless loin pork chops
Freshly ground white pepper
About 1 tablespoon butter (optional)
1 beerwurst, pricked with a skewer and blanched briefly, *or* about ¾ to 1 pound kielbasa, cut into large pieces
4 small lightly smoked sausages, pricked with a skewer and blanched briefly (about 1 pound)
1 to 2 roast bratwurst, pricked with a skewer
4 to 6 small bockwurst *or* 2 to 3 weisswurst (about 1 pound)
Chopped fresh parsley
Assorted mustards
Hot steamed small new potatoes (about 2 pounds) *or* mashed potatoes

Soak the sauerkraut briefly in cold water to cover. Drain and squeeze dry.

Preheat the oven to 325°F. Line the bottom of a large heavy casserole with strips of lean salt pork or bacon, and add the sauerkraut. Bury the whole onion, hocks and the cut-up salt pork, if using, in the kraut. Add the chopped apple, thyme and bay leaves. Scatter the garlic, juniper berries and peppercorns over all. Add the wine and chicken stock and bring to a simmer. Cover the casserole, transfer to the oven and bake for 30 minutes. Turn the ingredients and spoon a little sauerkraut over them; bake 30 minutes more.

(Continued)

Melt the fat in a large skillet and slowly sauté the chopped onion until soft and golden. Mix with the sauerkraut and add the smoked butt, if using. Return the casserole to the oven and cook 30 minutes to 1 hour more.

Sprinkle the pork chops with freshly ground pepper and brown them on both sides in the skillet, adding more butter if necessary to the fat in the skillet. Turn the chops frequently and when richly colored, transfer to the casserole. Spoon some of the sauerkraut over them and continue to bake, covered, about 45 minutes. Turn the pork chops and other ingredients once during this time and add the beerwurst or kielbasa. About 15 minutes later, add the lightly smoked sausages.

After the *choucroute* has baked 3 hours, the oven can be turned off and the casserole left undisturbed until time to resume cooking. If there is to be a considerable time lapse, remove it from the oven and allow it to cool.

To finish the *choucroute,* transfer the casserole to the stove top. Over low heat, return the *choucroute* to the barest simmer. Just before serving, add the more fragile sausages: the roast bratwurst, bockwurst or weisswurst. Cook only long enough for these delicate sausages to become piping hot. Check the sausages frequently, turning them in the hot sauerkraut. Take care that they do not burst.

TO SERVE

Remove the meats from the casserole and set aside on a hot platter. Carve the slab salt pork, smoked butt and beerwurst into thick slices. Remove the rind and partially bone the hocks for easier serving. Keep the meats warm while mounding the sauerkraut in the center of a large hot platter, pressing it gently to remove excess liquid.

Arrange the sausages around the sauerkraut and sprinkle with parsley. It may be easier to serve the chops and larger sliced meats on their own warm platter. Serve at once, piping hot, accompanied by an assortment of mustards.

If there is room, new potatoes may be cooked buried among the meats and sauerkraut; otherwise, steam them separately.

NOTE   Omit the smoked butt if the *choucroute* is for only 6 persons, but be sure to include it if ham hocks are unobtainable.

VARIATION

·

Mini Choucroute

Only a real love of sauerkraut could motivate a person to revise a recipe designed for a minimum of six to serve two!

Rather than forgo a perfect winter meal (because everyone else is as snowbound as yourself), I have adapted the *choucroute* to serve two. Since the ingredients will have to be limited, choices must be made regarding the meats. There will be too much sauerkraut, but it is not expensive and a minimum of 2 pounds is needed to make a sufficient bed for the other ingredients.

Line a casserole with roughly 8 ounces lean salt pork, then cut the amounts of sauerkraut, wine, stock, onion, apple and spices in half. Proceed according to directions in the master recipe, being sure to include the sautéed chopped onion.

In selecting the meats, remember that a *choucroute*—even on a small scale—will be enhanced by one smoked meat.

A combination I like is 2 extra-thick center-cut pork chops, well trimmed of fat and browned in a little butter and oil. After the sauerkraut has cooked 1 hour, add the chops and cook 1 hour longer. Then turn the meat, add 2 lightly smoked sausages and cook another hour. Three hours in all will be sufficient cooking time.

Another combination is 2 small ham hocks added at the beginning with the sauerkraut. Later, after 1½ to 2 hours, add 1 beerwurst or a large piece of kielbasa. Continue to cook 1 hour longer.

Andouillette Maconnaise

Andouillette is a white sausage made from pork tripe (chitterlings) that is popular in many parts of France. It is a specialty of the Beaujolais region where Macon is the principal town. The wine used in its preparation would most likely be a Macon blanc, a drinkable dry white *vin ordinaire* of the locality.

This is a vanity recipe. For many years, I was able to purchase andouillette from a specialty sausage store located on Ninth Avenue in New York City. After a few tries, I was unabashedly proud of being able to recreate this classic dish of Beaujolais in my own kitchen.

If you cannot find andouillettes in any specialty store that sells uncommon sausages, I do *not* encourage making them yourself. Locating a butcher who will sell you the pig's stomach or mesentery and the large intestine—and then cleaning them—is more than a bit daunting, and the preparation is lengthy. (Before the casings are filled, the tripe has to be cut into squares and simmered for hours in a strong stock redolent of onion, herbs and spices.)

There really is no substitute for andouillette, but the recipe is a good one and you may wish to try making it with another white sausage, such as bockwurst or weisswurst (see note).

SERVES 2

2 medium andouillettes (about ¾ pound)
Freshly ground white pepper
About 1½ to 2 cups dry white wine
About 2 heaping tablespoons slightly
    stale homemade bread crumbs
1 to 2 tablespoons butter
2 shallots, finely chopped

2 rounded teaspoons imported Dijon
    mustard, preferably *extra-forte*
⅔ cup very finely chopped fresh parsley
⅓ cup chopped fresh chervil *or*
    additional parsley
Crusty French bread

Preheat the oven to 425°F. Place the andouillettes in a shallow flameproof casserole or gratin dish. Sprinkle with freshly ground pepper and moisten with just enough wine (about ½ to ¾ cup) to cover the bottom of the casserole, reaching about ⅛ inch up the sides of the sausages. Sprinkle the sausages lightly and evenly with bread crumbs, then dot with small pieces of butter.

Roast the andouillettes 10 minutes. Transfer them to the broiler, keeping them a fair distance from the heating element. Cook 5 minutes per side, or until nicely but not overly colored. (Baste once, when turning them, scooping up crumbs from the bottom of the casserole. Add a few more crumbs, if desired.) Transfer the sausages to a hot plate and cover to keep warm.

Skim off the excess fat, and place the casserole on the stove top. Over low heat, add the shallots to the casserole and cook, stirring, until softened. Stir in the mustard and pour in 1 cup of the wine. Raise the heat and reduce the wine, stirring constantly. If the bread crumbs thicken the sauce too much, add another ½ cup of wine. When the sauce has reduced to a creamy combination, stir in half the parsley.

When satisfied with the consistency of the sauce, return the andouillettes to the casserole with their accumulated juices. (It is not too late to add a little more white wine if after the sausages are added the sauce seems too thick.) Add the rest of the parsley and spoon the sauce over the sausages. Sprinkle the chervil over all.

Divide the andouillettes between 2 very hot plates and spoon all the sauce from the casserole around them. Accompany the sausages with lots of good crusty bread to mop up the sauce as well as to temper the richness and pleasant indigestibility of this classic dish.

In some parts of France, andouillette is accompanied with mashed potatoes as well as bread.

NOTE   When I made this recipe using bockwurst and weisswurst, I found that 5 minutes total cooking time under the broiler was enough. These sausages brown faster than andouillette and there is a risk that if cooked any longer, they would split their casings. No other changes in the recipe are necessary.

Veal Breast Stuffed with Pork, Ham, Swiss Chard and Mushrooms

Stuffed veal is delicious served hot or cold. You can count on it for two meals. It also makes an attractive addition to a large buffet, in which case cook a whole breast and double all the ingredients.

SERVES 6

1¼ cups (about 1 ounce) imported dried
   cèpes or porcini mushrooms
About 1½ pounds Swiss chard *or*
   spinach

GROUND-PORK FILLING

½ pound lean ground pork
1 extra-large, lightly beaten
2 tablespoons minced shallots
½ teaspoon minced garlic
1 tablespoon Madeira
½ teaspoon fresh thyme leaves *or*
   a pinch of dried thyme

Half a boneless breast of veal, bones
   reserved (about 3 pounds)
Coarse salt
Freshly ground pepper
2 tablespoons minced shallot
¼ pound smoked ham, cut into fine
   julienne strips
4 tablespoons butter

4 tablespoons olive oil, in all
2 tablespoons pine nuts

1 teaspoon fresh tarragon leaves, finely
   chopped, *or* 1 teaspoon dried tarragon
   leaves, crumbled
¼ teaspoon salt
Freshly ground pepper to taste

3 cloves garlic, unpeeled
2 onions, thinly sliced (about 3 cups)
1 cup dry white wine
1¼ cups chicken stock
1 bay leaf, sprigs parsley, thyme and
   rosemary or tarragon, tied together
   (bouquet garni)
2 tablespoons Madeira

ADVANCE PREPARATION

Soak the dried mushrooms for several hours or overnight in lukewarm to cool water. If sandy, change the water several times.

Strip the Swiss chard leaves from the stems. Save the stems for another dish. Rinse the leaves thoroughly in cold water, drain and pat dry with paper towels.

Heat 2 tablespoons of the olive oil in a large heavy pot and add the pine nuts. As they begin to color, add the chard and toss until it is limp and has reduced in volume. Press the leaves gently in a sieve to remove excess moisture.

Combine the ingredients for the ground-pork filling and mix well. Take about a third of the mushrooms, squeeze out the water and chop them. Add to the filling and mix again.

If your butcher has not done this, trim away the fat and every bit of fine white membrane attached to the veal breast. Pull apart the natural pocket and spread open the veal. Do not worry if part of the meat separates from the rest. Sprinkle with salt, pepper and 1 tablespoon of the minced shallot.

STUFFING THE VEAL

Spread the pork mixture over the meat, leaving a slight margin on all sides. Arrange the strips of ham, lengthwise, on top of the pork. Take 1 cup or more of the chard and spread it as a band down the center of the meat.

If any part of the veal has become separated from the rest of the breast, lay it centered over the chard. Bring the veal together in a long roll, with edges overlapping. Use small skewers and string to tie the meat together. Tuck the ends inside so the filling does not leak out. If available, additional fresh herbs that are suggested for the bouquet garni can be tucked under the string. Otherwise, sprinkle the meat with any dried herbs you like.

COOKING THE VEAL

Heat 3 tablespoons of the butter with the remaining olive oil in a large heavy pot. When hot, brown the veal well on all sides. Allow about 30 minutes for this. After the veal has been turned once, add the garlic. Adjust the heat to be sure that neither the veal nor the garlic burns.

Before the veal has finished browning, add the bones from the veal and brown them also. After the bones have been turned once or twice, add the sliced onions and turn them with the bones until soft and golden. Add the wine and bring to a boil. Boil rapidly for 5 minutes, while basting the veal with wine and onions. Add the stock and the bouquet garni. Reduce the heat, partially cover and simmer 3 hours. During this time, baste and turn the meat frequently. When done, remove the veal and bones from the pot. Extract the skewers and discard the string. If serving hot, keep the veal warm.

TO SERVE HOT

Skim off as much fat from the broth as possible, then strain it through a fine sieve, pressing down on the garlic and onions; set aside. In a saucepan, briefly sauté the remaining tablespoon of the shallot in the remaining butter. Add the

(Continued)

1 8 6

rest of the mushrooms, squeezed dry. (If large, cut them into smaller pieces.) Stir together until the shallot has softened. Add the Madeira and pour in the strained broth. Cook until the broth is reduced to the point of being slightly thickened.

Slice the veal and arrange it on a hot serving platter. Spoon the sauce over it. Accompany the veal with plain buttered noodles or mashed potatoes.

TO SERVE COLD

Instead of making a sauce, strain and degrease the broth. If you like, clarify the broth and pour it into a shallow pan. Chill until set. Chop this aspic to garnish the meat.

Serve the veal, sliced, on a platter surrounded by sprigs of watercress, quarters of hard-boiled egg and cherry tomatoes. Spoon the aspic in a line down the center of the meat.

Veal and Ham Rolls with Mozzarella and Fresh Tomato Sauce
SALTIMBOCCA

To increase this recipe, allow five to six ounces of veal per person and another ounce or so of ham. The sauce is for two and should be adjusted accordingly.
SERVES 2

12 ounces thin slices veal scaloppine
Freshly ground pepper
2 ounces prosciutto *or* cooked ham
Fresh mozzarella
Fresh rosemary leaves *or* dried rosemary
Flour
Olive oil
1 scant tablespoon butter
2 large cloves garlic, chopped
1 large shallot, coarsely chopped
2 or 3 large fresh porcini, cèpes or shiitake mushrooms, cut into long slivers, *or* ½ to 1 ounce dried mushrooms (½ to 1 cup), soaked

½ to ⅔ cup dry white wine
2 to 2½ cups peeled and coarsely chopped fresh ripe plum tomatoes *or* canned Italian plum tomatoes
½ cup chicken stock
2 tablespoons chopped fresh parsley
6 to 8 ounces hot cooked fettuccine, tagliatelle or gnocchetti

THE USEFUL PIG

Spread out the slices of veal on your work surface. If they are very large, divide them in half, lengthwise, so they are long enough to roll. Depending on size, there should be 2 to 3 slices of veal per person. Sprinkle the veal with freshly ground pepper (no salt), then lay a thin slice of prosciutto over each piece. The prosciutto should be cut so the slices do not fully cover the veal.

Add a slice of mozzarella, cut as thin as possible. Keep the cheese well within the border of the ham, or it will leak out while cooking (no real harm done if this happens). Strew a little coarsely chopped fresh rosemary over the cheese. Roll the veal into tight packages, securing each one with a toothpick. Set aside.

When ready to cook, dip the veal rolls into the flour, coating them on all sides. Shake off all excess flour. Lightly coat a heavy enameled cast-iron skillet with olive oil, adding a small dab of butter. When the skillet is hot, add the veal rolls and cook, turning them until evenly browned on all sides. (Adjust the heat to be sure they do not burn.) Remove them from the pan and keep warm.

Add the garlic and shallot to the oil remaining in the skillet (add a little butter if needed), then the mushrooms. When softened, pour in the wine, raise the heat and cook until greatly reduced. Add the tomatoes and cook until they form a thick sauce. Add the chicken stock. (With the prosciutto and stock, it is possible no salt will be needed.) Simmer the sauce until only slightly reduced and arrange the veal rolls in the skillet. Spoon the sauce over them.

Partially cover the pan and cook about 30 minutes, turning the veal twice. Add a little water if more liquid is needed. Just before serving, stir in 1 tablespoon of the parsley.

TO SERVE

Remove the toothpicks and nest the rolls on a bed of hot pasta. Spoon the sauce over all and sprinkle with the remaining parsley.

Spaghetti Baked in Parchment with Mushrooms, Pancetta and Tomatoes

The excitement of this simple dish begins when the parchment is opened and an incredible waft of vapor, intense with the woodsy aroma of mushrooms, fills the room. For this reason, it would make a memorable first course to start off a festive evening.

It is important to note that in this recipe aluminum foil cannot be substituted for parchment paper. The results will not be the same. Foil is helpful, though, in protecting the parchment package, which becomes vulnerable as the sauce weakens the paper. Also note that in terms of handling, unless the parchment is wider than a standard fifteen-inch roll, the pasta should be divided between two packages.

Since the spaghetti is to be cooked further, when boiling it, drain and stop the cooking just before it reaches the al dente stage. For the same reason, choose spaghetti over vermicelli or other fine pasta. The risk of overcooking is too great.

SERVES 4 AS A MAIN COURSE OR 6 TO 8 AS A FIRST COURSE

1¼ cups (1 ounce) imported dried mushrooms, preferably porcini or cèpes
¼ cup olive oil
3 large cloves garlic, flattened and peeled
About 2 ounces pancetta, in one slice, *or* 2 thick slices lean salt pork or bacon, blanched to remove smokiness
2 large shallots, chopped
1 cup (3 ounces) sliced fresh mushrooms
2 ounces ham, cut into julienne strips, about 1½ inches long

¼ cup dry white wine
2 pounds ripe tomatoes, peeled and chopped, *or* 3½ cups canned Italian plum tomatoes with juices
Freshly ground black pepper
3 tablespoons chopped fresh parsley
Coarse salt
2 tablespoons dry marsala
¾ to 1 pound spaghetti
Freshly grated Parmesan cheese

ADVANCE PREPARATION

Several hours before cooking, soak the dried mushrooms in a bowl of luke-warm-to-cool water. (Hot water steals the flavor.)

Later, without disturbing the water, remove the mushrooms. Rinse, pat dry with paper towels and, if whole, slice them. Set aside.

Strain the soaking liquid through a fine, tightly woven cloth or plain white paper towel. Only ½ cup will be needed, but reserve 1 cup.

COOKING

Pour the oil into a casserole and add the garlic. Over low heat, turn the garlic frequently until golden brown but not burned. Remove, cut into slivers and set aside.

Cut the pancetta into small dice and add to the casserole. Render the fat over low heat, turning the pieces frequently, until very lightly browned. Raise the heat slightly, add the dried mushrooms and cook about 1 minute. Stir in the shallots and when softened slightly, add the fresh mushrooms, stirring to coat. Add more oil if needed.

When the mushrooms are lightly browned, add the ham. Stir briefly. Add the wine, raise the heat and deglaze the casserole. Cook until the wine evaporates, stirring constantly. Pour in ½ cup of the mushroom liquid, leaving any residue at the bottom of the cup. Bring to a boil and reduce slightly.

Add the tomatoes, slivers of garlic and a generous grinding of pepper. Cook the sauce over high heat until slightly thickened. Add 2 tablespoons of the parsley and salt to taste. Lower the heat and continue to cook about 15 minutes.

Preheat the oven to 475°F.

Stir in the marsala and remaining parsley and keep warm while cooking the pasta. (I have found 5 minutes to be about right for imported dry spaghetti; much less time for fresh pasta.)

Meanwhile, tear off 2 large sheets of heavy-duty aluminum foil. Cut 2 sheets of parchment paper to about 15 x 20 inches. Center each sheet over one of aluminum foil.

FINISHING THE SPAGHETTI

Drain the pasta. Return it to the hot pot in which it was cooked. Pour over the sauce and toss until well combined. Divide the pasta between the 2 sheets of parchment.

Start to fold the parchment like an envelope by turning in the 2 opposite corners; then continue to bring in the corners, allowing enough leeway to crimp them together and fold tightly to seal each package completely. Fold the protective aluminum foil loosely around the packages and arrange them on a baking sheet. Place in the hot oven and bake exactly 7 minutes.

Discard the foil and place the parchment packages on a hot serving platter. Bring to the table at once, open the packages and serve from the wrapping.

Pass the cheese separately.

Pasta with Meat Filling

CANELONES

Years ago, in Spain, this dish was reserved for special occasions. The tribute is still warranted. If extra chicken livers were unavailable, three or four ounces of fine smooth pâté, bought from a charcuterie in a nearby town, was used to supplement two livers garnered from chickens cooked for another course. This can still be done.

In Spain, one could purchase small square sheets of *canelone* at most grocery stores. *Canelones* are more delicate than the pasta used for Italian *cannelloni*. I usually make my own pasta, but this does make the recipe very time-consuming. Recently I tested a shortcut used by many chefs when making ravioli—substituting wonton skins, which are the right size and have sufficient delicacy. Though I still prefer homemade pasta, the wonton skins work quite well. Cook more than needed to allow for any that might become damaged during cooking.

Make the filling first so it can cool thoroughly. Later, fill the *canelone*, then prepare the Béchamel Sauce. The *canelones* can be refrigerated overnight before baking.

SERVES 8 TO 10

MEAT FILLING

7 tablespoons butter
1 pound ground pork
4 cups finely chopped onions
    (about 4 onions)
4 to 6 ounces chicken livers (about
    5 livers), filament removed
2½ pounds ripe tomatoes, peeled and
    finely chopped *or* 4½ cups canned
    Italian plum tomatoes
3 cloves garlic, finely chopped
¾ to 1 teaspoon coarse salt
Freshly grated nutmeg

2 pounds fresh pasta dough *or* enough
    wonton skins to make about 40
    canelones
Salt
1 tablespoon olive oil

1 tablespoon chopped fresh oregano or
    marjoram leaves *or* 1 teaspoon dried
    oregano
2 teaspoons chopped fresh tarragon
    leaves *or* 1 teaspoon dried tarragon
    leaves
2 tablespoons chopped fresh parsley,
    or more if dried herbs are used
2 tablespoons flour
1 cup milk
¼ teaspoon ground cinnamon
¼ teaspoon finely ground white pepper

Béchamel Sauce (page 192)
About ½ cup freshly grated Parmesan
    cheese

PREPARING THE FILLING

Prepare the filling several hours in advance or the day before. Melt 2 table-spoons of the butter in a large skillet over medium heat. Add the pork and cook, stirring frequently, until the meat loses its redness. Add the onions and continue to cook until very soft and translucent, stirring frequently. If neces-sary, lower the heat to prevent the onions from browning.

Raise the heat slightly and add the chicken livers. Brown them quickly, taking care to keep them soft and pink in the center. Remove the livers and finely chop them. Return them to the skillet along with the tomatoes, garlic, salt, a generous grating of nutmeg, the oregano or marjoram, tarragon and parsley. Cook together over moderate heat, stirring frequently. After the ex-cess tomato juices have cooked away, skim off any residue of fat.

Meanwhile, prepare a binder for the filling. Melt 2 tablespoons of butter in a small saucepan, over low heat. Stir in the flour and when well blended, add the milk, a little at a time, and the cinnamon and pepper. Cook until very thick, then stir into the meat and tomato mixture. Over low heat, continue to cook 15 minutes longer. Taste for seasoning, then let cool completely.

MAKING THE *CANELONES*

Roll the homemade pasta dough quite thin, using the #1 setting on a manual pasta machine (1 notch thicker than the thinnest #0 setting on most ma-chines). Use a ruler and knife to cut the sheets into near-squares, 3 x 3¼ inches. Forty are needed to use up all the filling.

Drop portions of *canelones* or wonton skins into a large pot of rapidly boiling salted water to which a little oil has been added. Cook briefly until they appear to blister slightly (little beads will appear on the dough), then remove and drop them into a large bowl of cold water to stop the cooking. Drain each one separately and lay it out on a soft kitchen towel to absorb the rest of the water. Wonton skins must *not* overlap.

Place a cylinder-shaped spoonful of filling in the center of each square of pasta. Then roll to close and lay seam side down in a shallow baking dish greased with a little of the butter. Arrange the *canelones* side by side (use more than one baking dish if necessary). Refrigerate while preparing the Béchamel Sauce.

Preheat the oven to 425°F.

Spoon the béchamel over the *canelones,* then sprinkle with cheese and dot with tiny pieces of the remaining butter. Bake 30 minutes, or until the surface is lightly browned. Serve the *canelones* piping hot.

Béchamel Sauce

MAKES 4 CUPS

1 quart milk
1 large onion, sliced
1 clove garlic, flattened and peeled
½ teaspoon salt
½ teaspoon cinnamon

½ teaspoon finely ground white pepper
8 tablespoons (1 stick) butter
6 tablespoons flour
Freshly grated nutmeg
½ to ¾ cup heavy cream

Combine the milk, onion, garlic, salt, cinnamon and pepper; bring almost to a simmer. Over very low heat, let the spices steep in the milk for about 20 minutes, or long enough to impart their flavor.

Melt the butter in a saucepan over low heat. Stir in the flour and blend with a wooden spoon until perfectly smooth. Strain in the hot milk, a little at a time. When most of the milk has been added and the béchamel begins to thicken, give the sauce a generous grating of nutmeg and taste for seasoning. More salt and pepper may be desired.

Continue to cook the sauce over low heat for about 30 to 40 minutes, or until very thick. Stir frequently, scraping the bottom and sides of the pan with the spoon. Before removing from the heat, add the heavy cream little by little; keep the consistency thick.

Cool slightly before using, but not too much, or it will not flow properly when spooned over the *canelones*.

Pork Chili

If the chili is served over rice or combined with beans, it will serve eight. This dish improves with reheating.

SERVES 4 TO 8

3 tablespoons olive oil
1¾ pounds boneless pork, cut into large dice
2 teaspoons cumin seed
3 cups chopped onions
1 small red bell pepper, seeded and finely chopped
3, or more, fresh jalapeño peppers, seeded, veins removed and finely chopped
½ head garlic, chopped (8 to 10 cloves)
6 tablespoons, or more, depending on hotness, best-quality pure chile powder

3 teaspoons ground cumin
2 teaspoons dried oregano leaves, crumbled
1 scant teaspoon celery seed
2 large bay leaves
2 cups beef stock
3 tablespoons strong red wine vinegar
About 1 quart boiling water
About 1 teaspoon coarse salt
Rice *and/or* beans (optional)

ACCOMPANIMENTS

Chopped onion
Sour cream
Chili-Raisin Sauce (page 194)
Diced ripe tomato (optional)

Diced avocado marinated in lime juice (optional)
Salsa cruda (optional)
Shredded cheese (optional)

Heat the oil in a large pot. Add the pork, raise the heat and cook, stirring frequently, until the meat begins to brown. Do this in several batches to prevent the pork from stewing in its own juices. If the meat gives off too much liquid, spoon off the excess but save it to return, little by little, after the onions and peppers have been added.

Add the cumin seed and onions and continue to cook, stirring frequently, until the onion has softened. Add the bell pepper, jalapeño peppers and garlic; cook a few minutes longer.

Sprinkle the meat with chile powder and ground cumin and turn it until well coated. Add the oregano, celery seed, bay leaves, stock and vinegar, and bring to a brisk simmer. Cook, uncovered, 30 minutes to 1 hour, or until the stock is greatly reduced and the sauce becomes thick.

(Continued)

Add 1 cup boiling water, stir, and continue to cook. If excessive pools of fat form on the surface of the chili, skim from time to time. As the chili thickens, continue to thin the sauce with boiling water, as needed.

After 2 hours, taste for hotness and seasoning. Add salt and more chopped jalapeños, if the heat is not sufficient. (Additional chile powder can only be added if it is first cooked separately in a little oil.)

After 4 hours, the granular texture of the chile powder should have cooked away. When the flavor and consistency of the chili begins to satisfy, turn the heat as low as possible and cook, covered, 1 hour longer. Do not add more water, unless the chili thickens too much.

If you like, accompany the chili with rice and/or beans. Include a bowl each of chopped onion and sour cream. Pass Chili-Raisin sauce, which is especially good with the rice. Other accompaniments include diced ripe tomato, diced avocado marinated in lime juice, salsa cruda and shredded cheese.

Chili-Raisin Sauce

MAKES ABOUT 1½ CUPS

½ cup sauce from Pork Chili (page 193), without meat
½ cup chicken stock

1 tablespoon tomato paste
1 teaspoon red wine vinegar
3 tablespoons yellow raisins

Thin the sauce from the chili with stock, stir in the tomato paste, vinegar and raisins. Simmer together over low heat for about 20 minutes, or until the raisins are plump. Serve the sauce separately.

Pork with Eggplant and Vegetables

This typical Spanish preparation is used with both freshly cooked and leftover pork. Meat that has already been cooked should be added to the vegetable sauce shortly before serving.

SERVES 4

1 medium eggplant (about ¾ pound)
Coarse salt
1 pound ripe fresh plum tomatoes
1 lean boneless pork butt, cut into 1-inch cubes, *or* cooked pork, cut into thick slices (about 1¾ pounds)
Freshly ground pepper
Olive oil
6 large cloves garlic, unpeeled
1½ cups chopped onion
1 large sweet red frying pepper, cut into long thin strips

1 small green frying pepper, cut into long thin strips
2 large cloves garlic, peeled and chopped
1 large sprig fresh oregano *or* 4 large fresh basil leaves, chopped, *or* 1 heaping tablespoon chopped fresh parsley
1 cup dry white wine
3 tablespoons chopped fresh parsley
½ cup small black imported olives, pitted (optional)
Large croutons *or* fried potato wedges

ADVANCE PREPARATION

Cut the eggplant into small cubes. Sprinkle well with coarse salt and place in a colander for 1 hour, tossing from time to time.

Blanch, peel and chop the tomatoes, retaining the juices. Set aside.

COOKING

Sprinkle the meat with coarse salt and freshly ground pepper. Coat a large skillet generously with olive oil and heat. Add the garlic cloves to the skillet and then the meat. Brown well on all sides. Allow about 20 minutes for this. Leaving the garlic in the pan, remove the meat and set it aside.

Add the onion and peppers to the skillet and cook, stirring frequently, until softened slightly. Pat the eggplant dry with paper towels, wiping off any salt, and add to the pan. Cook, turning the eggplant, until the flesh loses its pale greenish hue. Add a little more oil if needed. When the skillet becomes dry and the vegetables risk burning, stir in the chopped garlic, oregano or basil or 1 tablespoon parsley and the tomatoes.

(Continued)

Raise the heat and cook, stirring the vegetables and scraping the bottom to deglaze the pan. When the tomatoes thicken, add the wine and 1 tablespoon of the parsley. Bring the sauce to a boil and cook briefly. Return the meat to the pan and spoon the sauce over it. Reduce the heat to a low simmer, cover and cook 1 hour, or until the pork is tender.

Every 15 minutes, turn the meat and eggplant and spoon the sauce over all. If desired, add the olives 15 minutes before serving. When ready to serve, stir another tablespoon of chopped parsley into the sauce, then sprinkle the remaining parsley over all.

Serve surrounded by large thick croutons to dip in the sauce or with crisp wedges of potato fried in olive oil.

Romano Beans with Potatoes and Bacon

Romano beans resemble oversize flat green beans. Like any green bean, when truly fresh they are a treat that can be enjoyed as a meal by themselves. Depending on the season, toss the hot beans with thin slices of crisp Vidalia onion or bulbous spring onions just before serving. In summer add slices of sweet red onion and a diced vine-ripened tomato.

SERVES 4 TO 6

1 pound small new potatoes, unpeeled
Coarse salt
1 pound Romano beans, trimmed and
    cut into 3-inch lengths
¼ pound very lean salt pork, sliced

2 tablespoons butter
Freshly ground black pepper
1 tablespoon chopped fresh dill
1 tablespoon chopped fresh parsley

Put the potatoes in a large saucepan and cover with several inches of cold salted water. Bring to a boil and cook 10 minutes, uncovered. Drop in the Romano beans and boil 10 minutes longer.

While the potatoes and beans are cooking, coarsely chop the slices of salt pork. Melt the butter in a medium casserole and sauté the salt pork over low heat until slightly crisp.

When the beans and potatoes are done, drain and cut the potatoes in half. Combine the vegetables with the warm butter and salt pork and sprinkle generously with freshly ground pepper (salt should not be necessary). Cover tightly and let stand until ready to serve (see note). Shake the casserole from time to time.

When ready to serve, reheat the casserole if necessary. At the last moment, sprinkle the beans and potatoes with dill and parsley. Toss briefly and serve.

NOTE   The beans and potatoes can wait 15 to 30 minutes, if other dishes need your attention. They should not, however, stand long enough to get cold.

Stuffed New Potatoes from Spain
PATATAS RELLEÑOS DE CATALINA

This rustic dish, cooked on a trivet over an open fire, was one of the special-ties of a farm woman I knew in rural Mallorca. The stuffed potatoes can be set aside and reheated later. A short rest actually contributes to the flavor.

SERVES 4 TO 6

1 large eggplant (1 to 1½ pounds)
Coarse salt

STUFFING

1 pound lean ground pork
1 extra-large egg, lightly beaten
1 or 2 large cloves garlic, finely chopped
1 tablespoon chopped fresh oregano
  leaves *or* 1 teaspoon dried oregano
  leaves, crumbled
Freshly ground pepper

1 egg, lightly beaten, *or* 1 egg yolk,
  beaten with 2 teaspoons water
Good-quality olive oil for frying
1 large onion, coarsely chopped
1 or 2 large sweet frying peppers, seeded
  and cut into long strips, about ½ inch
  wide
1¾ to 2 pounds vine-ripened tomatoes,
  peeled and coarsely chopped

2 round, evenly shaped new potatoes per
  person (3 to 4 ounces each)

½ teaspoon coarse salt
½ cup finely chopped onion
½ cup fresh bread crumbs, soaked in ⅓
  cup milk or cream and squeezed dry
Finely grated zest of 1 small lemon
1 tablespoon dry sherry (optional)

1 bay leaf
1 large sprig oregano *or* bouquet of
  marjoram *or* parsley sprigs, tied
  together
2 cloves garlic, chopped
Freshly ground pepper
Coarse salt
Green olives, pitted and blanched
  (optional)

ADVANCE PREPARATION

Cut the eggplant into 1-inch-thick slices, then cut each slice into large chunks. Place them in a colander and sprinkle well with salt. Let stand 1 hour, or longer, to release any bitter juices. Toss occasionally.

Peel the potatoes and use a small spoon with a sharp edge to hollow them out. They should resemble small round bowls. Work through the broad-est area and scrape out as much as possible, while taking care not to puncture the walls of the shell. Drop them into a bowl of ice water until ready to stuff.

Combine the stuffing ingredients and mix thoroughly, adding sherry only if the mixture seems too dry.

Dry the potatoes well with a towel and stuff them with the meat mixture, letting it mound up. Brush the surface with a little beaten egg.

COOKING

Use a skillet that will hold the potatoes in one layer, side by side, so they keep each other upright. Heat about ½ inch of oil and when very hot, arrange the potatoes in the pan, meat side down. Fry, turning them, until well browned on all sides. Remove and set aside.

Dry the eggplant well with paper towels. Drop the chunks into the oil used to fry the potatoes. When browned on all sides, remove and drain on paper towels. Pour off most of the oil remaining in the skillet, but leave a generous coating of about 3 tablespoons.

Add the onion and, after a minute, the peppers. Cook over medium heat until the onion is soft and golden. Add the tomatoes, bay leaf, oregano and garlic. Sprinkle with freshly ground pepper and add salt to taste. When slightly thickened, pour the sauce into a shallow flameproof cassserole and add the potatoes, arranged meat side up. Spoon a little of the sauce in the casserole over them. Bring the sauce to a boil, reduce the heat and simmer, covered, about 30 minutes, or until the potatoes are done when tested with a fork.

Add the eggplant, turning it in the sauce. When the eggplant is hot, add olives, if you like, and serve.

THE TRADITIONAL PIG

Roast Pork on a Bed of Potatoes

·

Roast Pork with Pan-Glazed Vegetables and Red Wine Sauce

·

Game Marinade

·

Roast Loin of Pork Stuffed with Prunes and Apricots

·

Loin of Pork Braised in Milk with Garlic and Fennel Sauce

·

Braised Pork with Black Salsify and Mushrooms

·

Pork Chops with Apples and Cream

·

Roast Fresh Ham with Wine and Mustard Sauce

·

Classic Baked Smoked Ham

·

Ham Braised in Wine with Aromatic Vegetables

·

Mustard Sauce

·

Roast Suckling Pig with Herb Basting Sauce

I cannot forget the wonderful *cerdo* of Spain and the shops abounding with every kind of pork product—from head to tail—not to mention sausages and hams. On the hillside farm where I lived, trees heavy with figs and apricots hung over the pigpens. In those days the fruit was considered too perishable to be worth marketing, so the animals were often nourished on nature's windfall, supplemented by bruised oranges and other fruits of the land.

After a slaughtering, the country people went to work immediately boiling the intestines for casings in caldrons over open fires and preparing sausages for sustenance through the winter. Lacking refrigeration, a great feast was soon to follow, the centerpiece of the occasion being the *lomo del cerdo* (loin of pork). We would gather eagerly, tables pushed together and made respectable by embroidered cloths, to feast on this delicious product of our own landscape, feeling, rightly, that a meal that included pork was always a celebration.

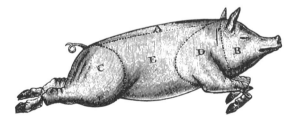

WORKING WITH A CENTER-CUT PORK ROAST

You can save money by buying a whole loin of pork and dividing it to suit your needs. A whole piece weighs roughly ten to eleven pounds. Boned, the meat weighs about six to seven pounds. To count portions, allow one full rib per person.

If you are buying the meat boned, ask the butcher to save the bones for you to use for sauces. (Roast them first, then make a stock.) Unless requested to do otherwise, the butcher will usually roll and tie the meat. Let him do this as it makes the meat easier to divide; then cut it as you wish. If the pork is to be stuffed, it is easy enough to open up the meat and retie it.

A full loin is unwieldy and easier to handle in two pieces. Divided, each boneless piece will weigh around three pounds and serve six to seven persons. If these amounts are too large, cut off thick medallions, retie each piece compactly and cook them the same way as bone-in chops—either barbecued or sautéed in a skillet.

These center-cut roasts are good prepared in any manner described for whole pieces of pork. With their low fat content, they do not shrink as much as the shoulder butt cuts. It is wise at some point during the cooking to insert a meat thermometer. This is not so much to be sure that the pork is well cooked as to avoid overcooking, which will result in dryness. The trichina parasite is killed at 140°F.; even though the American Meat Institute suggests that those who are wary cook pork to an internal temperature of 170°F., this is considerably more than enough. A temperature between 150° and 160°F. is sufficient. A brief rest before carving will allow the juices to settle evenly in the meat.

Barbecuing a center-cut roast is explained in detail on page 121.

Roast Pork on a Bed of Potatoes
RÔTI DE PORC À LA BOULANGÈRE

This is a classic French recipe, its origins dating back to a time when it was the custom for women to bring their special dishes to the commodious oven of the local bakery, assembled and ready for roasting. Someone would then return to the bakery at the appointed hour and rush the dish, piping hot, home to an expectant family.

This recipe is one that is easy to increase or decrease, the only major change being the size of the pan to accommodate the amount of pork and potatoes. For two to three persons, a boneless pork butt, which is smaller, is delicious cooked in this manner.

SERVES 6

1 center-cut loin of pork, boned and tied
    (about 3½ pounds)
Coarse salt
Freshly ground white pepper
Sprigs fresh thyme and fresh rosemary
    or ½ teaspoon each dried thyme
    and rosemary
3½ pounds baking potatoes, very thinly
    sliced (about 7 large potatoes)
About 6 tablespoons butter
1 large mild Spanish onion, thinly sliced

1 large leek, thinly sliced
3 large cloves garlic, finely chopped
2 teaspoons fresh thyme leaves, rubbed
    from the stem, *or* 1 teaspoon dried
    thyme
About 2 tablespoons finely chopped fresh
    parsley
2 bay leaves, broken in half
About ¾ cup chicken stock
Applesauce (page 129), optional

Sprinkle the pork roast with coarse salt and freshly ground pepper. Tuck several sprigs of thyme and rosemary under the string used to tie the meat or sprinkle the roast with dried herbs. Save a few sprigs of thyme for the potatoes. Bring the meat to room temperature before cooking.

Several hours before cooking, soak the potato slices in cold water, changing the water once, to rid them of excess starch. When ready to cook the pork, drain the potatoes and pat dry in a towel.

Preheat the oven to 450°F. Grease a large 3-quart oval gratin dish or other baking pan about 16 to 17 inches long lavishly with about 2 tablespoons softened butter. Spread the onion rings over the bottom of the pan. Arrange slightly overlapping layers of potatoes, fanned out over the onions, and interspersed with the leek, garlic, and thyme leaves. Strew a little of the parsley over a few of the layers and sprinkle coarse salt and freshly ground pepper on the first layer and the last. Place the pork on top of the potatoes and tuck the bay leaves around it. Pour ½ cup of the chicken stock evenly around the pan and dot the potatoes and meat generously with butter.

Roast the pork and potatoes about 2 hours. After the first 30 minutes, baste the potatoes and the meat every 15 minutes. Tilt the pan and press down on the potatoes to gather the juices and, occasionally, loosen them from the bottom with a spatula. Add the remaining chicken stock as needed. After the pork has cooked 1 hour, turn it and dot the unbrowned side with a little more butter. (If desired, the meat can be turned several times during the cooking and the potatoes under the meat redistributed.)

Lower the oven temperature to 425°F. after 1½ hours, or if using a meat thermometer, when the internal temperature reaches 140°F. Pork is safely cooked through at 150°F.

When the meat is done, transfer it to a carving board, cover with aluminum foil and let stand 10 minutes before carving. During this time, return the pan of potatoes to the oven so that those buried under the meat have a chance to color.

Remove the string, carve the pork and arrange it, slightly overlapping, over the potatoes. Sprinkle with a line of finely chopped parsley and serve from the pan.

If the spirit moves you, accompany this meal with a bowl of warm freshly made Applesauce.

Roast Pork with Pan-Glazed Vegetables and Red Wine Sauce

This makes a highly festive winter platter, ideal for any special occasion. For a rewarding visual presentation, allow ample time for the arrangement. This one-dish meal will require a very large platter for serving.

Despite its length, this recipe is not overly complicated. Most of the vegetables can be nearly ready in advance. The chestnut and fruit garnishes only need reheating. What is important is to check the clock for timing the additions and, later, to keep a watchful eye when making the sauce.

Do not feel compelled to prepare all the fruit and vegetable garnishes. Indeed, the limited season of chestnuts may prevent it; celery root might not be available, or you may prefer to increase the potatoes and eliminate the turnips. Do, however, choose a fruit for one of the garnishes and, if possible, include a green vegetable. My first choices would be pears or prunes, onions, carrots, potatoes and Brussels sprouts.

Do the advance preparation as it suits you, but allow two and a half to two and three-quarter hours for the pork: two hours cooking time, half an hour for the juices to settle (while making the sauce), then a few minutes for carving and assembling the platter.

SERVES 6 TO 8

1 center-cut pork roast, boned and nicely
    trimmed (3½ pounds)
Freshly ground black pepper
Coarse salt

FRUIT GARNISHES

12 to 16 whole chestnuts, peeled
    and cooked
2 tablespoons strong meat stock
3 firm slightly underripe pears
    (Anjou or Bartlett)

Sprigs fresh rosemary *or* 1½ teaspoons
    dried rosemary leaves
About 12 tablespoons (1½ sticks) butter
8 to 10 large cloves garlic, unpeeled

½ lemon
Pinch of sugar
6 to 8 large pitted prunes
Red wine
½ orange, sliced

VEGETABLE GARNISHES

12 small white boiling onions, peeled
1 large knob celery root (about 12
   ounces), cut into sticks, about ½ inch
   x 2½ inches (optional)
1 pound Brussels sprouts (optional)
3 to 4 carrots, cut into 3-inch pieces and
   in half lengthwise if large

2 large baking potatoes (8 ounces each),
   cut into small wedges and soaked in
   cold water until ready to cook
2 turnips (about 5 ounces each), cut into
   sticks, ¼ inch x 2½ inches

SAUCE

2 tablespoons butter
1 large shallot, chopped
¼ cup cognac *or* brandy

1 tablespoon chopped fresh parsley

1 cup dry red wine
About 1 cup strong meat stock
1 tablespoon red *or* black currant jelly

ADVANCE PREPARATION

Sprinkle the inside of the boned pork with freshly ground pepper and a little salt. Reserve a few sprigs of rosemary for the pan; chop the leaves from the rest and strew in a line across the meat. Roll the roast together and tie it securely with string.

Rub a roasting pan (preferably nonaluminum) with about 2 tablespoons of softened butter; sprinkle the pan with a little salt and freshly ground pepper. Make a bed of garlic in the center of the pan and arrange the meat, seam side down, on top. Set aside.

Except for the Brussels sprouts, prepare all the fruit and vegetable garnishes you wish to serve.

Sauté the chestnuts in 2 tablespoons of butter and moisten with 2 tablespoons of stock. Cook just until glazed. Peel the pears, wipe with ½ lemon and cut into ¼-inch-thick slices. Sauté in 2 tablespoons butter with a pinch of sugar and ½ cup water. Cook until the water evaporates and the pears are glazed. Marinate the prunes in enough red wine to cover along with the orange slices. Drain and gently heat in 1½ tablespoons butter.

Sauté the onions in 2 tablespoons butter with ¼ teaspoon sugar until nicely glazed. Blanch the celery root for 5 minutes, drain and rinse in cold water. Trim the Brussels sprouts and put to soak in cold salted water until ready to cook.

(Continued)

ROASTING THE PORK

Preheat the oven to 350°F. Roast the pork for 15 minutes. Turn, baste and roast 15 minutes longer. Lower the heat to 325°F., turn the meat and baste again. Roast another 30 minutes, turning the meat and basting every 15 minutes.

When the pork has cooked 1 hour, add the carrots, the reserved rosemary sprigs and, if the pan seems dry, a little more butter. Baste and roast another 15 minutes, then raise the heat back to 350°F. and add the potatoes, drained. Turn them in the pan juices until coated. Place the meat fat side up, baste and continue to cook.

When the potatoes have cooked 15 minutes, add the turnips, if using, and the onions. Baste again and roast 15 minutes longer. When the pork has only 15 minutes left to cook, add the celery root, if using, and turn all the vegetables in the pan juices.

When the pork is done, place on a carving board and cover with heavy-duty aluminum foil. Transfer all the vegetables, except the garlic, to a smaller roasting pan. Return them to the oven. Raise the heat to 400°F. while making the sauce.

If cooking Brussels sprouts, drop them at this time into a large pot of boiling salted water. Cook about 8 minutes, depending on size. Drain and return them to the warm pot. Add 2 tablespoons of butter, cover and set aside. Gently reheat them at the last moment before serving.

Pour off any fat remaining in the roasting pan. Add 2 tablespoons of butter and the shallot. Sauté the shallot until softened. Deglaze the pan with cognac. When it has all but disappeared, add the red wine and bring to a boil. Cook until reduced to about ⅓ cup, then add ½ cup of the stock and continue to reduce. Taste for seasoning, add a little more stock and reduce again. Strain the sauce into a small saucepan, pressing down hard on the garlic. Stir in the currant jelly and simmer over very low heat. As the sauce simmers, continue to add more stock, a little at a time.

Gently reheat the fruit garnishes and carve the pork.

TO SERVE

Arrange the pork down the center of a warmed serving platter, slices overlapping. Without crowding, surround the meat with small arrangements of vegetable and fruit garnishes. Keep the fruits toward one end of the platter and the vegetables toward the other. Alternate them with a focus on color.

Spoon a little sauce over the meat, then sprinkle a line of chopped parsley down the center. Pass the rest of the sauce separately.

Game Marinade

I have used this marinade for venison and wild game birds ever since I can remember. It is also perfect for pork. For a larger amount of meat, such as a fresh ham, double the recipe.

MAKES ENOUGH FOR ONE 4- TO 5-POUND PORK ROAST OR 6 LARGE, THICK CHOPS

½ teaspoon white peppercorns, crushed coarsely

½ teaspoon juniper berries, crushed slightly

1 cup dry white wine

⅓ cup white wine vinegar, preferably tarragon-flavored

⅓ cup olive oil

2 bay leaves, broken

½ teaspoon coarse salt

2 large cloves garlic, flattened, peeled and thinly sliced

¼ cup coarsely chopped fresh parsley

2 teaspoons coarsely chopped fresh rosemary leaves *or* 1 teaspoon dried rosemary

Several sprigs fresh thyme *or* ½ teaspoon dried thyme

1 large shallot, coarsely chopped (about ¼ cup)

1 small onion, thinly sliced

1 carrot, thinly sliced

½ cup celery leaves, coarsely chopped

Combine the ingredients in a shallow glass or ceramic baking dish or bowl.

Place the meat in the marinade, turning it and spooning the herbs and spices over it. When weather permits, a cold room is preferable to the refrigerator for marinating meat. Turn the meat and baste it as often as possible.

Roast Loin of Pork Stuffed with Prunes and Apricots

Much of the work is done in advance, making this festive dish deceptively easy. Serve the pork with some form of crisp roasted potatoes and a green vegetable.

SERVES 6 TO 8

1 center-cut loin of pork, boned
   (3 to 4 pounds)
Game Marinade (page 209)
6 to 8 large prunes
6 to 8 dried apricots
1 to 1½ cups dry red wine

1 sweet navel orange, thinly sliced
3 to 5 thin slices lemon
1 whole clove
Flour
Olive oil

AROMATICS

2 medium onions, cut into thick slices
10 whole cloves garlic, unpeeled
½ Granny Smith apple, unpeeled, cored
   and cut into large dice
1 carrot, sliced
1 stalk celery, coarsely chopped

8 small sprigs fresh rosemary *or*
   1 teaspoon dried rosemary
Several sprigs fresh thyme *or* 1 teaspoon
   dried thyme
Several sprigs parsley (optional)

1¾ cups dry white wine
¼ cup dry Madeira

2 cups strong meat stock

ADVANCE PREPARATION

Start marinating the pork at least 2 days before you intend to cook it. If the pork roast has been tied, remove the string and spread it open. Combine the marinade in a rectangular glass or earthenware casserole and place the pork in it. Roll it in the marinade and let marinate in the refrigerator for several days, turning and basting it daily.

    The day before cooking, pit the prunes and drop them into a bowl with the apricots. Add enough red wine to cover the fruit, along with the slices of orange and lemon and the clove. Let the fruits steep at room temperature, turning them as they plump in the wine.

    Early in the day of cooking, remove the pork from the marinade; discard the marinade. Look on the underside of the meat for a thin seam of fat running the length of the roast. Using a small sharp knife, follow the seam across the meat to work open a natural pocket. Take care not to cut all the way through. Spread open the pork and arrange a line of prunes, end to end, deep within the pocket. Then tuck an apricot under each prune. To make closing the pocket easier, temporarily bring it together with skewers and string. Secure the roast for cooking by tying it tightly at 1-inch intervals. Extract the skewers. If a piece of fruit pushes its way out of the end of the roast, block it with a piece of stale bread (to be discarded after cooking). Return the pork to the refrigerator, but bring it to room temperature 1 or 2 hours before cooking.

ROASTING THE PORK

Preheat the oven to 350°F. Pat the roast dry with paper towels and roll it lightly in flour, brushing off any excess. Coat a flameproof roasting pan liberally with olive oil and place it on the stove top. When hot, brown the meat on all sides, taking care not to let the flour burn. When finished, transfer the roast to a platter and pour off the excess oil, leaving enough to keep the vegetables from sticking.

Scatter the aromatic vegetables, apple and herbs over the bottom of the roasting pan and place the pork on top, fat side up. (If fresh rosemary and thyme are unavailable, sprinkle the pork and vegetables with dried rosemary and thyme and add several sprigs of parsley to the roasting pan.) Place the pork in the oven and roast about 1 hour and 15 minutes, or until a meat thermometer registers 150°F. During the roasting, tilt the pan and baste the meat every 15 to 20 minutes.

When done, remove the roast from the pan and place on a warmed platter or carving board. Cover the pork tightly with heavy aluminum foil and let rest in a warm place 15 to 30 minutes before carving.

Set the roasting pan on the stove top and add 1 cup of the wine. Bring to a boil and reduce, stirring the wine and aromatics, until the bottom of the pan is almost dry. Add the rest of the wine and boil down by about half. Stir in the Madeira and cook briefly. Add half the stock and simmer, stirring and pressing down on the vegetables. As the broth reduces, lower the heat to a bare simmer and add the rest of the stock, little by little.

Continue to cook until the broth is reduced to barely 2 cups. Taste for seasoning. Strain the sauce through a fine sieve into a saucepan, pressing down hard on the vegetables. Keep the sauce warm while carving the pork.

Snip and remove all string from the meat; carve into ½- to ¾-inch slices. Arrange them, slightly overlapping, on a warmed platter. Spoon some of the hot sauce over the pork and serve at once. Pass the rest of the sauce separately in a hot sauceboat.

Loin of Pork Braised in Milk with Garlic and Fennel Sauce

Allow three and a half to four hours for cooking this dish. The slow process of browning the pork and sautéing the onions will take about one hour. After the long simmering in milk, the pork will be incredibly moist and juicy. The pork is also excellent served cold (without the sauce), very thinly sliced.
SERVES 4

1 center-cut loin of pork, well trimmed, boned and tied (2 pounds)
Coarse salt
Freshly ground white pepper
5 sprigs fresh rosemary *or* 1½ teaspoons dried rosemary
2 tablespoons butter
1 tablespoon olive oil
2 medium onions, sliced
1 whole head garlic, cloves separated, flattened and peeled

1 bay leaf
1 small fennel bulb
4 cups milk
1 baking potato, peeled and cut into wedges (about 6 ounces)
1 tablespoon freshly squeezed lemon juice
1 teaspoon Pernod or Ricard (optional)
1 tablespoon finely chopped fresh parsley
8 large thick croutons, about 3 x 3 inches

Sprinkle the pork liberally with salt and freshly ground pepper. Tuck a sprig or two of rosemary under the string used to tie it, or scatter dried rosemary evenly over all.

Over moderate heat, melt the butter and oil in a heavy oval casserole roughly the shape of the meat. Slowly brown the pork well on all sides without allowing the butter to burn. Surround the meat with the onions and reduce the heat to low. Cook, covered, about 15 minutes, or until the onions have softened. Lift the lid and stir occasionally to redistribute the onions so they cook evenly. Add the garlic, bay leaf and remaining sprigs of rosemary. Cook 10 minutes more, covered.

Cut off the top stalks of the fennel, but reserve the fine leaves. Cut the bulb into large dice. (There should be about 2 cups.) Add to the casserole and cook, covered, 10 minutes longer. Stir occasionally. Pour in the milk and add the potato wedges. Bring to a simmer and cook, partially covered, 2½ hours. Turn and baste the meat from time to time.

Fifteen minutes before the pork has finished cooking, preheat the oven to 450°F.

FINISHING THE SAUCE

Remove the pork from the casserole and place it in a shallow ovenproof baking dish. Roast 10 minutes to glaze the surface. Transfer to a carving board and remove the string.

Skim all fat from the surface of the sauce. If the milk has not reduced and thickened considerably, boil it down slightly. There should be about 2 cups. Pour the sauce into the workbowl of a food processor or blender and puree until smooth.

Turn the puree into a saucepan and, over very low heat, stir in the lemon juice, Pernod and fennel leaves, chopped. Taste for seasoning.

Carve the pork and arrange the slices, overlapping, on a hot platter. Sprinkle with parsley and surround the meat with croutons. Run a narrow band of sauce around the platter, only partially covering the croutons. Pass the rest of the sauce separately. Serve at once.

NOTE There may be more of this delicious sauce than you need. Leftover sauce can be frozen and reheated at another time. It makes a nice accompaniment to smoked pork.

Braised Pork with Black Salsify and Mushrooms

The flavor of salsify—white or black—reminds me of white asparagus. Peeled, it looks like parsnip but retains the firmness of carrot. Italians know black salsify as *scorzonera*.

If interesting fresh mushrooms are unavailable, substitute dried cèpes, porcini or shiitake mushrooms. Save their soaking liquid, filtering it to remove all traces of sand, and use it in place of about 1 cup of the stock.

SERVES 4

1 pound black salsify
¼ cup distilled white vinegar
1 center-cut pork roast, boned and tied (about 2 pounds)
Sprigs fresh rosemary *or* ½ teaspoon dried rosemary
Sprigs fresh thyme *or* ½ teaspoon dried thyme
Coarse salt
Freshly ground white pepper
3 tablespoons olive oil
6 small cooking onions, cut into rings, ¼ to ½ inch thick
12 large cloves garlic, unpeeled, preferably purple-hued

1 tablespoon butter
4 to 6 ounces fresh shiitake mushrooms, stems trimmed and caps cut into thick slices
1 tablespoon freshly squeezed lemon juice
2 tablespoons Madeira
1 cup dry white wine
About 2 to 3 cups strong stock
1 rounded tablespoon finely chopped fresh chervil *or* parsley
Fresh egg noodles *or* mashed potatoes (optional)

Peel the salsify, trimming the ends and cutting them into 3-inch lengths. Drop the pieces into a bowl of cold acidulated water.

Thread sprigs of rosemary and thyme through the strings tying the meat or scatter dried herbs evenly over all. Tuck some of the thyme deep into the crevice where the meat comes together. Sprinkle the pork with salt and freshly ground pepper.

Heat the olive oil in a large casserole and sear the pork on all sides. When it has colored evenly, reduce the heat to low and add the onions and garlic. Continue to cook, allowing about 30 minutes to finish browning the meat. Stir the onions and garlic frequently so they do not stick to the pan. Remove the meat, onions and garlic and set aside.

Preheat the oven to 350°F. Drain the salsify and pat dry with paper towels. Add it to the casserole and cook, turning the pieces until lightly colored on all sides. When finished, the casserole will be somewhat dry. Remove the salsify and add the butter.

When the butter has melted, add the mushrooms. Toss them until they need moistening, then sprinkle lemon juice over them. Toss again and add the Madeira. Cook, stirring, until the bottom of the casserole is dry. Remove the mushrooms and set aside.

Return the salsify, meat, onions and garlic to the casserole and pour in ½ cup of the white wine. Raise the heat and reduce until the wine barely coats the bottom of the casserole. Then pour in 1 cup of the stock and reduce by about half.

Cover the casserole tightly and place in the oven. After 30 minutes, baste the meat, adding ½ cup stock to the casserole. Lower the heat to 325°F. and cook 1 hour longer, turning and basting the meat after 30 minutes and adding more stock as needed.

After 1½ hours total cooking time, add the mushrooms to the casserole and continue cooking 30 minutes longer. Add more stock as needed. After 2 hours in all, transfer the meat and vegetables to a warm platter and cover to keep warm.

Return the casserole to the stove top and add the remaining ½ cup white wine. Reduce the liquid in the casserole by half, then add about ½ cup more stock. Continue to reduce, keeping the volume of sauce to about 1 to 1½ cups. Taste for seasoning.

Transfer the meat to a carving board, remove the string and cut the pork into thin slices. Arrange them, slightly overlapping, down the center of a warmed serving platter. Surround the meat with the vegetables and spoon the sauce over the slices. Sprinkle a narrow band of chervil the length of the platter and serve at once.

Fresh egg noodles or mashed potatoes make a nice accompaniment.

Pork Chops with Apples and Cream
CÔTES DE PORC NORMANDE

This dish shows off the products for which Normandy is famous—apples, cream, calvados, and, yes, a little butter. In that region, the pig would have been nurtured on the same apples it would be cooked with. Here, it is a perfect recipe to celebrate the arrival of autumn.

SERVES 4

4 double-thick pork chops, bone in
   (about 12 ounces each)
Coarse salt
Freshly ground white pepper
Flour
2 to 3 tablespoons olive oil
3½ tablespoons butter
1 sprig fresh tarragon *or* 1 small bay leaf
1 pound onions, thinly sliced (about 4
   heaping cups)

3 large cloves garlic, cut into thin slices
2 or 3 Granny Smith *or* other tart crisp
   apples, peeled and cut into slices
   about ¼ inch thick
3 tablespoons sherry vinegar
⅓ cup calvados
About 1½ cups strong chicken stock
1 tablespoon imported Dijon mustard
⅓ cup heavy cream (optional)
1 tablespoon chopped fresh parsley

Sprinkle the chops with salt and freshly ground pepper, then dust with flour, shaking off the excess. Coat a large 12-inch skillet with olive oil and add 1 tablespoon of the butter. Heat the oil and when the butter sizzles, arrange the pork chops in the pan. Slowly brown the chops on both sides, turning them frequently and adjusting the heat so the flour does not burn. When the chops are nicely colored, transfer them to a large shallow casserole. Add the tarragon or bay leaf and set aside.

Preheat the oven to 350°F. Pour off the oil, but save it. Add 1 tablespoon of butter to the skillet. Add the onions and cook, stirring frequently over low heat, until softened. (Add a little of the reserved oil, if needed.) Then add the garlic and continue to cook until very soft and golden. Push the onions to the side and add another tablespoon of butter to the pan.

Add the apples and cook, stirring constantly. Keep them separate from the onions. Raise the heat slightly and turn the onions as necessary. From time to time, switch places between the onions and apples so each cooks in the other's juices. When the onions show signs of browning, remove and spoon them over the pork chops. When the apples are nicely colored, transfer to a plate.

Off heat, add 2 tablespoons of the vinegar to the hot skillet. It will evaporate as it hits the pan (if it is hot, there will not be a trace left). Follow with ¼ cup of the calvados. Stir the calvados briefly and return the apples to the pan. Cook over low heat, stirring, until there is little, if any, liquid left. Remove the apples and arrange them around the edge of the casserole, separate from the chops.

Add 1 cup of the stock to the skillet and boil down by about a fourth. Pour the stock over the chops, then place the casserole in the oven and bake 30 minutes. Keep the skillet handy; it will be used again.

After 10 minutes, baste the chops. If the bottom of the casserole seems dry, add a little more stock. Baste every 10 minutes and rotate the casserole occasionally so the chops cook evenly.

After 30 minutes, remove the casserole from the oven and return the chops, but not the onions, to the skillet. Place the skillet in the turned-off oven to keep warm. Transfer the apples to a small hot skillet with a dab of melted butter. Set aside.

Stir the mustard into the casserole with the onions. Add the remaining tablespoon of vinegar and bring to a boil. Stir in the remaining calvados and adjust the heat to a simmer. Add ½ cup of stock and cook, stirring frequently, until the sauce thickens. Thin with enough stock to make enough sauce to coat the chops. Taste for seasoning and slowly add the cream to thicken the sauce, if desired. Reduce the heat to very low and return the chops to the casserole, spooning the sauce over them.

Cook the pork chops 10 minutes, keeping the sauce at a low simmer. Turn them once and spoon the sauce over them as they cook. If it thickens too much, add more stock. During the last few minutes, reheat the apples, turning them until they are nicely glazed.

TO SERVE

Discard the tarragon or bay leaf and serve from the casserole, or transfer the chops to a warmed serving platter and spoon the onions and sauce over them. Sprinkle each one with a little chopped parsley, then divide the apples, arranging them over the chops or, if serving on a platter, to the side. Do not let them bathe in the sauce or they will lose their identity.

Roast Fresh Ham with Wine and Mustard Sauce

A fresh uncured ham is perfect for feeding a large number of people, especially when the serving time cannot be precisely predicted. This is one reason for their abundance in the markets around the holidays.

White Beans Provençal (pages 272–273), cooked with lardons, tomatoes and a profusion of fresh herbs, makes a good accompaniment and you can make it in advance. Applesauce (page 129) may also be in demand.

Even half a fresh ham goes a long way. The directions are the same for half or whole, except that half a ham will be done a little sooner.

SERVES 10 TO 20

1 fresh ham, half or whole, bone in
   (10 to 16 pounds)
About 6 cloves garlic, cut into thin slivers
Coarse salt

Freshly ground pepper
Game Marinade (page 209), double
   recipe for a whole ham

AROMATICS

2 large onions, sliced
1 carrot, sliced
1 large stalk celery, sliced
1 large leek, sliced

1 head garlic, unpeeled, cloves separated
1 Granny Smith apple, unpeeled, cored
   and coarsely chopped

1 cup dry white wine

MUSTARD SAUCE

1 tablespoon imported Dijon mustard
1 level tablespoon flour
1 cup dry white wine

About 1¼ cups strong chicken stock *or*
   meat stock

1 or 2 tablespoons chopped fresh parsley

ADVANCE PREPARATION

Three or 4 days before cooking, start marinating the ham. If the butcher has not already done so, score the rind of the ham. Puncture the skin all over with the point of a small sharp knife. At regular intervals, stud the ham with slivers of garlic, using the knife to help push them in. Rub the ham all over with coarse salt and fine freshly ground pepper, pressing it into both scoring and puncture marks.

Combine the marinade. Place the ham in a large bowl or baking dish, pour in the marinade and turn the ham in it until well coated. Place it in the refrigerator or other cool place; let it marinate several days. Each day turn the ham and baste it. On the day of cooking, bring it to room temperature at least 2 hours before roasting.

ROASTING THE HAM

Preheat the oven to 400°F. Strew the aromatics, except for the apple, over the bottom of a roasting pan (for half a ham a large shallow casserole may be more suitable than a rectangular roasting pan). Remove the ham from the marinade and pat dry with paper towels. Remove a few onions and carrots from the marinade and add them to the roasting pan. Rest the ham over the bed of aromatics and place it in the oven. (If cooking half a ham, use toothpicks to tack a piece of sturdy aluminum foil over the cut end so it stays moist.)

You will need to roast the ham from about 4½ hours for half a ham up to 5 hours or longer for a whole ham. Rely on a meat thermometer to check when it is done. Start by roasting the ham 45 minutes, then turn it and lower the heat to 350°F. Roast 45 minutes longer. At this time (after 1½ hours), add the apple to the aromatics, baste with fat from the pan and cook 1 hour longer.

After the ham has cooked 2½ hours, remove the pan from the oven and tilt to spoon off all the fat. Turn the ham again and pour over ½ cup of the white wine. Return the pan to the oven and lower the heat to 325°F. Roast 1 hour.

After 3½ hours roasting time, pour over the remaining ½ cup of wine and insert a meat thermometer deep into the thickest part of the meat (without touching the bone). Continue to roast another hour, or until the thermometer registers 165°F. (Baste the ham and check the thermometer after 30 minutes.)

When the ham is done, remove it from oven and turn off the oven. Transfer the ham to another pan, platter or several layers of heavy aluminum foil. Return it to the warm oven and let stand 1 hour before carving. (While the juices settle in the meat, there will be ample time to make the sauce.) If the ham needs to wait longer, set the oven to 200° or 250°F. to keep it warm until ready to carve.

(Continued)

PREPARING THE SAUCE

Prepare the sauce while the ham rests. Leave the vegetables in the pan, but skim off every last bit of fat. Place the roasting pan over low heat and stir mustard into the remaining juices.

When the mustard is blended in, sprinkle flour over the vegetables and stir until well blended. Add the wine to the pan, raise the heat and simmer until thickened. Add the stock and continue to cook, stirring and pressing down on the vegetables. As the sauce begins to thicken, taste for seasoning. Strain the sauce through a sieve into a saucepan. Press down hard on the vegetables to release as much of their essence as possible.

Keep the sauce warm over very low heat until ready to serve.

TO SERVE

Transfer the ham to a carving board and cut away the rind and all excess fat. Slice the meat and set aside some of the crispiest parts of the skin for those who like it. Add accumulated carving juices to the sauce.

Arrange the meat on a warmed serving platter and moisten with a little of the sauce. Sprinkle freshly chopped parsley over all and bring the platter to the dinner or buffet table, depending on how many people are present. Serve the rest of the sauce separately.

Classic Baked Smoked Ham

This recipe is not for the aged country hams of the South, which require a long soaking and a good scrubbing before cooking by an entirely different method.

The secret of a well-prepared baked ham lies mainly in its quality (not too salty or too fat), oven temperature and length of cooking time. Most hams in supermarkets are precooked, meaning cooked to an internal temperature specified by the USDA. Nothing else has been done to the ham to give it any special quality. Although they can be eaten as is, a majority of people would find them greatly lacking in flavor and texture. I believe in cooking these hams the same length of time as for an uncooked ham and, while unnecessary, as long as feasibly possible, starting with a minimum of 4 hours for half a ham. Keep the oven temperature low—250° to 300°F.

As to the rest, here is what I often do, but the garnishes and basting sauce are variable.

SERVES A LARGE NUMBER OF PEOPLE

1 whole smoked ham (about 22 to 25 pounds) or half a smoked ham, preferably shank end (11 to 12 pounds)

Several teaspoons powdered English mustard

About 1 cup brown sugar

Whole cloves

Unsweetened slices fresh or canned pineapple (optional)

About 1 cup slightly sweet white wine, such as Gewürztraminer, Chenin Blanc or California Riesling (optional)

About 1 cup ginger ale

Mustard Sauce (page 223)

Preheat the oven to 250°F. or, if pressed for time, 300°F.

Remove the rind from the ham and most of the fat, leaving an even layer about ⅛ inch thick. Place the ham in a baking pan lined with heavy-duty aluminum foil to eliminate a nasty clean-up later.

Score the fat, making a diamond pattern. Rub the ham all over with powdered mustard, followed by a little brown sugar pressed into the cut marks. Stick a whole clove in the center of each diamond. If desired, use toothpicks to attach pieces (whole slices or segments) of pineapple to the ham. Do not overwhelm the meat with fruit; the idea is flavor, not decoration. When the ham has finished cooking, most of the pineapple will have colored too much to make an attractive garnish.

If preparing half a ham, cover the cut end with heavy-duty aluminum foil, secured by toothpicks, to keep the meat from drying out.

Bake the ham, fat side up, as long as possible, from 4 hours to all day. Baste every 30 minutes with equal parts wine and ginger ale, or ginger ale only. Later in the cooking, baste with pan juices.

Let the ham stand 30 minutes before carving. Then cut into slices, as thin as possible.

Serve the Mustard Sauce separately.

Ham Braised in Wine with Aromatic Vegetables

The mirepoix (finely diced aromatic vegetables) makes a nice addition to the platter of sliced ham. If pressed for time, simply add the vegetables to the kettle and eliminate the butter and oil. If cooking a whole ham, double the amount of vegetables. The liquid should remain about the same.

SERVES 12 TO 16

½ large smoked ham with rind, shank
    end (about 11 pounds)
Veal knuckle bones, cut into several
    pieces

2 tablespoons butter
1 tablespoon olive oil

AROMATICS

1 large onion, cut in half and thinly sliced
2 large carrots, thinly sliced
1 large leek, thinly sliced
1 stalk celery with leaves, chopped
6 cloves garlic, unpeeled

2 large bay leaves
Several sprigs fresh thyme *or* 1 teaspoon
    dried thyme leaves
Several large sprigs fresh tarragon *or*
    rosemary

½ teaspoon black peppercorns
Several sprigs parsley, tied together
About 2 bottles dry white wine
    (about 7 to 8 cups)
1½ to 2 quarts mild chicken stock

Watercress and cherry tomatoes for
    garnish (optional)
Mustard Sauce (page 223) *and/or*
    assorted mustards

Soak the ham for 1 hour in cold water to cover.

Place the veal bones in a kettle with cold water to cover. Bring to a boil and simmer a few minutes; drain and rinse with cold water.

Melt the butter in oil in a large kettle or stockpot over low to medium heat. Add all the aromatic vegetables and herbs. Cook, stirring frequently, until slightly softened. If desired, cover the kettle to speed up this operation.

Wipe the ham with paper towels and poke the rind all over with a skewer. Arrange the ham on top of the vegetables. Add the veal bones, peppercorns and parsley and pour over enough wine and stock, in equal parts, to almost cover the shank. Bring the liquid to a boil, reduce the heat to a gentle simmer, cover and cook 2½ to 3 hours (3½ hours, if cooking a whole ham) over low heat. If the ham is not completely submerged, turn it once or twice during the cooking.

When done, leave the ham in the broth until ready to carve.

TO SERVE

Remove the rind and excess fat. You will not be able to carve the ham into the usual large slices. After braising, the shank will probably divide into several parts. Carve each piece separately, against the grain, into slices as thin as possible.

Arrange the slices on a large platter and spoon a little of the cooking broth (skimmed of fat) and vegetables over them. Serve the ham while still warm and as soon as possible after slicing so the meat does not dry out.

If you wish, decorate the platter with sprigs of watercress and cherry tomatoes. Have a bowl of warm Mustard Sauce on the table and/or an assortment of mustards.

Mustard Sauce

This is a pale custardlike sauce, not at all timid where the flavor of mustard is concerned. It was a recipe of my mother's and has been passed around for more than 50 years. Surprisingly, I've never encountered another like it.

My own contribution is to add a good pinch of chopped fresh tarragon or dill.

SERVES 10

2 extra-large eggs
2 slightly rounded tablespoons sugar
2 level tablespoons flour
¾ teaspoon salt
2 tablespoons powdered English mustard
¾ cup distilled white vinegar

¾ cup milk
3 tablespoons butter, cut into small
  pieces
Coarsely chopped fresh tarragon *or* dill
  (optional)

Break the eggs into a saucepan and mix vigorously with a wire whisk. Then beat in the sugar, flour, salt and mustard. Mix well after each addition. Over low heat, stir constantly with a wooden spoon while adding the vinegar, followed by the milk. When the sauce begins to thicken, add 2 tablespoons of the butter. Off heat, stir in the remaining butter and the tarragon or dill, if using.

This sauce can be served warm or at room temperature, but not ice cold. It will keep for several weeks in the refrigerator.

Roast Suckling Pig with Herb Basting Sauce

This version of roast suckling pig is notable for its unusual basting sauce. I learned to make the sauce long ago when living in Spain. It was a tradition for the butcher who slaughtered the pig to assist in its preparation and cooking the next day. Early on the day of cooking he would begin to assemble this amazing combination of ingredients for basting the pig. Using a coarse stone mortar and pestle, he ground the herbs, little by little, first moistening them with a drop of water and then adding the odd mélange of ingredients to follow. The crisp quality of the pig's skin that resulted from this witch's brew leaves no room for improvement. It can also be applied to fresh ham and it's easy to imagine other uses. His method was quite tedious. Nowadays, I cheat—a food processor is perfect for making a laborious job fairly easy.

The quality of the meat of a suckling pig is unique. Certain parts are so meltingly tender the meat can be cut with a spoon. Also, it retains a moistness not always found in the leaner pork of today. The only disappointment is discovering that, for all its weight, there is not a lot of meat: a sizeable amount of the weight is due simply to its head and bone structure.

A suckling pig is best appreciated unsauced (not even mustard will be needed). Aside from crisp chunks of sautéed potatoes, other accompaniments should be pungent and fruity or spicy—Applesauce (page 129) is a must and spiced red cabbage ideal. Follow with a simple green salad and a fruit dessert.

Consider a garland of bright cranberries strung with shiny green jalapeños, flowers—daisies, pansies and nasturtiums, or even classy gardenias—a wreath of evergreens held together by a scarlet ribbon, small branches of kumquats or tiny lady apples woven together, for decoration of the pig. For the eye sockets, I prefer something dark and glossy—like black olives or prunes—to the cherries frequently used. Have your decoration ready when the pig has finished roasting.

A word about oven and pan sizes. Most wall ovens are too small to accommodate a suckling pig. A large standard range, 30 inches wide with an oven about 23 inches wide, will do just fine. The minimum size rectangular pan would be 20 inches. Larger is better and also makes it easier. If you have an oval baking ban, it can be placed at an angle in the oven; this will give you at least two more inches leeway than a rectangular pan. Do *not* use a flimsy aluminum foil pan. The utensil must be sturdy to hold the weight of the pig without incident.

If possible, rest the pig in the pan in a crouched position on its belly with haunches folded under. If the pan is too cramped, arrange the pig on its side, then turn it several times during the roasting. At times, a crouched pig may slip during cooking and end up on its side. If this happens, do not lose time trying to maneuver it to an upright position. Proceed with the roasting, turning the pig to the other side to ensure that the skin crisps evenly.

SERVES 10 TO 16

1 suckling pig (15 to 20 pounds), eyes removed
Distilled white vinegar
Coarse salt

Finely ground black pepper
3 large cloves garlic, peeled and cut into thin slivers
Olive oil

STUFFING

3 large Granny Smith apples, cored and cut into thick slices
1 large orange, sliced, then slices cut in half
2 large stalks celery with leaves, coarsely chopped
4 large onions, sliced
1½ inches fresh unpeeled ginger, sliced
1½ to 2 cups coarsely chopped fresh parsley
8 small sprigs fresh rosemary, cut in 1 inch pieces, or 1 scant tablespoon dried rosemary

About ½ cup fresh oregano, coarsely chopped, or 2 teaspoons dried oregano
About ½ cup fresh mint leaves, coarsely chopped, or 1 tablespoon dried mint leaves
1 loaf French or Italian bread, cut into cubes

BASTING SAUCE (see note)

1 cup (packed) fresh parsley leaves
1 cup (packed) fresh mint leaves
½ cup (packed) fresh fennel ferns
½ cup (packed) fresh oregano leaves
5 large cloves garlic, peeled
Scant ⅓ cup freshly squeezed lemon juice

1 teaspoon coarse ground black pepper
1 teaspoon coarse salt
1½ cups cognac or brandy
About 1¼ cups milk

Olive oil for the pan
4 large onions, sliced
2 or 3 large carrots, sliced

1 large celery stalk, coarsely chopped
10 large cloves garlic, unpeeled
1 small firm lemon

Large branches mint, parsley and oregano, tied together for basting brush

Olives for the eye sockets (optional)
A cranberry and jalapeño necklace or other decoration (optional)

(Continued)

ADVANCE PREPARATION

Put the pig in the kitchen sink and using a mix of water and vinegar, scrub it with a coarse vegetable brush. If any hairs were missed, shave them off with a single-edged razor blade. Dry the pig thoroughly with paper towels and lay it on a large tray or baking sheet that will fit in the refrigerator.

Using the point of a small sharp knife, puncture the skin all over. Keep the knife on a diagonal to make shallow pockets rather than stabbing deeply into the flesh. Rub the pig all over, inside and out, with coarse salt and finely ground pepper. Cut the slivers of garlic into splinters, if necessary, and insert them here and there in the tiny pockets.

The aromatics are used to enhance the flavor of the pig, not to be eaten as stuffing. Combine the stuffing ingredients in a large bowl and put them in the cavity. Most likely there will be room left; this should be filled with cubes of bread. Close the cavity tight, using skewers and string. Wipe the skin all over with olive oil and cover lightly with wax paper or aluminum foil. Refrigerate the pig from overnight to 2 days.

PREPARATION ON THE DAY OF COOKING

Early in the day, prepare the basting sauce. Combine the parsley, mint, fennel and oregano and grind them to a paste in the food processor, adding them in small amounts. When about half have been processed, begin to include the garlic, and continue to add the remaining herbs. Moisten with the lemon juice and transfer the paste to a large mortar and pestle or a bowl with a round bottom. Add pepper and slowly blend in the salt, 1 cup of the cognac and ⅔ cup of the milk. Press down hard on the herbs at the bottom of the mortar or bowl. When finished, set aside to steep.

Three hours before cooking, bring the pig to room temperature.

Coat the bottom of an extra-large roasting pan liberally with olive oil and cover it with the onions, carrots, celery and garlic. Arrange the pig in a comfortable position on top of the vegetables. With the help of a heavy-duty screwdriver, pry open the jaws of the pig and insert a lemon in its mouth (an apple is too big). If the snout protrudes over the edge of the roasting pan, arrange a piece of aluminum foil under its chin so the juices flow back into the pan. For cooking only, insert a few stubs of carrots in the eye sockets and protect the ears with aluminum foil (the ears will still brown).

ROASTING THE PIG

Preheat the oven to 450°F. Roast the pig 3 hours in all. Allow 1 hour for the juices to settle in the meat, then about 30 minutes for carving.

Place the pig in the hot oven and roast, undisturbed, 30 minutes. Then baste the pig, using the brush of herbs to slather the sauce over all. Roast 15 minutes longer, rotate the pan 180° and baste again (turn the pig if it is on its side).

After 1 hour, baste again and lower the heat to 350°F. During the next 2 hours, baste the pig every 30 minutes and rotate the pan once or twice to ensure even cooking. It is likely that the basting sauce will soon be depleted, but a good residue of herbs will remain both in the mortar and on the brush. Replenish the sauce with ½ cup milk and ¼ cup olive oil, mixing well. If it needs replenishing again, add ½ cup cognac, blend in a little more milk and stir in a spoonful of olive oil.

When the cooking time is up (a thermometer inserted into the thickest part of the rump should read close to 170°F.), baste once more. Turn off the oven. If using an electric oven, leave the oven door partially open to release some of the heat and reset the oven temperature to warm (150°F.). Let the pig rest 1 hour.

TO SERVE

Transfer the pig to a large board, tray or platter. Remove the foil from the ears, press olives into the eye sockets and give the pig a good send-off with a garland that suits your fancy and pays the pig a fine tribute. Before carving, either trot the pig out for viewing or invite your friends into the kitchen, but make the show brief so the pig can be carved while it is still hot.

Remove the forelegs and hindquarters, then cut a slit down the back and pull away the skin. Cut away any pockets of fat and slice out the meat from around the ribs. Carve the hind legs, but don't bother with the forelegs. Cut the skin into potato-chip-size pieces. (A scissors works best for this.) Arrange the meat on a warmed serving platter and distribute the crisp skin over all. Serve at once.

NOTE   Dried herbs are not acceptable; if necessary, use more of the fresh herbs that are available.

THE ECLECTIC PIG

Braised Loin of Pork with Onions and Hot Peppers

·

Pork with Ancho Pepper and Green Tomato Sauce

·

Pork Chops with Mint and Citrus Sauce

·

Pork Chops with Tomato Vinegar Sauce

·

Curried Pork Chops with Fresh Tomato

·

Braised Pork Chops with Cucumber and Tomato

·

Pork Chops, Mediterranean Style

·

Scallops of Pork with Garlic and Lemon Sauce

Preserved Lemons

·

Pork Hips with Garlic, Ginger and Quince

·

Pork and Rice with Preserved Lemon and Olives

·

Braised Pork Nuggets with Black Beans in Red Wine and Pepper Sauce

·

Winter Vegetables Wrapped in Ham with Curry Sauce

·

Steamed Red Snapper with Pork and Mushrooms

·

Crispy Whole Fried Fish with Pork and Mushrooms

This porcine gathering offers unexpected flavors and surprising combinations. These eclectic recipes gather the best from diverse resources.

In China pork is often used to garnish seafood, transforming a simple fish into a dish worthy of a banquet. The taste of the Mediterranean dominates when pork is enhanced by tomatoes, olives, quince, herbs and citrus, all creating memorably distinctive sauces. Pork is also well suited to long simmering in sauces redolent of spices associated with Middle Eastern cooking—coriander, cumin, cardamom—and all the pungent herbs and spices carefully blended to compose a first-rate curry.

This chapter offers a variety of cures for the jaded palate.

Braised Loin of Pork with Onions and Hot Peppers

A small portion of a boneless center-cut roast is just right for two persons, but since it is very good cold, more makes for delicious leftovers.

SERVES 2

About 2 tablespoons olive oil
1 small center-cut pork roast, trimmed of fat, boned and tied (about 1½ to 2 pounds)
Coarse salt
Freshly ground white pepper
1 teaspoon cumin seed
1 large mild Spanish onion, cut in half and thinly sliced
4 to 5 large thin slices fresh ginger, about 1½ inches in diameter
½ head garlic, cloves peeled and left whole

3 to 4 long fresh hot red peppers, seeded and cut into 1- to 1½-inch lengths
1 large bay leaf, broken
¼ cup freshly squeezed lime juice
⅔ to ¾ cup dry white wine
About ½ cup chicken stock
About ½ cup hot water
1 tablespoon chopped fresh parsley *or* coriander leaves
Sautéed rice (optional)

Heat the olive oil in a heavy oval casserole, tilting the casserole to coat the bottom evenly. When hot, add the pork roast and brown it on all sides. Turn the meat frequently, adjusting the heat, and as it browns, sprinkle each side with salt, freshly ground pepper, and cumin.

When the meat has colored nicely, push it toward one end of the casserole and add the onions. Lower the heat, and cook the onion, turning the slices until softened. Scatter the ginger, garlic, hot peppers and bay leaf around the end of the casserole near the pork, away from the onions. Adjusting the heat, continue to turn the onions at one end and the aromatics at the other. Combine the onions with the ginger, garlic and peppers and arrange them around the meat. During this time, try to keep the underside of the meat free of vegetables so that it glazes nicely.

Preheat the oven to 425°F. When the onions have taken on a rich color from the meat juices, tilt the casserole and skim off any excess fat; save it. Raise the heat and add the lime juice. Cook briefly, pour in the wine and reduce until almost, but not quite, syrupy.

Baste the meat and onions. Place half the broken bay leaf on top of the meat; keep the other half buried in the onions. Place the casserole in the oven, reduce the heat to 375°F. and roast 20 minutes, uncovered.

Baste the pork and add a little of the chicken stock, lower the heat to 325°F. and roast 60 to 80 minutes more, basting frequently, switching from stock to hot water. Add just enough to keep the onions and peppers in the juicy state of a confit.

TO SERVE

When finished, transfer the pork to a carving board, remove the string and slice the meat. Serve the pork arranged over the vegetables on a hot serving platter. Sprinkle with freshly chopped parsley or coriander.

The pork would be nice accompanied by sautéed rice. Use a little of the reserved fat from the casserole to sauté the rice, supplementing it with as much olive oil as needed.

Pork with Ancho Pepper and
Green Tomato Sauce

Instead of a center-cut pork roast, you may use a boneless butt or fresh picnic, whole or cut into one-inch cubes. The cubed meat would be cooked and served in its sauce like a stew.

SERVES 6

MARINADE AND SAUCE

3 dried ancho chile peppers
1¾ cups canned Mexican green tomatoes *(tomatillo entero)* and their liquid
1 large clove garlic, chopped
1 cup chopped onion
1 small sweet green pepper, coarsely chopped

1 center-cut pork roast, boned and tied (about 3 pounds)
2 large cloves garlic, cut into thin slivers
3 tablespoons olive or peanut oil
⅓ cup chicken stock

2 fresh hot green chile peppers, seeded and chopped
½ cup packed fresh coriander leaves
½ cup parsley leaves
½ cup freshly squeezed orange juice, strained

3 tablespoons dark rum *or* sherry
Sprigs fresh coriander and orange slices or segments for garnish
Spicy Black Beans (pages 270–271)
Hot cooked rice

ADVANCE PREPARATION

The day before you plan to cook, prepare the marinade. Remove the stems from the ancho chiles and scrape out the seeds. Tear the chiles into strips and put them in a bowl. Pour in enough boiling water to just cover and let stand 2 hours. Press down on the peppers from time to time.

Put the chiles and their liquid in a blender or food processor and puree them. Blend in the remaining marinade ingredients, one at a time.

With the point of a knife, poke small holes all over the meat and insert slivers of garlic. If using cubes of pork, chop the garlic and combine with the meat. Place the meat in a deep dish and pour over the marinade. Turn it in the marinade until well coated, then refrigerate from overnight to about 24 hours.

COOKING THE PORK

Remove the pork from the marinade and dry thoroughly with paper towels. Reserve the marinade.

Heat the oil in a casserole just large enough to hold the meat. Brown the pork on all sides, about 20 minutes. The same applies to cubes. Adjust the heat to keep any marinade from burning. Place the pork on a plate while you remove excess oil and any burnt particles, then deglaze the casserole with chicken stock. Turn the heat very low, put the pork back in the casserole and cover it tightly; cook the pork 15 minutes. More juices will accumulate during this time.

Pour the reserved marinade over the pork and cook 2 hours, partially covered. Keep at a bare simmer and turn and baste the meat every 20 minutes. When ready to serve, stir in the rum or sherry.

TO SERVE

Transfer the meat to a carving board and let stand 5 minutes. Keep the sauce warm over low heat. Remove the string and slice the pork as thin as possible. Arrange on a warmed platter with the slices overlapping slightly.

Spoon a long narrow ribbon of sauce over the meat and surround with sprigs of coriander interspersed with orange slices or segments. Pass the rest of the sauce separately.

If preparing cubes, transfer them to a deep platter and pour the sauce over them. Arrange coriander and orange slices as described above.

Black beans and rice are a nice accompaniment to this dish. Cold leftover pork is ideal for making Pork and Avocado Tostados (page 274).

Pork Chops with Mint and Citrus Sauce

CÔTELETTES DE PORC SAUCE AGRUMES

Inspiration for this recipe can be credited to the *frères* Troisgros of Roanne. My improvisations include decreasing the butter in favor of olive oil, using boneless pork chops, freshly squeezed orange juice instead of orange segments and fresh shiitake mushrooms if available.

This is a dish that can be prepared in advance, kept warm, covered, then gently reheated before serving.

SERVES 4

4 very thick boneless pork chops, cut
    from the loin and well trimmed of fat
    (about 7 ounces each)
Coarse salt
Freshly ground white pepper
A few tablespoons olive oil
1 tablespoon butter
Dried mint leaves (optional)
1 large onion, coarsely chopped
4 cloves garlic, thinly sliced
Handful fresh shiitake mushrooms
    (about 3 ounces)
1 medium-size ripe tomato *or* 2 large
    plum tomatoes, unpeeled and cut into
    small wedges

⅓ cup combined freshly squeezed orange
    and lemon juices
8 to 10 large fresh mint leaves
About 1½ cups *demi-glace de tomate*
    (strong concentrated stock with
    tomato essence) *or* 1 teaspoon tomato
    paste stirred into simmering strong
    meat stock
Mint leaves *or* chopped parsley for a
    garnish
Noodles, buttered rice *or* mashed
    potatoes

Sprinkle the chops with coarse salt and freshly ground pepper. Use enough olive oil to barely coat the bottom of a large cast-iron or enameled cast-iron skillet; add the butter. Heat the oil and butter together and arrange the chops in the skillet, side by side. Sear them on each side, lower the heat, and finish cooking, turning the chops several times during the cooking and basting with the pan juices. If using dried mint, sprinkle the crushed leaves over the chops after they have been turned once; fresh mint goes in later. When done, transfer the chops to a plate and set aside in a low oven (150° to 200°F.) to keep warm.

Add the onion and garlic to the skillet and cook over low heat, stirring constantly, until the onion takes on a rich amber color. Tilt the pan and press down on the onion with a spoon to release excess fat. Pour off most of the fat from the pan, but save it in case more is needed later.

Cut off the hard part of the mushroom stems and slice the caps into thick strips. Add to the pan and cook, turning with the onion and garlic, until softened.

Add the tomato wedges, raise the heat and cook, stirring, until the skillet needs moistening. Pour in the citrus juice, add the fresh mint leaves and reduce until the juice is the consistency of a glaze.

Pour in the *demi-glace* and reduce until the sauce is syrupy. Over low heat, return the chops to the pan and spoon the sauce over them. Simmer about 15 minutes, turning the chops repeatedly in the sauce. Add more stock, if necessary.

When ready to serve, transfer the chops to a hot serving platter. Boil down the sauce until quite thick, then spoon it over the chops. Add a garnish of additional mint leaves or chopped parsley to each chop.

Serve with noodles, buttered rice or mashed potatoes.

Pork Chops with Tomato Vinegar Sauce

SERVES 4

¾ pound ripe tomatoes, preferably plum
    tomatoes, peeled
2 tablespoons red wine *or* sherry vinegar
4 tablespoons olive oil
Coarse salt
Freshly ground white pepper
4 large thick center-cut pork chops, bone
    in, well trimmed (about 10 ounces
    each) *or* 8 rib chops
Flour
1½ tablespoons butter
2 bay leaves, broken
1 sprig fresh tarragon *or* 1 teaspoon
    dried tarragon leaves, crumbled

2 large cloves garlic, peeled and thinly
    sliced
2 to 3 shallots, coarsely chopped
1 cup chicken stock
1 pound slim carrots, cut into 3-inch
    pieces, boiled 8 minutes and refreshed
    in ice water
¾ cup freshly shelled peas, blanched 30
    seconds and refreshed in ice water
1 heaping tablespoon coarsely chopped
    fresh mint leaves
Hot rice *or* noodles
Green salad

ADVANCE PREPARATION

Chop the tomatoes into small dice, then combine with the vinegar, 2 tablespoons olive oil, a good pinch of salt and freshly ground pepper. Let stand
several hours or overnight. Stir occasionally.

COOKING THE CHOPS

Sprinkle the chops with pepper and dust with flour, shaking off the excess.
Heat the butter with the remaining 2 tablespoons oil in a skillet over medium
to high heat. Brown the chops well on both sides, keeping the heat high
enough to sear the meat without allowing the butter to burn. Turn the chops
frequently and when well browned, lower the heat and scatter bay leaves,
tarragon and garlic over all. Cover tightly and let the meat simmer in its own
juices. After 10 minutes, turn the chops and baste, spooning the garlic and
herbs over them. Cook, tightly covered, 10 to 15 minutes longer.

FINISHING THE SAUCE

Remove the chops from the skillet and set aside. If there is excess fat in the pan, remove some of it.

Add the shallots and cook 1 minute, or until softened. Add the tomato-vinegar mixture, raise the heat, and bring to a boil. Reduce the sauce, stirring frequently, until glossy and thickened. Add ½ cup of the stock and return to a boil. Lower the heat to a bare simmer and as the sauce reduces, add the rest of the stock.

Return the chops to the skillet and spoon the sauce over them. Cover the pan and let simmer 10 minutes over low heat. Taste for seasoning, then add carrots and peas. Cook only until heated through. Sprinkle with freshly chopped mint leaves and serve at once.

Hot rice or fresh noodles and a sprightly green salad would be perfect accompaniments.

Curried Pork Chops with Fresh Tomato

SERVES 4

4 thick center-cut pork chops, bone in (about 10 ounces each)

Coarse salt

Freshly ground white pepper

3 tablespoons, or more, butter

1 tablespoon olive oil

3 or 4 small dried red chile peppers, broken

1 heaping cup finely chopped onion

1 small sweet red bell pepper, cut into thin strips

1 small stalk celery, finely chopped

2 tablespoons finely chopped fresh ginger

4 large cloves garlic, finely chopped

2 rounded tablespoons curry powder

1 rounded teaspoon ground cumin

2 rounded teaspoons ground coriander

1 rounded teaspoon ground cardamom

1 large bay leaf

½ Granny Smith apple, peeled and finely chopped

4 tablespoons freshly squeezed lime juice

About 2 cups peeled and coarsely chopped ripe tomatoes or plum tomatoes cut into long strips or 6 canned Italian plum tomatoes and their juices

1 cup chicken stock

1 rounded tablespoon coarsely chopped fresh mint leaves (optional)

1 rounded tablespoon thin shreds fresh basil leaves (optional)

Rice, plain or sautéed

Sprinkle the chops with salt and freshly ground pepper. Melt 3 tablespoons butter in the oil in a heavy skillet and when the butter sizzles, brown the chops slowly on both sides. Adjust the heat and turn the chops frequently to be sure they do not burn. Remove and set aside.

Add the dried chiles to the skillet and before they blacken, add the chopped onion, followed by the sweet pepper, celery, ginger and garlic. Cook over low heat, stirring frequently, until the onion has softened. (Covering the skillet will speed this operation.) Reduce the heat to very low and add the curry powder, cumin, coriander, cardamom and bay leaf. Stir constantly until the spices have dissolved into a paste. (Add more butter if needed.) Add the apple and moisten with lime juice. After a few minutes, stir in the tomatoes, raise the heat and bring to a boil.

Cook, stirring frequently, until the tomato juices are slightly reduced, then add the chicken stock. Adjust the heat, maintaining the sauce at a bubble, and cook several minutes. Lower the heat, partially cover the pan and simmer 20 minutes, stirring occasionally.

Return the pork chops to the skillet and spoon the sauce over them. Cook 1 hour, partially covered. Check frequently to be sure the sauce remains at a simmer, turning and basting the meat each time.

When ready to serve, stir in the mint and basil, if available. (Do not substitute dried herbs.) Accompany with rice, plain or sautéed.

Braised Pork Chops with Cucumber and Tomato

This is a nice meal to make toward the end of summer when the nights are cool again.

SERVES 4

4 boneless center-cut pork chops, about
   1½ inches thick (6 to 8 ounces each)
Freshly ground white pepper
Coarse salt
Flour
Olive oil
1 tablespoon butter
2 or 3 large cloves garlic, chopped
1 large shallot, chopped
Several sprigs fresh rosemary *or* 1
   teaspoon dried rosemary

1 cup dry white wine
2 cups Fresh Tomato Sauce (page 132)
   or 1 pound ripe plum tomatoes,
   peeled and chopped
1 large cucumber (about 8 ounces)
About ½ cup chicken stock
1 tablespoon chopped fresh parsley
2 teaspoons chopped fresh mint leaves
Garlic-flavored mashed potatoes
   (optional)

Sprinkle the chops with freshly ground pepper and a little coarse salt, then dip them lightly in flour, shaking off the excess.

Coat a large heavy skillet with the olive oil and add the butter. When the skillet is hot, add the chops and cook, turning them periodically, until each side is nicely browned. Shortly before they have finished, add the garlic, shallot and several sprigs of fresh rosemary (or sprinkle the chops with dried rosemary). When the chops are nicely browned, remove and set aside on a warm plate. Leave the garlic, shallot and rosemary in the pan.

Deglaze the skillet with white wine. Bring to a boil; stir and continue to cook until greatly reduced and syrupy. Add either Fresh Tomato Sauce or fresh plum tomatoes. If fresh tomatoes are used, cook them until they become somewhat saucelike in appearance. If sauce is used, just bring to a simmer.

(Continued)

Meanwhile, peel the cucumber, quarter it lengthwise and scrape out the seeds. Cut each quarter into pieces about ⅝ inch long. Add them to the sauce, stir and return the chops to the skillet, spooning the sauce over them. Reduce the heat to a gentle simmer and cover the skillet.

Cook the chops about 1 hour, turning them every 15 minutes. As the sauce thickens, thin it occasionally with a little chicken stock. Taste for seasoning.

When ready to serve, arrange the chops on a hot platter, spoon the sauce and cucumber segments over them and sprinkle with freshly chopped parsley and mint.

Garlic-flavored mashed potatoes are a nice accompaniment.

Pork Chops, Mediterranean Style

The addition of preserved lemon gives this dish a taste of Morocco, while the rest of the ingredients imply the best of the whole Mediterranean region.
SERVES 4

4 thick loin pork chops, bone in (about 10 ounces each) *or* without bone (8 ounces each)
Coarse salt
Freshly ground white pepper
2 to 3 tablespoons olive oil
1 very large onion, quartered and thinly sliced (about 3 cups)
7 cloves garlic, flattened slightly, peeled and thinly sliced
About 2 tablespoons thin slivers fresh ginger
1 sweet red pepper, cut into long thin strips
4 to 6 mild fresh green chile peppers, seeded and cut into large pieces
1 large bay leaf
1 rounded teaspoon ground cumin
2 rounded teaspoons ground coriander

1 cup dry white wine
About 2½ cups peeled and coarsely chopped ripe plum tomatoes
1 cup chopped fresh basil, mint and parsley, combined
1 Preserved Lemon, rinsed (page 245)
About 1 cup chicken broth
1 to 2 cups very small young artichoke hearts, cooked, trimmed and quartered, *or* frozen artichoke hearts, defrosted
1 small zucchini, cut into small sticks, about ½ inch x 2½ inches (about 6 ounces)
A heaping ½ cup small black Gaeta olives, drained
Sautéed rice *or* crisp sautéed or roasted potatoes *or* crusty bread

Sprinkle the pork chops lightly with salt and generously with freshly ground pepper. Heat just enough oil to lightly coat the bottom of a heavy skillet. Fry the chops, turning them until nicely browned on both sides. Remove and transfer to a shallow casserole. Pour off any excess fat, leaving just enough to fry the onion.

Add the onion to the skillet and sauté over low heat, stirring frequently until partially softened. Add the garlic and ginger and, after a minute, the sweet red pepper, green chiles and bay leaf. Continue to cook until the onion (not the peppers) has softened completely. Push the vegetables to the side of the pan and add the cumin and coriander. Stir the spices in the oil and juices, then combine with the vegetables. Stir together until the skillet needs moistening, then pour in the wine and raise the heat. As the wine reduces, remove the vegetables (but not the bay leaf) with a slotted spoon and set aside on a plate. When about half the wine has cooked away, add the tomatoes with half the herbs. Adjust the heat to a simmer and cook, uncovered, until the tomatoes achieve a saucelike consistency.

Meanwhile, cut away some of the pulp from the preserved lemon; cut the rind into long strips and add it to the tomatoes. If needed, moisten the tomatoes with a little chicken broth. Lower the heat, cover the skillet and cook 10 minutes. Return the vegetables to the pan and cook 5 minutes longer, covered.

Pour the sauce and vegetables over the pork in the casserole. Maintaining the heat at a gentle simmer, cover and cook the chops 20 minutes. During this time, turn them occasionally and thin the sauce with chicken broth as needed.

After the pork is fully cooked, the casserole can be left to simmer over very low heat for 1 hour. During this time the sauce may need to be thinned periodically with a little chicken broth.

Ten minutes before serving, add the artichoke hearts, zucchini and olives. Simmer, covered, about 10 minutes, or until the zucchini is tender, but still firm. During the last minute of cooking, stir in the remaining herbs. This is a dish that can be served from the casserole in which it was cooked. It should be left within reach for those who would like more sauce.

Serve the pork with sautéed rice, crisp potatoes or simply good crusty bread to dip in the sauce.

Scallops of Pork with Garlic and Lemon Sauce

Slices of boneless pork work very well in a sauce usually reserved for veal scaloppine. Pork is so well suited to this preparation that I hardly think of it as an economical substitute. In fact, since it is cooked longer, it absorbs more flavor of the sauce.

Use the best-quality pork for this dish, boneless tenderloin or center-cut loin, trimmed of all but the thinnest line of fat. Do not pound the meat as you would for veal scaloppine.

SERVES 4

2 tablespoons butter
About 2 tablespoons olive oil
1½ to 1¾ pounds lean boneless pork,
  cut into thin scalloppinelike slices,
  ¼ to ⅜ inch thick
Coarse salt
Freshly ground white pepper
Flour
1 large shallot, chopped
2 cloves garlic, chopped

1 bay leaf, broken
1 sprig fresh rosemary (optional)
½ cup dry white wine
½ cup chicken stock
1 lemon, fluted from end to end and
  thinly sliced
4 large fresh mushrooms, cut into thick
  slices (about 4 ounces)
1 tablespoon chopped fresh parsley
Mashed potatoes *or* buttered pasta

Over medium heat, melt the butter in just enough oil to coat the bottom of a large skillet. Sprinkle the pork slices lightly with salt and generously with freshly ground pepper. Dust with flour, shaking off the excess. When the butter sizzles and begins to color, brown the slices slowly, turning them until each side is nicely colored; remove them and set aside.

Over low heat, add the shallots and stir until softened. Add the garlic, bay leaf and rosemary. (Omit if fresh rosemary is unavailable.) Continue to cook about 1 minute, without letting the garlic brown. Pour in the wine, raise the heat and bring to a boil. Cook until the wine is reduced to about 3 tablespoons and the juices are nicely caramelized.

Add the stock and simmer briefly. While there is still ⅓ to ½ cup of sauce left in the skillet, return the pork and accumulated juices. Baste, lower the heat, cover and cook 10 minutes.

Turn the meat, baste and cook, covered, another 10 minutes. Adjust the heat so the sauce does not cook away. After 10 minutes, arrange the lemon slices over the slices of pork, cover the skillet and simmer 5 minutes longer.

At this time, add the mushrooms, tucking the slices around the meat. Cover and cook about 3 minutes longer. Turn the scallops and mushrooms, rearranging the lemon slices on top. Cook briefly, uncovered, tilting the pan to gather sauce for basting the meat.

Transfer the pork, lemon slices and mushrooms to a warmed platter. Spoon over the sauce, sprinkle with parsley and serve.

Either mashed potatoes or buttered pasta make a nice accompaniment.

Preserved Lemons

These lemons impart a unique flavor that makes them irreplaceable in any dish calling for preserved lemon.

Since they must be made in advance, pick a time of the year when the price of lemons is reasonable. The lemons can be kept for several months at room temperature in a cool kitchen; thereafter, store them in the refrigerator, where they should keep for a year, often longer. Make sure the lemons are always covered by juice.

MAKES 1 QUART

About 6 unblemished lemons,
   not too large
About ½ cup coarse salt

Enough freshly squeezed lemon juice to
   cover the lemons completely (about
   10 lemons)

Wash the lemons well, then drop them into boiling water. Blanch 20 seconds, drain and dry with a clean towel.

Place 1 tablespoon of salt in the bottom of a sterilized, wide-mouthed, 1-quart canning jar. Put the rest of the salt in a small round-bottomed bowl.

Quarter the lemons, stopping about ½ inch from the base. Holding each one over the bowl, dredge the interior with salt, allowing about 1 tablespoon per lemon. Then press the quarters closed to reshape the lemon and place it in the jar. Pack the lemons into the jar as tightly as possible, literally wedged together. Add enough freshly squeezed lemon juice to cover the lemons completely with about ½ inch to spare, then seal the jar.

Let the lemons stand at room temperature for 2 weeks before using. Turn the jar from right side up to upside down daily, letting it remain in each position for 12 to 24 hours.

Before using a lemon, rinse it thoroughly to remove excessive salt. If preferable, discard the pulp and use the rind only.

Pork Hips with Garlic, Ginger and Quince

Pork hips are the connecting meat between the end of the loin and the ham. These small delicate morsels can be found in custom butcher shops, particularly those specializing in pork products. They may not be available in supermarkets; in that case, substitute boneless pork loin or tenderloin, trimmed of all fat.

SERVES 4

1½ to 2 pounds boneless pork, cut on a slight angle into slices about ½ inch thick (about 2 large hips)
Coarse salt
Freshly ground white pepper
Flour
2 tablespoons butter
2 to 3 tablespoons olive oil
2 teaspoons fresh rosemary leaves, chopped, *or* 1 teaspoon dried rosemary

2 tablespoons long thin slivers fresh ginger
2 tablespoons long thin slivers garlic
¼ cup freshly squeezed lime juice
2 to 3 large shallots, coarsely chopped
1 small ripe quince, peeled, cored and cut into thin slices (about 1½ cups)
½ cup dry white wine
1 cup strong chicken *or* veal stock
Mashed potatoes *or* White Beans Provençal (pages 272–273)

Sprinkle the pork slices on both sides with coarse salt and freshly ground pepper, then dip lightly in flour, shaking off the excess.

Melt the butter in the oil in a large skillet over medium to high heat. Without crowding, brown as many slices as possible, cooking them in several batches if necessary. When the meat has been turned once, sprinkle with rosemary leaves, then turn again. Add half the ginger and garlic, adjust the heat and cook briefly. When the slices are nicely browned, transfer them to a warm platter and sprinkle them with half the lime juice.

Add the remaining garlic and ginger and the shallots to the pan. Stir briefly and add the quince. Cook, stirring and turning the slices of quince, until nicely colored. Deglaze the pan with the remaining lime juice, stirring to loosen all particles. When the lime juice has evaporated, add the wine and boil until greatly reduced. Add half the stock and reduce again.

Add enough of the remaining stock to make a thin sauce. Return the pork to the pan. Baste well with sauce, cover the pan and cook about 1 hour over very low heat, basting once.

Serve the pork slices on a warm serving platter, well coated with sauce and garnished with slices of quince.

Accompany the pork with mashed potatoes or White Beans Provençal.

Pork and Rice with Preserved Lemon and Olives

You would expect to find any meat except pork in a recipe heady with the flavor of Morocco, but if you favor pork, I can assure you it is delicious.

This is an excellent one-dish meal, needing nothing more than a salad and fruit to complete it.

SERVES 4

1 lean boneless fresh pork butt
    (about 2 pounds)
Coarse salt
Freshly ground pepper
About 3 tablespoons olive oil
4 large cloves garlic, chopped
1 heaping tablespoon thin slivers
    fresh ginger
Several sprigs fresh rosemary *or* fresh
    oregano *or* fresh parsley
1 large onion, quartered and thinly sliced
1 small sweet red pepper, cut into thin
    strips
2 long green chile peppers, seeded and
    cut into small pieces
1 bay leaf
1 heaping cup peeled and chopped ripe
    tomatoes (½ pound)
½ cup dry white wine

1 Preserved Lemon (page 245), rinsed,
    pulp discarded and rind cut into long
    thin strips
¾ pound fresh baby artichokes, trimmed,
    cooked and quartered, *or* frozen
    artichoke hearts, cooked as directed
    (9-ounce package)
4 tablespoons chopped fresh parsley
About 2 to 3 cups chicken stock,
    simmered with ¼ teaspoon saffron
    threads
1 very small zucchini, cut into medium
    dice (about ¾ cup)
¾ cup pitted green olives, blanched
    and drained
1 cup medium-grain rice (see note)
¾ cup fresh peas *or* 1 cup fresh fava
    beans, blanched 1 to 2 minutes and
    skins slipped off

Cut the pork into ½-inch cubes, trimming away any fat. (If preferable, the meat can also be cooked in slices, like small steaks.) Sprinkle with salt and pepper. Heat 2 tablespoons of the oil in a large heavy skillet or casserole and lightly brown the cubes on all sides. Allow about 15 minutes for this. When almost finished, add the garlic, ginger and rosemary to the pan, combining them with the pork. Remove and set aside.

Add the onion to the skillet with a little more oil, if needed. When the onion begins to soften, add the red pepper, chile peppers and bay leaf. Continue to cook, stirring frequently, until the onion is translucent, then add the tomatoes and raise the heat. Cook, stirring, until the tomatoes are incorporated. Pour in the wine. Cook until the wine is greatly reduced and the sauce has thickened slightly. Lower the heat, return the pork to the pan and scatter the preserved lemon strips over all. After a moment, add the arti-

(Continued)

chokes, 2 tablespoons of the parsley and 1 cup of stock. Cover and simmer 15 minutes, stirring occasionally.

Add the zucchini and drained olives to the skillet, then the rice, carefully distributed to fill in the spaces. Pour in enough hot stock to cover the rice with liquid, then cover the skillet tightly and cook 20 minutes. Scatter peas or fava beans evenly over all, gently prodding them into the rice. The rice will not yet be fully cooked; if more stock is needed to finish it, add just enough to prevent the rice from sticking to the pan. (When done, the rice will have a texture somewhat like risotto.)

Continue to cook until the rice is tender, but not mushy. Check the rice frequently, add more stock if needed and taste a few grains to see if they are done. When ready, sprinkle with the remaining parsley and serve from the skillet or casserole.

NOTE   Medium-grain rice is grown in California and sold in Asian markets.

Braised Pork Nuggets with Black Beans in Red Wine and Pepper Sauce

Instead of serving the usual bowls of rice as an accompaniment, I spoon this dish over a soft and crisp fried noodle nest.

SERVES 4 TO 6

1 boneless fresh pork butt, cut into 1-inch cubes (2 to 2½ pounds)
½ teaspoon freshly ground black pepper
2 to 3 tablespoons peanut oil
2 slightly rounded teaspoons crushed dried red chile peppers
½ head garlic, peeled (10 large cloves)
2 inches fresh ginger, cut into thin slices, about 1 inch in diameter
8 scallions, cut into ¼-inch pieces, white and green parts separated
5 long fresh chile peppers, seeded and cut into narrow strips, about 1½ to 2 inches long (set aside 2 of the peppers)
¾ pound ripe tomatoes, peeled and cut into small wedges

2 tablespoons salted black beans, soaked in 2 tablespoons dry sherry
2 teaspoons brown sugar
2 tablespoons red wine vinegar
2 tablespoons mild imported soy sauce
¼ cup strained tamarind liquid (page 29) or pomegranate juice or lime juice
⅔ cup dry red wine
About ¾ cup fresh coriander leaves
6 large fresh basil leaves
1 large sprig fresh mint, leaves stripped
Fringed cucumber slices and small wedges vine-ripened tomato for garnish (optional)
Hot rice or a fried noodle nest (pages 260–261)

Toss the cubes of pork with a liberal amount of freshly ground pepper. Heat the oil in a large heavy pot and when hot, add the meat, all at once. Cook the pork until it loses its redness, turning the cubes on all sides. Sprinkle with dried chile peppers and toss together until the peppers are evenly distributed. Cook until the meat begins to take on color. Add the garlic, ginger and three-quarters of the white part of the scallions. Lower the heat and continue to toss the pork. Before the pork and aromatics begin to stick to the bottom of the casserole, add 3 of the fresh chiles, followed by the tomatoes. When the tomatoes are well incorporated, pour over the black beans with the sherry soaking liquid.

Stir, lower the heat and sprinkle with brown sugar. Continue to stir until the sugar dissolves, then add the vinegar and cook until it has evaporated. Moisten with soy sauce, followed by the tamarind liquid or pomegranate or lime juice. When the sauce is dark and syrupy, pour in the red wine. Cook until the wine has reduced by about a third, then add ½ cup of water. Return the liquid to a boil and reduce the heat to a gentle simmer.

Partially cover the pot and cook 2 to 3 hours. During this time, stir the pork frequently, making sure it does not stick to the bottom. As the sauce thickens and reduces, replenish it with small amounts of water, up to about 2 cups total. It may be necessary to reduce the heat to as low as possible.

After 2 hours, taste the sauce and a small piece of meat. The pork should be fork-tender. If the sauce is too thin, cook a little longer, uncovered, or if too thick, thin with a little more water. When satisfied, remove it from the heat until almost ready to serve. (At this time, the pork can be finished, but both the pork and the sauce will benefit from standing at room temperature for several hours and then being reheated. The stew can also be refrigerated overnight and reheated with the remaining ingredients added the next day.)

As serving time approaches, reheat the pork and sauce over very low heat. At this time, add the remaining peppers, remaining white part of the scallions and about half the green part. Coarsely chop the rest of the scallion tops with the coriander, basil and mint leaves. Near the end of cooking, stir half of this herb mixture into the sauce.

When ready to serve, transfer the pork nuggets to a warmed deep serving platter. If desired, surround the meat and its dark sauce with a garnish of crisp cucumber slices and small tangy wedges of ripe tomato. Sprinkle the remaining herb mixture over all.

Winter Vegetables Wrapped in Ham
with Curry Sauce
GRATIN DE LEGUMES D'HIVER AU SAUCE CURRY

Endive, leeks, celery and fennel all prove to be excellent choices and all interchangeable in this dish. Once, I combined them in one baking dish so the family could choose. The winner happened to be leeks, but all were good and each contributed to the flavor of the sauce.

As a main course, little is needed to complete the meal other than buttered rice and a simple green salad. With portions scaled down, the vegetables could also be served as a first course.

SERVES 4 AS A MAIN COURSE OR 6 TO 8 AS A FIRST COURSE

4 large endives *and/or* 8 medium to large leeks *and/or* 4 small celery hearts *and/or* 2 fennel bulbs (about ½ pound each)

CURRY SAUCE

4 tablespoons butter
1 medium leek, including some green, thinly sliced
1 small onion, chopped
2 very small zucchini, cut into large dice (about 1½ cups)
Coarse salt
Freshly ground white pepper
2 teaspoons chopped fresh mint leaves *or* 1 teaspoon dried mint, crumbled

8 large thin slices cooked ham (about ½ pound)

1½ to 2 cups mild chicken stock
3 tablespoons freshly squeezed lemon juice
1 tablespoon butter, softened

1 slightly rounded tablespoon curry powder
1 slightly rounded teaspoon ground cardamom
1 level tablespoon flour
3 tablespoons freshly squeezed lemon juice
½ to ⅔ cup heavy cream

About ¾ cup coarsely shredded Gruyère cheese

PREPARATION OF THE VEGETABLES

Remove any blemished leaves from the endives. Cut about ½ inch off the tops; trim the base without detaching the leaves. Cut the endive in half, lengthwise, and arrange, cut side down, in a shallow flameproof baking dish or gratin dish.

Trim and split the leeks, stopping about ¾ inch from the base. Rinse thoroughly and tie together in bundles of 2. Arrange in the baking dish.

Quarter the celery hearts and trim the tops of the stalks to an even length of about 6 inches. Arrange, cut side down, in the baking dish.

Cut off all of the green stalks of fennel and remove any blemished outer layers. Carefully trim the base and cut the bulbs into quarters, lengthwise, using the heart and base to hold the layers together. Arrange, cut side down, in the baking dish.

Pour the chicken stock over the vegetables. There should be enough to come about two-thirds of the way up the sides or for leeks, enough to cover when pressed down. Squeeze lemon juice over all.

Cut a piece of wax paper to fit the baking dish and grease liberally with softened butter. Set aside. Bring the stock to a boil, reduce the heat to a simmer and baste the vegetables. Cover with the buttered wax paper (it will help to keep them from discoloring) and cook 15 minutes.

When the vegetables are done, carefully pour off all the stock and reserve it. Leave the wax paper in place. Set the dish aside while preparing the sauce.

PREPARATION OF THE SAUCE

Melt 3 tablespoons of the butter in a casserole and add the leek and onion. Cook over medium heat, stirring frequently, until slightly softened. Add the zucchini and sprinkle with salt and freshly ground pepper. Lower the heat and cook, covered, for about 15 minutes or until the zucchini is almost tender. Add the mint leaves and remaining butter to the casserole, along with the curry powder, cardamom and flour. Cook 3 to 5 minutes, stirring constantly. Raise the heat slightly and add the reserved stock, a little at a time. Let the sauce thicken between additions; when all the stock has been added, simmer 20 minutes. Stir frequently and taste for seasoning, adding lemon juice, if necessary. Let cool 10 minutes.

Puree the sauce in a blender or food processor and return it to the casserole. Add the cream and reheat without allowing it to boil. Set aside.

FINISHING THE GRATIN

Preheat the oven to 450°F. and preheat the broiler, if separate.

Remove the wax paper and wrap each serving of vegetables in a slice of ham. If preparing endive or leeks, gently squeeze out any stock remaining in the leaves. Return the vegetables to the baking dish. (The gratin could also be finished in individual ovenproof dishes.)

Spread the sauce over all and sprinkle with cheese. Bake about 10 minutes, or until faintly bubbling around the edges. Transfer to the broiler and broil just until brown spots appear on the surface of the sauce.

Serve directly from the baking dish.

Steamed Red Snapper with Pork and Mushrooms

Red snapper usually arrives in our markets gutted. If you buy a whole fish, though, increase the weight by about one-half pound. If a steamer needs to be improvised (see note), allow about twenty inches for the length of the fish. Porgy can replace red snapper and two fish can be cooked to serve four.
SERVES 2

1 red snapper, with head and tail
    (about 1½ pounds)
1 bunch fresh coriander
¼ cup imported soy sauce
2 tablespoons mild rice vinegar
½ cup peanut oil
6 to 8 ounces thin slices pork, about
    ½ inch x 4 inches
1¾ cups (1 ounce) dried shiitake
    mushrooms, soaked and cut into thick
    strips *or* 4 ounces fresh shiitake
    mushrooms

3 to 4 fresh hot red cherry peppers,
    seeded and cut into strips, *or* green
    chiles, seeded and cut into pieces
5 pickled shallots *or* 2 large fresh
    shallots, coarsely chopped
About ⅓ cup long slivers fresh ginger
8 scallions, cut into ¾-inch pieces, white
    and green parts separated
Hot rice

Have the fish scaled, gills removed and fins cut off. If possible, leave the head and tail on. (This will depend on the size of your steamer.)

Using a cleaver, make 3 to 4 shallow slashes diagonally on each side of the fish. Stuff the cavity loosely with some of the coriander and arrange the fish on a platter or in a shallow baking dish. Before steaming, mix the soy sauce and vinegar together and dribble just a little of it over each side of the fish. Using your fingers, smear it evenly over all and in the slashes.

When ready to cook (20 minutes before serving time), bring water to a boil in a steamer. Set the fish platter on the steamer rack, cover tightly and steam 20 minutes. Test the fish for doneness before serving; if the fish flakes easily along the thickest part of the dorsal area, it is ready.

While the fish steams, heat the oil in a wok or skillet (a skillet with a pouring lip works best for this) and fry the pork. When the slices have been turned once, add the mushrooms. After a moment or two, add the hot peppers. Stir frequently until the pork is fully cooked. Remove the pork, mushrooms and peppers, leaving the oil in the skillet.

When the fish is ready to be served, reheat the oil and return the pork, mushrooms and peppers to the skillet along with the shallots, about two-thirds of the ginger, all the white part of the scallions and half the green part.

Remove the fish from the steamer and pour off the accumulated liquid or transfer the fish to another platter. Press the remaining ginger and scallion tops into the slashes, then pour over the rest of the soy-vinegar mixture. Follow *immediately* with the hot oil, distributing the pork, mushrooms and aromatics *evenly* over the fish.

Add a generous garnish of fresh coriander leaves and accompany the fish with bowls of hot rice. Needless to say, this dish should not wait.

NOTE It is not difficult to improvise a steamer. Place 1 or 2 cake racks in a deep roasting plan, raising them from the bottom with short hollow cans (both ends removed) or pastry cutters. Add water, keeping the level just below the rack, and bring to a boil. Arrange the platter on top of the rack and cover the pan tightly. Adjust the heat as necessary so there is sufficient steam, but do not allow the water to boil too vigorously. Check the water level occasionally.

Crispy Whole Fried Fish with Pork and Mushrooms

This is a wonderful dish that can be made with either one large sea bass or red snapper or several smaller sea bass or red snappers, allowing one per person.

Deep-frying whole fish in a wok should be done only on a stove or cooking top with a strong gas flame. Do not use an electric wok or electric burner; if the bottom of the wok has no direct contact with a flame, it will not be able to maintain a large volume of oil at the continuous high temperature necessary for deep-frying. A strong charcoal fire on an outdoor barbecue can be used successfully by embedding the wok in the hot coals.

SERVES 2 TO 4

2 to 4 small whole fish (¾ to 1 pound each) *or* 1 large fish (2½ to 3½ pounds)

MARINADE

1 extra-large egg, beaten
¼ teaspoon sugar
⅛ teaspoon finely ground white pepper
½ teaspoon coarse salt

1 tablespoon dry sherry
1 tablespoon grated or minced fresh ginger

SAUCE

1 cup chicken broth
1 tablespoon strong rice vinegar
1 rounded teaspoon sugar

3 tablespoons imported soy sauce
2 tablespoons dry sherry

Sifted cornstarch
Peanut or corn oil
5 to 10 dried red chile peppers (not the tiniest variety), broken in half if longer than 2 inches
1 rounded tablespoon finely chopped garlic
1 rounded tablespoon finely chopped fresh ginger
8 scallions, cut into 1½-inch pieces
7 to 8 ounces lean boneless pork, cut into thin slices, ½ inch x 4 inches *or* 6 to 12 ounces cooked pork, cut into long thick strips

1¾ cups (about 1 ounce) dried shiitake mushrooms soaked and cut into thick strips, *or* 5 large fresh shiitake mushrooms, cut into thick strips
2 scant tablespoons cornstarch, mixed with 2 tablespoons cold water
½ cup chicken broth
2 teaspoons imported sesame oil (optional)
3 whole scallions, thinly sliced
A large handful fresh coriander leaves for garnish
Hot rice

ADVANCE PREPARATION

Cut shallow slashes on a diagonal across each side of the fish. If using a large fish, score it, cutting in both directions. Combine the marinade ingredients in a large shallow baking dish and turn the fish in the marinade until saturated. Press some of the ginger into the slashes. Marinate the fish about 2 hours, turning it occasionally.

Combine the sauce ingredients in a bowl and have everything assembled. Just before heating the oil for deep-frying, dredge the fish in cornstarch. Dust the cavity as well.

COOKING THE FISH

Heat a large volume of oil in a wok to 375°F. Carefully lower the fish into the oil in the wok. Small fish will take about 10 to 12 minutes to cook, 5 minutes per side and 2 more turns in the oil to ensure a crisp golden color. For large fish, allow 10 minutes per side.

While the fish is cooking, coat the bottom of a skillet with oil. When the oil is hot, add the dried chile peppers, stirring until they are browned; remove them and set them aside. Lower the heat, add the garlic, chopped ginger and scallion pieces to the skillet and stir briefly. Add the pork and cook, stirring, until it loses its redness. (If using cooked pork, add it after the mushrooms, just before the sauce.) Add the mushrooms and as soon as they soften, return the chile peppers. Pour in the sauce mixture and bring to a boil. Reduce the heat to a simmer and, when the pork is fully cooked, stir in the cornstarch dissolved in cold water. Keep the heat under the sauce very low and, as it simmers, thin it with chicken broth, adding a little at a time. Before serving, stir sesame oil and sliced scallions into the sauce.

When the fish is done, carefully lift it from the wok and drain it on paper towels arranged over a warm serving platter. Slip the paper towel out from under the fish and pour over the sauce, distributing the pork and mushrooms evenly over all.

Garnish the platter with fresh coriander leaves and serve at once, accompanied by bowls of hot rice.

THE PRACTICAL PIG

Twice-Cooked Pork with Soft and Crisp Noodles

·

Stir-Fried Cabbage with Pork and Noodles

·

Roast Pork with Bean Sprouts

·

Fried Rice with Pork and Shrimp

·

Pork Enchiladas with Green Sauce

·

Mexican Green Tomato Sauce

·

Pork and Potatoes with Green Tomato Sauce

·

Chili Tostados

·

Spicy Black Beans

White Beans Provençal

·

Pork and Avocado Tostados with Black Beans

·

Fresh Bean Casserole

·

Spanish Flat Potato Omelet

·

Potato and Zucchini Tortilla with Ham and Mozzarella

·

Tagliatelle Verde with Spinach and Herb Sauce

·

Burgundy Pork and Potato Pie

Dorthy Parker may have defined eternity as "two people and a ham," but with the many uses for a leftover ham, or any cooked pork for that matter, it is more often the source of inspiration. Combining simplicity with the imagination is a ham sandwich under a brilliant sky, feet dangling in an aqua sea, or a late-afternoon repast where home-cured sausage, oily black olives and hard cheese taken under an olive tree in the hills with a wine skin become a meal for kings, or at least for poets.

In the early 1960s, out in the countryside with neither car nor refrigeration, the pig made a significant contribution to my well-being and, as it has throughout history, the ritual fall slaughtering saw many a family in the same region through the hardships of winter. The cured or cooked meat in whatever guise—a leftover roast, sausages or a shank hanging in the larder—could be counted on to transform a plate of rice, pasta, beans or winter vegetables into a satisfying meal.

A practical meal, despite its leanings toward rusticity, is more than a plain white plate set out upon a bare wood table. Rewarding dishes and good times are to be gained from leftover meats. Besides sandwiches, omelets and hash, enchiladas and all their garnishes make a festive dinner party. Stir-Fried Cabbage with Pork and Noodles is certain to delight the family, as will Twice-Cooked Pork with Soft and Crisp Noodles. The phrase "making a silk purse out of a sow's ear" is sure to come to mind when a regal Burgundian *tourte* is placed upon the table.

Twice-Cooked Pork with Soft and Crisp Noodles

In this dish, noodles are fried in a large skillet, giving them the appearance of a big nest. The top and bottom crusts are slowly fried until crisp, while the interior remains soft. The noodles are then transferred to a large round serving platter and the sauce of pork strips and mushrooms poured over it. Cut and serve the noodles like a pie.

There are other dishes that work very well served over fried noodles. Braised Pork Nuggets with Black Beans in Red Wine and Pepper Sauce (pages 248–249) is one to remember.

SERVES 4

¾ pound thin Oriental egg noodles (the size of spaghetti), preferably fresh
Coarse salt
About 7 tablespoons peanut oil
About 1 tablespoon imported sesame oil
1 pound boneless cooked pork, preferably from the loin
1½ ounces salt pork, cut into small dice (optional)

About 8 scallions, sliced, white and green parts separated
2 tablespoons chopped fresh ginger
2 long green fresh chile peppers, seeded and sliced
6 large fresh shiitake mushroom caps, cut into long strips (about 4 ounces)

SAUCE

1 cup strong Spicy Chicken Stock (page 77)
2 tablespoons imported soy sauce

A large handful fresh coriander leaves

1 rounded teaspoon chili paste with garlic

ADVANCE PREPARATION

Drop the noodles into a large pot of boiling salted water to which 1 tablespoon of peanut oil has been added. (If the noodles are frozen, defrost completely before cooking.) Cook only a few minutes, no time at all for fresh noodles. Test noodles frequently to catch them as they are just cooked. Drain in a colander and rinse with cold water. While draining, drizzle another tablespoon of peanut oil over the noodles and toss to prevent them from sticking together. (Add more oil, if necessary.) Transfer the noodles to a bowl and add 1 tablespoon sesame oil. Toss again and when well combined, set aside.

PREPARING OF THE SAUCE

Cut the cooked pork into thin slices, then cut in half again to make long strips. Reserve about 2 heaping tablespoons of diced fat trimmed from the meat or substitute salt pork. Add 1 tablespoon of peanut oil to a wok and render the fat until crisp.

Push the cracklings to the side of the wok and add the white part of the scallions, the ginger and chile peppers. Stir briefly, add the mushrooms and when combined, the pork strips; mix together. Combine the stock, soy sauce and chile paste and pour in. Simmer over low heat while frying the noodles.

FRYING THE NOODLES

Add about 3 tablespoons of peanut oil to a 13-inch cast-iron skillet. When the skillet is hot, arrange the noodles in it, working from the rim toward the center. Adjusting heat, fry the noodles until the bottom is nicely colored and slightly crisp (about 7 minutes). Take care not to let the noodles stick to the bottom of the skillet. Add a little more peanut oil to the skillet or drizzle a little sesame oil over the noodles, if needed. Press down slightly on the noodles with the back of a spatula to make them compact. Then cover the skillet with a large lightweight pan or tray and carefully invert the noodles so the bottom becomes the top. (If this action is too difficult, flip the noodles, using 2 large spatulas. If they come apart, no real harm will be done.) Add another tablespoon of peanut oil to the skillet, then slide the noodles back into the pan.

Continue to cook until the noodles are nicely colored on the bottom. Transfer to a warm serving platter.

TO SERVE

Spoon the hot sauce evenly over the noodle nest and strew green scallion tops over all. Scatter fresh coriander leaves around the rim of the platter and serve at once.

Stir-Fried Cabbage with Pork and Noodles

Because this dish uses cooked pork, its character will vary depending on whether the meat was simply roasted or barbecued with a basting sauce. The results from either method, though different, are interesting and very good.

If Chinese egg noodles are unavailable, substitute regular egg noodles or fettuccine.

SERVES 4

1 small head green or white (not Chinese) cabbage (about 2 pounds)
About 4 tablespoons peanut oil
¼ cup diced fattier parts of cooked pork *or* salt pork (about 4 ounces)
1 tablespoon chopped garlic
1 tablespoon thin slivers fresh ginger
1 scant cup (½ ounce) dried Chinese mushrooms, soaked, squeezed dry and cut into long slivers, *or* about 5 thinly sliced fresh shiitake mushrooms (2 or 3 ounces)

1 large leek, including some of the green, thinly sliced
3 to 4 fresh mild green chile peppers, seeded and thinly sliced
1 large stalk celery, thinly sliced
About ¼ teaspoon coarse salt
½ to ¾ pound cooked pork, cut into thin strips, about ½ inch x 2 inches

SAUCE

½ cup chicken stock
2 tablespoons mild imported soy sauce

2 tablespoons mild rice vinegar

¾ pound hot cooked wide Chinese egg noodles

2 whole scallions, thinly sliced
1 tablespoon roasted sesame seeds

Quarter the cabbage, cutting out most of the core. Separate the leaves in multiples and cut out all thick pieces of core. Stack the leaves and cut them into pieces, approximately 1½ inches square, and set aside.

Add 2 tablespoons of oil to the wok and render the fattier pieces of pork over medium heat until slightly crisp. Add the garlic and ginger and, after a moment, the mushrooms. Cook briefly, stirring, until the garlic and ginger start to color, then add the leek and peppers.

Stir-fry until the leek begins to soften. If needed, add 1 or 2 tablespoons more oil; then add the celery and cabbage. Sprinkle lightly with salt and cook until the cabbage leaves become glossy and slightly translucent. Add the cooked pork. Combine the stock, soy sauce and vinegar and add the mixture to the wok. Raise the heat and stir until the ingredients are well combined and the pork is heated through.

TO SERVE

Spoon the cabbage and pork into the center of a large warmed platter and surround with hot noodles. Scatter scallions over all, then sprinkle the noodles with sesame seeds.

NOTE   A tasty variation of this dish can be made by combining any leftover pork and cabbage mixture with the noodles and frying them in a skillet to which just a little oil has been added. Allow the noodles to brown a bit before serving.

Roast Pork with Bean Sprouts

I remember limp bean sprouts in a gloppy sauce as one of the clichés of Chinese take-out cuisine. None of the ingredients are exotic or anywhere in the realm of the combinations that titillate our palate today. There is not even any garlic! However, in a spate of nostalgia, my husband insisted we try cooking this questionable classic at home, and in an old-fashioned way it *was* good.

The essentials: crisp fresh bean sprouts, purchased the day they arrive in the market, and lots of prepared English or Chinese Hot Mustard, without which this dish would not be the same.

This recipe provides an agreeable answer for leftover fresh ham.

SERVES 2 OR 3

2 tablespoons peanut oil
About 2 rounded tablespoons diced fat
   from roast pork
1 heaping tablespoon thin slivers
   fresh ginger

7 scallions, cut into pea-size pieces,
   white and green parts separated
12 to 14 ounces roast pork, cut into
   thin strips

SAUCE

½ cup strong meat stock
2 tablespoons imported soy sauce
2 tablespoons mild rice vinegar

Scant 2 teaspoons cornstarch, mixed
   with 2 teaspoons cold water
¾ pound fresh crisp white bean sprouts,
   rinsed and well drained

1 tablespoon dry sherry
1 tablespoon imported sesame oil

English or Chinese Mustard (page 41)

(Continued)

Heat the oil in a wok with the diced fat. Adjusting the heat, render the fat until crisp and golden brown. Add the ginger and the white part of the scallions and stir briefly. Raise the heat and add the pork strips. Stir-fry until well combined. Combine the sauce ingredients and pour in. When it comes to a boil, lower the heat and cook, stirring, until all ingredients are well combined. Push the pork to the side of the pan and stir the dissolved cornstarch into the sauce.

As soon as the sauce is slightly thickened (the consistency should be thin), add the bean sprouts and toss together only until the sprouts are combined with the sauce. They must remain crunchy. Add all but 1 heaping tablespoon of the green part of the scallions and continue to toss just until piping hot.

Turn the pork and bean sprouts out onto a deep warmed platter and sprinkle with the remaining scallion tops. Serve at once.

Have plenty of mustard for each person to add according to taste.

Fried Rice with Pork and Shrimp

Barbecued pork is especially good here, but it can be replaced by diced ham or sausage. The rice must be completely cold before it is fried.

SERVES 6

6 to 8 ounces medium shrimp, peeled and deveined

Finely ground white pepper

2 tablespoons dry sherry

About 4 tablespoons peanut oil

2 extra-large eggs, beaten

1 scant cup (about ½ ounce) dried shiitake mushrooms, soaked, squeezed dry and thinly sliced, stems removed

6 scallions, sliced, white and green parts separated

1 fresh hot chile pepper, seeded and thinly sliced

1 clove garlic, finely chopped

SAUCE

4 tablespoons mild imported soy sauce

½ teaspoon sugar

2 teaspoons imported sesame oil

6 ounces cooked pork, cut into thin strips, about 2 inches long

¾ cup freshly shelled peas

4 to 5 cups cold cooked rice

Cut each shrimp in half or, if large, into several pieces. Sprinkle with pepper and sherry and marinate from 30 minutes to 2 hours, tossing occasionally.

Heat 1 tablespoon of the peanut oil in a wok or cast-iron skillet and add the eggs. Tilt the pan to make a thin pancake. When fully cooked, but not browned, remove and set aside. When cool, roll up like a jelly roll and cut into thin strips, ¼ inch thick.

Add 3 tablespoons of oil to the wok (more for the skillet) and cook the shrimp quickly, just until they start to turn opaque. Remove and drain.

If necessary, add a little more oil to the wok, then add the mushroom slices. Sear them over high heat. Lower the heat and add the white part of the scallions, the chile pepper and garlic. Combine the soy sauce, sugar and sesame oil and pour in. Return the shrimp to the wok and stir in the pork and peas.

Bring the sauce to a boil and add the rice, broken into small clumps. When the rice is well combined and has taken on the color of the sauce, mix with the egg strips and scallion tops. Serve the rice mounded on a hot platter.

Pork Enchiladas with Green Sauce
ENCHILADAS DEL CERDO CON SALSA VERDE

Shoulder butt or fresh picnic is ideal for this recipe. If the meat was poached, braised or stewed, it may be possible to pull it apart, instead of cutting it.

The Mexican Green Tomato Sauce and filling can be made in advance, but it is best not to fry and stuff the tortillas too far ahead because they may become soggy.

SERVES 8

About 4 cups Mexican Green Tomato Sauce (page 267)

FILLING

½ cup sour cream
4 ounces softened cream cheese, cut into pieces
4 ounces soft white cheese, such as queso blanco or fresco or Monterey Jack or Muenster, shredded

About 1½ pounds boneless cooked pork, preferably poached (page 175), cut into thin strips

½ cup heavy cream
16 corn tortillas
About ½ cup peanut or corn oil
About 4 ounces soft white cheese, shredded

About ½ cup freshly grated Asiago or Parmesan cheese
About ½ cup chopped sweet onion

ACCOMPANIMENTS

Sour cream
Mexican Green Tomato Sauce or uncooked tomato salsa

Spicy Black Beans (pages 270–271)

Prepare the Mexican Green Tomato Sauce and set aside.

To make the filling, use a fork to work the sour cream into the cream cheese. Work in the shredded cheese and 1 cup of the Mexican Green Tomato Sauce. Cut or tear the pork into small pieces; combine it with the cheese mixture.

Preheat the oven to 425°F. Mix ⅔ cup of Mexican Green Tomato Sauce with ½ cup heavy cream in a pie plate and place next to the stove.

Fry the tortillas in oil only until softened. Do *not* let them become crisp. As each tortilla is fried, drain briefly, then dip in and out of the tomato sauce and cream mixture, coating each side. Do *not* soak. Transfer to a plate, stacking one on top of the other.

When all the tortillas are fried, place a heaping tablespoon of filling in the center of each one, then roll each into a neat cylinder. Arrange side by side, seam sides down, in a shallow baking dish. Do not crowd. (If necessary, use 2 baking dishes.)

Pour the rest of the Mexican Green Tomato Sauce evenly over the enchiladas, sprinkle with shredded cheese, followed by the grated cheese. Scatter chopped onion over all (see note).

Bake the enchiladas about 15 minutes, or until bubbling hot. Serve at once with a bowl of sour cream passed separately and, if desired, make additional Mexican Green Tomato Sauce or an uncooked tomato salsa. Spicy Black Beans are the perfect accompaniment.

NOTE   If you are sure the onion is sweet, scatter it over the enchiladas *after* baking.

Mexican Green Tomato Sauce
SALSA TOMATILLO

This sauce keeps well in the refrigerator. If storing for longer than two or three days, however, bring to a simmer on the second day. It can also be frozen, but should be returned to a simmer after defrosting.
MAKES ABOUT 4 CUPS

1¾ cups canned green tomatoes
    (tomatillo entero) and their juices
1 clove garlic, chopped
1 cup chopped sweet onion
1 small sweet green pepper, seeded
    and chopped
2, or more, fresh hot green chile peppers,
    seeded and chopped
⅔ cup canned mild green chiles, left
    whole, stems removed

1 cup coarsely chopped fresh
    coriander leaves
½ cup coarsely chopped fresh parsley
    leaves
½ cup chicken stock
Salt (optional)

Combine ingredients, one by one, in a blender or food processor, running the machine after each addition. Puree until smooth, then taste for seasoning.

Pork and Potatoes with Green Tomato Sauce
CERDO CON PATATAS Y SALSA TOMATILLO

Fresh or smoked pork can be used for this dish. For a number of servings, it can be prepared in a large shallow casserole; for fewer people, individual two-cup gratin dishes can be used. That is how I usually make it for myself, most often with a smoked butt that made its debut in a Boiled Dinner (pages 176–177) a day or so earlier.

These portions are for a shallow individual gratin dish. For a casserole, use only as much butter and oil as necessary, but keep the amounts of pork and potatoes, per person, roughly the same. A little less sauce will be needed and only enough cheese to scatter lightly over all.

SERVES 1

1 small baking potato, unpeeled
1 small bay leaf
Salt
1 teaspoon butter, softened
4 to 6 very thin slices cooked pork
About 2 tablespoons olive oil

⅔ cup Mexican Green Tomato Sauce
 (page 267)
2 to 3 tablespoons heavy cream
¼ cup freshly grated imported
 Swiss cheese

Put the whole potato and bay leaf in a pan of cold salted water, bring to a boil and cook 10 minutes. Drain and when cool enough to handle, peel and cut into slices about ¼ inch thick. Grease a shallow gratin dish lightly with butter. Spread the slices of pork over the bottom, overlapping slightly.

Preheat the oven to 425°F. Coat the bottom of a skillet with olive oil and fry the potatoes until lightly browned. Drain on paper towels and arrange over the pork.

Combine the Mexican Green Tomato Sauce and cream and pour it over the potatoes. Some of the sauce should moisten the pork. Scatter the cheese over all and bake about 20 minutes, or until the sauce is bubbling and the cheese is golden brown. Let stand a few minutes before serving.

VARIATION

Instead of frying the potatoes, simmer the slices in milk with a clove of garlic, freshly ground white pepper, a bay leaf and salt. Cook until tender, then drain. (If making a large casserole, this would be the easiest method.)

Chili Tostados

These tostados are topped with a cooling salad to quench the fire of the chili. The salad is dressed with only a little vinaigrette to keep the lettuce crisp and the flavors distinct.

SERVES 4

8 flour tortillas
4 cups Pork Chili (pages 193–194)

2 to 3 tablespoons Chili-Raisin Sauce (page 194), optional

VINAIGRETTE

1 rounded teaspoon Dijon mustard
2 teaspoons red wine or sherry vinegar
4 tablespoons olive oil

Freshly ground black pepper
A pinch of coarse salt (optional)

½ ripe California avocado
2 teaspoons lime juice for the avocado
1 or 2 crisp yellow hearts of Boston lettuce, shredded

2 small Belgian endives, sliced
3 large crisp radishes, sliced paper thin
Sour cream

Toast the tortillas under the broiler until crisp and colored with brown spots. Arrange on individual plates.

While the tortillas are toasting, heat the chili, adding a few tablespoons of Chili-Raisin Sauce, to taste. Cook the chili until very thick.

Mix the vinaigrette, adding the ingredients one at a time until well blended. Cut the avocado into large dice and coat with lime juice. At the last moment, when ready to assemble the tortillas, combine the vinaigrette with the avocado, lettuce, endives and radishes.

Spread each tortilla with about ½ cup of chili, then cover with a mound of salad. Spoon a line of sour cream over the lettuce and serve.

Pass additional sour cream separately.

Spicy Black Beans

FRIJOLES NEGROS

This dish welcomes all sorts of leftover meats. Served as is, the beans make a perfect side dish for many Mexican and Southwestern specialties. If not bolstered by extra meat, they can constitute a meal when accompanied with a plate of rice.

These beans get better and better with each reheating and should always be made at least a day before they are to be eaten.

SERVES 8

2 cups dried black turtle beans (1 pound)
1 whole onion, stuck with 2 cloves
1 carrot
Sprigs fresh thyme and parsley and
   1 large bay leaf, tied together
   (bouquet garni)
6 large cloves garlic, unpeeled
3 dried red chile peppers, broken
2 smoked ham hocks (pig's knuckles)
Chicken stock (optional)
2 or 3 tablespoons olive or peanut oil
1 large Bermuda onion, chopped

½ small sweet green or red pepper,
   finely chopped
1 large ripe tomato *or* 3 large plum
   tomatoes, peeled and diced
   (about 1½ cups)
Coarse salt
1 or 2 tablespoons red wine or
   sherry vinegar
1 tablespoon finely chopped garlic
2 tablespoons cornstarch
2 or 3 tablespoons dry sherry (optional)
Fresh coriander leaves

GARNISHES

Sour cream
Diced avocado sprinkled with lime juice

Diced tomato
Chopped sweet onion

ADVANCE PREPARATION

Rinse the beans and soak them overnight in a large pot or bowl of cold water to cover by several inches.

COOKING THE BEANS

Drain the beans and place them in a large heavy pot with 2½ quarts of fresh water. Add the onion, carrot, bouquet garni, garlic and chile peppers. Bury the smoked hocks among the beans and bring to a gentle simmer. Skim the surface as needed, cover and cook about 3 hours. It may be necessary to add a little more water or, if you prefer, chicken stock. The beans should remain covered by liquid. (If you are using additional meats, add them at the appropriate time to make sure they are fully cooked. Leftover meats should be added at the end, only to heat.)

When the beans show signs of becoming tender, remove the hocks, onion, carrot, bouquet garni and garlic cloves. Discard the rind and bone the hocks. Cut or tear the meat into small morsels and return it to the pot. Discard the onion, carrot and bouquet garni. Pinch out the soft pulp of the garlic cloves and stir it back into the beans. If additional meats need to be cut up or have their casings removed, do so at this time.

Heat the oil in a skillet and sauté the onion and sweet pepper. When the onion is soft and golden, stir in the tomato. Cook briefly over high heat, then add to the pot. Simmer 1 hour or longer. When the beans are completely tender, taste for salt and add the vinegar. Stir in the chopped garlic.

Mix the cornstarch with 2 tablespoons cold water and stir it into the beans to thicken the sauce. Simmer, uncovered, about 30 minutes, without letting the liquid come to a boil. If the broth becomes too thick, thin with a little water or stock. Stir frequently.

When ready to serve, stir in the sherry, if using, taste for seasoning and scatter a few coriander leaves over the surface of the beans.

If the beans are to be the main course, be sure to pass an assortment of garnishes. Include sour cream, diced avocado sprinkled with lime juice, diced tomato and always a bowl of chopped sweet onion.

White Beans Provençal

These beans are an excellent accompaniment to many pork dishes—from roast fresh ham to simple chops on the grill. The beans are best made ahead and given ample time to absorb the flavor of the herb-permeated tomato sauce. I like to prepare the beans a day in advance and let them stand overnight at room temperature. They are then reheated early in the day and once again shortly before serving.

Other meats (leftovers especially) or sausages can join the beans, making them substantial enough to serve as a main course. All that's needed to accompany them is a simple green salad and a piece of fruit for dessert.

SERVES 8 AS A SIDE DISH

2 cups small dried white beans, such as Great Northern *or* baby limas, *or* imported *flageolets*
6 ounces, or more, meaty bacon, in one piece
1 large onion, stuck with 2 cloves
1 large carrot, peeled
½ head garlic, unpeeled (about 10 large cloves)
1 bay leaf, celery leaves, sprigs thyme and parsley *and/or* fresh sage *or* rosemary, tied together (bouquet garni)
3 tablespoons olive oil

1 large onion, finely chopped
2 large cloves garlic, finely chopped
⅔ cup dry white wine
2 cups Fresh Tomato Sauce (page 132) *or* 3 cups peeled, seeded and chopped ripe tomatoes *or* canned Italian plum tomatoes, drained
About 1 cup chicken stock
Freshly ground white pepper
Coarse salt (optional)
About 1 cup combined chopped fresh mint, basil and parsley leaves (see note)

ADVANCE PREPARATION

Soak the beans overnight in enough cold water to cover by several inches.

COOKING

The next day, drain the beans and place them in a large heavy pot with fresh cold water to cover. Bury the bacon, whole onion, carrot, garlic cloves and bouquet garni in the beans and bring to a simmer. Skim the surface, then cook at a very low simmer for about 1 hour and 20 minutes, or until the beans are tender, but not mushy.

Let the beans remain in their cooking liquid until ready to sauce them. Then drain in a colander. Reserve the bacon, carrot, garlic cloves and bay leaf. Discard the rest.

Remove the rind from the bacon, but save it for flavoring the sauce. Cut the meat and fat into small dice. Place them in a clean casserole and add enough olive oil to supplement the fat. Render the bacon over very low heat until golden and slightly crisp. Add the chopped onion and cook slowly, stirring frequently, until softened. Add the chopped garlic and cook briefly, then pour in the wine. Cook over high heat until greatly reduced.

Add the tomato sauce or tomatoes, and reserved bay leaf and bacon rind and continue to cook until thickened. Lower the heat, thin with stock and simmer until the sauce is reduced slightly. Add a generous grinding of pepper and taste for seasoning. Salt may not be needed.

Chop the reserved carrot into small dice and add to the sauce with the drained beans. Press out the sweet soft pulp of the garlic cloves and stir into the beans, along with half the freshly chopped herbs. Cook the beans over very low heat, for as long as possible so that they take on the flavor of the sauce. Add small increments of stock, as needed. Best of all is to let the beans stand overnight, then reheat before serving.

Before bringing the beans to the table, sprinkle with the remaining chopped herbs.

NOTE   The flavor of mint is more important in this dish than that of basil.

Pork and Avocado Tostados with Black Beans

SERVES 4

½ pound cooked pork, preferably cooked in Ancho Pepper and Green Tomato Sauce (pages 234–235)

4 fresh corn or flour tortillas

About 4 tablespoons peanut or corn oil

About 2 cups Spicy Black Beans (pages 270–271), reheated

1 cup cooked Ancho Pepper and Green Tomato Sauce from the cooked pork, simmered until slightly thickened, *or* Mexican Green Tomato Sauce (page 267)

1 ripe California avocado, thinly sliced, sprinkled with lime juice

½ cup sour cream

Coarsely chopped fresh coriander leaves

Tomato-chile salsa (optional)

Cut the pork into long julienne strips. Set aside.

In a small skillet, fry the tortillas in the oil, one at a time, until crisp. Drain on paper towels.

Cover each tortilla with about ½ cup of hot black beans. Arrange the pork over the beans; then coat with several spoonfuls of thickened sauce. Top with slices of avocado and a small dollop of sour cream. Sprinkle with coriander leaves and serve.

If desired, pass a tomato-chile salsa separately.

Fresh Bean Casserole

Different varieties of fresh beans are available in the markets from early spring until the end of summer—beginning with cranberry and other white beans, continuing with green fava beans and, later, lima beans.

Three or four pounds unshelled beans will yield approximately four cups shelled. The amount of cooking time can vary from as little as 10 minutes for some of the green varieties to 30 minutes for harder white beans such as cranberry. Dried beans can be substituted for fresh, if first soaked overnight. Place in a pan of fresh water to cover by several inches and simmer gently with spices until tender.

If preparing this dish in summer, substitute fresh basil for half the amount of parsley. Chop the herbs together with one small clove of garlic.

SERVES 4

4 pounds unshelled fresh beans
Coarse salt
1 peeled carrot, 1 stalk celery, 1 bay leaf
    and several sprigs parsley, tied
    together (bouquet garni)
1 small onion, stuck with 2 cloves
About 2 tablespoons olive oil
1 large onion, chopped
1 small stalk celery, cut into small dice
    (optional)
1 bay leaf
1 sprig fresh rosemary *or* several sprigs
    fresh thyme *or* ½ teaspoon dried
    thyme
3 cloves garlic, chopped

1 to 1½ cups peeled and chopped
    tomatoes, fresh or canned, and their
    liquid
2 or 3 cups leftover smoked pork butt,
    ham *or* other cooked meats, cut into
    bite-size pieces (see note)
¾ cup dry white wine
Chicken stock
1 cup large dice zucchini *and/or* a small
    handful green beans, cut into 2-inch
    pieces and blanched 5 minutes
½ cup chopped fresh parsley
Freshly grated Parmesan cheese
    (optional)

Shell the beans and if they are favas, peel off the fine inner skin before adding to the casserole.

Bring 3 or 4 quarts of salted water to a boil with the bouquet garni and whole onion. Drop in the beans, reduce heat slightly, and boil gently until tender. Skim off any foam that rises to the surface and taste a bean from time to time to be sure they do not overcook.

When the beans are ready, drain, reserving the liquid and saving the carrot used in the bouquet garni. Coarsely chop the carrot and set aside.

(Continued)

Heat the olive oil in a large heavy pot and sauté the chopped onion over low heat until softened. Add the diced celery, if using, the bay leaf, rosemary or thyme and chopped garlic. After a minute, add the tomatoes and their liquid, bring to a simmer and cook 2 minutes.

Add the leftover pork and/or other meats, followed by the wine. When the wine has reduced slightly, stir in the beans. Add enough chicken stock or reserved cooking liquid from the beans (or both) to come to a level a little below the surface of the ingredients. Bring to a simmer, turn the heat to very low, cover and cook 30 minutes. Stir once or twice during this time.

When the level of liquid has greatly reduced and the flavor of the sauce has impregnated the beans (they should be tender, but not mushy), mix in the reserved chopped carrot, the zucchini and/or green beans. Cook 5 minutes longer, stirring frequently. This dish can be made to this point well in advance.

When ready to serve, stir in freshly chopped parsley. Pass a bowl of freshly grated Parmesan cheese for those who might like it.

Serve the bean mélange in deep plates, accompanied by good crusty bread and a green salad. Depending on the thickness of the sauce, soup-spoons might be in order.

NOTE   In addition to smoked pork and ham, you can also use morsels of hocks, roast pork, lean pork belly, sausage or, as in a cassoulet, lamb or duck. Any combination of these meats adapts very well to the beans.

VARIATIONS

Add 1 baking potato, cut into large dice, and 1 cup chicken stock when adding the wine.

A handful of shredded fresh spinach or Swiss chard can be stirred into the beans shortly before serving.

Spanish Flat Potato Omelet
TORTILLA

This is a typical omelet of Spain with earthy ingredients—potatoes, onions, peppers, ham and sausage—bound together with eggs. Such a tortilla is often the mainstay of a light supper or lunch; served at room temperature, it makes a tasty snack.

SERVES 3 TO 4

2 small to medium potatoes
 (about 8 ounces)
5 extra-large eggs
Coarse salt
Freshly ground white pepper
1 tablespoon chopped fresh parsley
 or basil
1 clove garlic, crushed slightly
¼ cup olive oil

1 large onion, chopped
2 large mild chile peppers *or* 1 frying
 pepper, seeded and cut into thin
 strips, about 1½ inches long
3 ounces cooked sausage, cut into small
 dice (about 1 cup)
2 cloves garlic, finely chopped
2 ounces cooked ham, cut into julienne
 strips (about ¾ cup)

Preheat the oven to 350°F. Peel the potatoes and slice into thin rounds, about ⅛ inch thick. Beat the eggs vigorously with a fork, add a good pinch of coarse salt, freshly ground pepper and the parsley or basil. Stir and set aside.

Rub a 12-inch cast-iron skillet with the crushed garlic and discard the garlic. Heat the oil in the skillet and when hot, spread the potato slices over the bottom of the pan. Cook the potatoes, turning them frequently and, at the first sign of coloring, lower the heat to medium. Do not allow the potatoes to brown. When done, they should be faintly crisp with a golden hue. Remove and set aside on paper towels.

Lower the heat and add the onion to the skillet with the hot or sweet pepper. Cook until the onion has softened, stirring frequently. Add the sausage and chopped garlic. Stir together and when the sausage is heated through, push it and the vegetables to the side of the pan.

Return the potatoes, spreading them out and spooning the sausage and vegetables over them. Without stirring, distribute the strips of ham over all. Carefully, holding the eggs back with a fork, slowly let them slide evenly over the vegetables and meats to bind them together. Tilt the skillet, but do not stir. If needed, prod the surface gently with the edge of a spatula to ease the eggs into bare spots, but leave the bottom of the omelet undisturbed.

(Continued)

Over low heat, let the eggs cook about 5 minutes. As they begin to set, slip a spatula around the rim of the skillet to keep them from sticking. To finish the eggs, transfer the skillet to the oven. Bake 5 minutes, or just long enough for the surface to set but for the interior to stay moist. Remove from the oven and loosen the bottom of the tortilla with a spatula. Cover the skillet with a large warmed plate and invert the pan, removing the tortilla, burnished bottom up.

Potato and Zucchini Tortilla with Ham and Mozzarella

This flat omelet, which can be served at room temperature, makes a good use of leftovers.

SERVES 2 AS A LUNCHEON DISH OR LIGHT SUPPER OR 4 AS AN APPETIZER

Olive oil
2 cloves garlic, flattened slightly
 and peeled
1 very small onion, thinly sliced
2 small zucchini, sliced paper thin
 (about 1 cup)
1½ to 2 cups cooked potato slices
 (see note)

2 or 3 thin slices cooked ham, cut into
 long strips, about ½ inch wide
3 extra-large eggs, lightly beaten
Coarse salt
Freshly ground white pepper
Thin slices fresh mozzarella
 (about 3 ounces)

Preheat the oven to 350°F. Coat a 10-inch cast-iron skillet liberally with olive oil. Add the garlic cloves and over low heat fry them until crisp and golden. Press down on the cloves, then discard.

Slowly sauté the onion slices until quite soft and translucent. Add the zucchini to the skillet, raise the heat slightly, and toss together until well combined and just a bit limp. The zucchini should remain sprightly looking. Remove and set aside.

Add a little more oil if needed, then spread out the potato slices in the skillet. Add some of the leeks, garlic and herbs that the potatoes were cooked with. Over low to medium heat, warm the potatoes, turning them on each side and letting them color slightly. Spread the slices of zucchini and onions over all. Maintain a very low heat under the skillet while adding the zucchini and the rest of the ingredients. Arrange strips of ham over the zucchini.

Beat the eggs with a little salt and a generous grinding of pepper. Slowly and evenly pour the eggs over all. Tilt the skillet to be sure the eggs are evenly distributed. Prod the vegetables gently with the tines of a fork to make sure the eggs seep into any pockets. Dot the surface of the omelet with slices of mozzarella and place in the oven.

Bake the omelet about 10 minutes, or until just set, then invert onto a round platter. Serve hot or warm, cut into wedges.

NOTE Any leftover potato from recipes in which the slices are baked in the oven with a scattering of thinly sliced leeks, chopped garlic and herbs, then either moistened with chicken broth or basted with butter, will do nicely for this omelet. See the *boulangère* recipe on page 204, for example.

Tagliatelle Verde with Spinach and Herb Sauce

It is imperative that the tomato in this recipe be of good quality and flavor, or it will not enhance the sauce. If unavailable, add a teaspoon of lemon juice or a few chopped sorrel leaves. If fresh basil is in season, be sure to include it.
SERVES 3 OR 4

Coarse salt
1 tablespoon olive oil
½ pound green tagliatelle or fettuccine
4 tablespoons butter
1 clove garlic, finely chopped
1 cup well-drained chopped cooked fresh spinach
¾ cup freshly grated Parmesan cheese
1 cup coarsely chopped vine-ripened tomato

Freshly ground pepper
1 egg yolk
1½ cups heavy cream
⅔ cup chopped smoked pork butt, hocks (pig's knuckles) *or* ham
½ cup chopped fresh parsley *or* basil *or* a combination of both
½ to ¾ cup fresh peas

Bring a large pot of salted water to a vigorous boil. Add the olive oil and the noodles and cook until al dente, then drain in a colander.

While the noodles are cooking, melt the butter and sauté the garlic in a large skillet over low heat. When the noodles are drained, turn them into the skillet and combine with the butter and garlic.

Add the spinach with half the cheese and toss briefly. Add half the tomato, the remaining cheese, and a generous grinding of pepper. Toss again to combine.

(Continued)

Mix the egg yolk with ½ cup of the cream and add to the noodles, then fold in the rest of the cream, the smoked pork, herbs and remaining tomato. Season to taste with coarse salt.

Continue to toss the noodles over low heat until the sauce thickens. If necessary, raise the heat slightly. At the last moment, add the peas.

Serve at once on warmed deep plates.

Burgundy Pork and Potato Pie

TOURTE AUX PORC ET POMMES DE TERRE BOURGUIGNONNE

Occasionally I cook meat specifically for this recipe, rather than use leftovers, and sometimes I cook both fresh and smoked pork together in the wine-fortified poaching broth for pork (page 175). The mixed meats combine nicely with their subtle but discernible differences in flavor. Remember that if freshly cooked, the meat must be cold in order to slice it thin.

Puff pastry or one based on lard would be traditional for the *tourte,* but I like the results of Sour Cream Pastry Dough. The amount of dough in the recipe will suffice for a ten-inch *tourte;* I prefer to make a double batch and use an eleven- to twelve-inch tart form or baking dish. This way there is ample dough to bring it up from the sides of the bottom crust and make a thick roll where it joins the top crust around the rim of the form. I then take some of the excess and cut it into fanciful shapes to decorate the lid of the *tourte.* Store the remaining dough, for there will be some left, in the freezer. This pastry is strong enough to support the *tourte* by itself; when baked, it will readily separate from the form. With this in mind, the *tourte* could even be made in a skillet and then transferred to an attractive platter.

SERVES 4 AS A MAIN COURSE OR 8 TO 10 AS AN APPETIZER

A double batch of Sour Cream Pastry
   Dough (page 46)
1½ to 1¾ pounds large baking potatoes
2 cups milk
1 large clove garlic, flattened and peeled
1 small bay leaf
Freshly ground white pepper
½ teaspoon coarse salt
1 leek, both white and green part,
   thinly sliced
2 tablespoons butter

2 heaping tablespoons chopped fresh
   chives, parsley, chervil and thyme
   leaves, combined
1½ to 1¾ pounds boneless cooked fresh
   or smoked pork, not barbecued,
   thinly sliced
¾ cup heavy cream
1 piece uncooked macaroni or penne for
   a "steam chimney"
1 large egg, beaten with 1 teaspoon
   cold water

ADVANCE PREPARATION

Roll out half the dough as thin as possible to make a circle several inches larger in diameter than the form that will be used. Lay the pastry over the form, pressing it in lightly around the sides. Leave an overhang of about 1½ inches around the rim, then trim evenly. Prick the bottom of the crust all over with the tines of a fork. Roll out the top crust as thin as possible and only slightly larger than the diameter of the form. Place on a sheet of wax paper, then roll out a portion of the remaining dough to use for decoration. Refrigerate until ready to proceed.

Peel the potatoes, slice thin, and chill in cold water. Combine the milk, garlic, bay leaf, a generous grinding of pepper and coarse salt in a large saucepan. Let steep while the potatoes soak. Later, drain the potatoes well in a colander and arrange in the saucepan, pressing down to submerge them in the milk. Bring to a simmer, keeping them submerged. Remove from the heat and let cool in the milk.

FINISHING THE *TOURTE*

Preheat the oven to 425°F. Sauté the leek in the butter in a small frying pan until softened.

Remove the form with the bottom crust from the refrigerator. Drain a few slices of potato at a time and arrange them, partially overlapping, to cover the bottom of the *tourte* shell. Scatter half the sautéed leeks and half the herbs over the potatoes, then arrange the sliced meats over all. Keep the meats in one layer, with slices overlapping as necessary. Top the meats with the rest of the potatoes, evenly arranged. Sprinkle the remaining leeks and herbs over them and very slowly pour the cream evenly over all.

Position the top crust over the potatoes and bring up the bottom crust to join it in a neat inward roll around the rim of the form. Press tightly together at regular intervals. Using the point of a small knife, break through the center of the crust and insert a small piece of macaroni to allow steam to escape.

Have fun with the remaining sheet of dough. Cut leaves, flowers, scallops or geometric shapes to decorate the *tourte*. Brush the surface of the pastry and the rolled border with egg wash, then attach the cut-outs and brush them also. (The egg will help them stick.) With the point of a small sharp knife, scratch leaflike patterns over the surface, piercing the egg wash.

Place in the oven and bake 30 minutes. Rotate the *tourte* 180° and bake 15 minutes more. Remove it from the oven and let it rest at least 15 minutes before serving. Cut the *tourte* like a pie, in large or small wedges.

I·N·D·E·X

INDEX

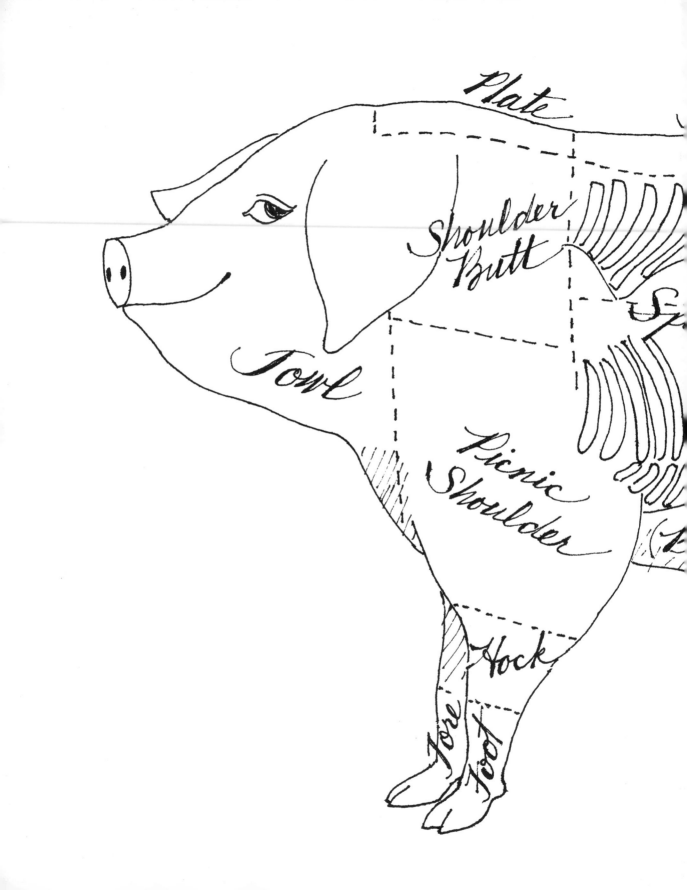